Malcolm Mann
Steve Taylore-Knowles

Laser B2

Student's Book

MACMILLAN

Contents

1

Relationships

Wordpower!

anger • annoy • argument
criticism • demand • hurtful

Starting point

What problems can people have with the following?

- relationships with brothers and sisters
- relationships with parents
- friendships
- professional/working relationships

1 **Look at the information surrounding the main text. What do you expect to read in this blog?**

2 **Read the main text quickly and find examples of relationship problems and solutions to them.**

Reading 1 1.01

www.relationshiphotline-blog.org

Relationship hotline ▶ Home

Relationship hotline

Go to:
What can possibly go wrong?
Making it work
Who's to blame?
Getting professional help
Learning to communicate
Making big decisions
Take control!

Tags
Breaking up (2)
Communication (4)
Professional advice (5)
Family (4)
Boyfriend/Girlfriend (3)
Marriage (5)

Get our newsletter
Send us feedback
Ask a question
Live updates
Add to favourites

Sites we like
I blame the parents
National Youth Hotline
What to do when …
Youth Medical

Welcome to our relationship blog. We have put together suggestions and advice on all kinds of relationship issues. In this blog, you'll find links to articles on many problems that people face. Our purpose is to help people deal with problems and have happier, more successful relationships. We hope you find what you're looking for and above all, we hope we can help. If you have a particular relationship problem that is not covered in these pages, feel free to contact us.

21st March – 2.06pm
What can possibly go wrong?
As we go through life, we develop a variety of relationships – with family, friends, teachers and, later, workmates and marriage partners. 1 ______ Sometimes, the problems that come up are of our own making, and sometimes they are out of our control.

EXAM EXPERT

How should you do the exam practice task?

a Don't worry about words in the sentences like *her*, *his*, *our*, etc because you don't know who they refer to so they can't help you decide.

b Look at words like *her*, *his*, *our*, etc carefully and try to work out who they refer to because they will help you decide.

Family issues make up a large number of the problems people approach us with. **2** But, just as our parents, brothers and sisters are usually the ones we share our happiest moments with, they are often the people we take it out on when things get bad. There's an old saying that we usually hurt the ones we love, and that can be very true in families. Friends, too, often go through rough patches. **3** In the early days of this blog, we received a question that is typical of the kind of things people are concerned about in their friendships. This is what the person had to say:

We became friends years ago, but recently I noticed something. I had a problem at home and I told my friend about it, but he wasn't interested. He just didn't want to know. When I thought about it, I realised that he never really cares about any problems that I have, but he expects me to listen to all of his problems. Why does he behave in this way?

The short answer to this question is that he was never really a good friend to begin with. **4** And they are rarely perfectly balanced – there is always one person who does more listening, or who needs more support, or who does things that annoy the other person. The real question here is about our expectations – what do we demand of a relationship?

Making it work

Expecting perfection in a relationship is always going to end in disappointment. **5** So we shouldn't demand of others something that we can't do ourselves. As soon as we accept that, we take the first step towards making things work in a relationship.

Our experience tells us that another key point is to learn to choose the right moment to say something, especially if it's negative. We are all human and it's natural that we get angry or feel hurt from time to time. **6** Something we say in anger cannot be taken back, so it's worth taking a deep breath and waiting for a better opportunity to sort things out. The same goes for criticism. Ask yourself what you want to achieve. **7** Is that even possible? Or is it better to change your attitude towards the situation?

Always remember that it takes two to have a relationship of any kind. Sometimes a problem will be the other person's fault – sometimes it will be our fault. But does it really matter who is to blame? Didn't we just say that everyone's human? We all make mistakes, so we really do need to learn to accept the other person for who they are. We might need to try a little harder to make the relationship work, but if the relationship is worth having, it's worth a little hard work.

3 exam practice

You are going to read a blog about relationship issues. Seven sentences have been removed from the blog. Choose from sentences A–H the one which fits each gap (1–7). There is one extra sentence which you do not need to use.

A But we all know that friendships are not as simple as that.
B However, it doesn't always help if we express these feelings straight away.
C This is perhaps not surprising, as we spend a great deal of our time with family members.
D All of these relationships have their own specific difficulties.
E Do you really want to change the other person?
F And, when he stopped to think about it, he saw that he was wrong.
G Nobody is perfect, and that includes us!
H No matter how much you have in common with someone, things can get in the way of a good friendship, and even end it.

4 Find words or phrases in the text or removed sentences which have a similar meaning to these words and phrases.

1 experience (paragraph 1)
2 arise; appear (paragraph 2)
3 contact (paragraph 3)
4 get angry with, and/or blame (paragraph 3)
5 share (eg an interest) (sentence H)
6 pausing (paragraph 7)
7 find an answer to a problem (paragraph 7)
8 responsible (paragraph 8)

WORK IT OUT!

Find these words and phrases in the text and underline them. Can you work out what they mean from the context?

saying • rough patches • typical • key
perfectly balanced • the same goes for

Have your say!

- Do you think many people would find a blog like this useful?
- What problems in relationships do you think are the most serious?
- Do you agree with the advice given in the blog? Can you add any suggestions of your own?

G Grammar 1

Present simple and past simple

Can one or both of these sentences contain the word *often*? Can one or both of these sentences refer to one specific occasion?

a *I go out with my friends.*
b *I went out with my friends.*

We use the present simple and the past simple:

- to show how often things happen.
  We never go out/went out during the week.
- for permanent situations.
  She lives/lived with her parents.
- for general truths and facts.
  Carl doesn't speak/didn't speak French.
- for states.
  Does Dana have/Did Dana have red hair?

We also use the present simple:

- for the future (in timetables).
  Term starts next Monday.
- for the future (in time clauses).
  I'll call you when I get back.

We also use the past simple:

- for single completed actions.
  I met our new neighbours yesterday.

Stative verbs

Stative verbs, such as *like, love, believe, see, appear, understand, know* are not normally used in continuous tenses because they don't describe actions.

☒ *I don't like the way you're talking to me.*
☒ *I am not liking the way you're talking to me.*

See *Grammar database 1* on page 174 for more information.

! Be careful!

Some verbs are stative with one meaning and non-stative with another meaning.

Stative: I **have** a lot of work to do at the moment.
Non-stative: They **are having** an argument at the moment.

1 **Look back at the blog on pages 6–7 and find an example of:**

- the present simple in the question form (paragraph 4).
- the emphatic present simple (paragraph 7).
- the past simple in the negative (paragraph 4).

2 **There are 10 mistakes with verb tenses and forms in this text. Find them and correct them.**

> My Sister
> Do you get on well with your sister? I get. My sister and I are best friends, even though Fiona's three years older than me. We do go out together almost every weekend, and we are always having fun. Fiona don't tease me or bully me. In fact, we've never had a serious argument! Of course, we aren't always agreeing about everything. Last Saturday, for example, Fiona wanted to go to the cinema, but I didn't fancied seeing a movie. It wasn't be a problem, though. While she and a couple of our friends were watching the film, I was going to an internet café and chatted online with some friends of mine in the USA. We all meet up afterwards and did went for a coffee. It's great – we have a very close but easygoing relationship.

3 **Use these verbs in the correct form to complete the sentences.**

go • know • meet • seem • get in • make • forget

1 Melina ____________ to invite Adam and he's really upset with her now!
2 Stan's girlfriend's train ____________ in half an hour so he's gone to pick her up from the station.
3 I ____________ my uncle and aunt who live in Germany for the first time recently.
4 Sheila ____________ lots of new friends at the party.
5 Dan and I ____________ out very often as we prefer to stay at home.
6 It's a shame we ____________ you were coming today – the kids would love to see you again.
7 Ollie ____________ to be annoyed with me for some reason at the moment.

4 **Write five questions you can ask someone about:**

a their family and friends.
b what they did last weekend.

5 **Ask your partner your questions. Now use your partner's answers to tell the class about him/her.**

! Be careful!

Who told you? = Someone told you something.
Who did you tell? = You told someone something.

Vocabulary

Feelings and situations

1 Make adjectives from these verbs and decide whether they describe feelings or situations.

bore • interest • excite • tire • please
scare • frighten • terrify • relax • annoy

Now use the adjectives to talk about the people you know.

2 Phrasal verbs

Use the correct form of these phrasal verbs about relationships to replace the words in bold. Be careful with word order.

bring up • grow up • let down
look after • put up with • take after

1 My parents **raised** me / ______________ to believe that family is the most important thing in the world.
2 As the kids **got older** / ______________ , it became easier to take them on public transport.
3 Simon **was just like** / ______________ his father. They were both mad about fishing.
4 I **took care of** / ______________ my neighbours' cat while they were on holiday.
5 I don't know how you **tolerated** / ______________ his rudeness for so long!
6 Diana really **disappointed** me / ______________. She'd promised to be there, but she didn't show up.

! Be careful!

Parents **bring up** children.
Children **grow up**.
Plants **grow**.

3 Word formation

Complete this table. Include all possible forms you can think of, including negative forms.

Noun	Verb	Adjective	Adverb
	help		
	relate		
friend	befriend		☒
	care		
	attract		
obedience			
	☒	honest	
	appear		
	☒	rude	
	☒	kind	
	☒	jealous	
	☒	nervous	

4 Confusable words

Choose the correct word to complete each sentence.

1 My mum gets so **nervous** / **annoyed** when I don't tidy my bedroom.
2 Freda's the most **sincere** / **honest** person I know. She never steals or tells lies.
3 I love being **alone** / **lonely** as long as I've got a good book to read.
4 That was so **kind** / **polite** of you to offer to help us move house.
5 We really **enjoyed** / **entertained** ourselves at the party.
6 The party was **funny** / **fun**. We danced all night!

5 Look at the incorrect answers in exercise 4. Why is each one incorrect?

6 Word patterns

Choose the correct word to complete each sentence.

1 Does your sister usually help you **at** / **with** your homework?
2 Why do adults always complain **for** / **about** what teenagers wear?
3 As a babysitter, I'm responsible **for** / **in** making sure the kids go to bed on time.
4 I don't approve **with** / **of** parents smacking their children.
5 Do you believe **about** / **in** love at first sight?
6 How can we prevent young people **from** / **for** getting into dangerous situations?
7 Your advice saved me **in** / **from** making a huge mistake!
8 Charlotte often borrows clothes **from** / **by** her older sister.

Listening

Starting point

Look at the pictures. Which people do you think are

- colleagues?
- acquaintances?
- friends?
- family members?
- strangers?
- neighbours?

Why do you think that?

1 1.02 **Look at the questions in exercise 2. Listen to a short excerpt from each of the situations 1–8. Which of the options might be wrong?**

EXAM EXPERT

How should you do the exam practice task?

a Choose an answer because it has a word you hear in the recording.

b Don't assume an answer is right just because it contains a word you hear in the recording.

2 1.03 exam practice

You will hear people talking in eight different situations. For questions 1–8, choose the best answer (A, B or C).

1 You hear two people talking. What is their relationship?
A colleagues **B** acquaintances **C** close friends

2 You hear this man talking about his daughter's boyfriend. What does the man think?
A He's looking forward to their engagement.
B He thinks his daughter should find someone better.
C He's not certain whether they will get married.

3 You hear this message from a friend on your answerphone. What does she ask you to do?
A buy an extra ticket
B put someone up for the night
C accompany her to a play

4 You hear two people talking about an exam. How does the woman feel?
A annoyed **B** nervous **C** jealous

5 You hear a girl describing her twin brother. In what way are they different?
A He's more sociable.
B He's more polite.
C He's more helpful.

6 You hear two people talking about their neighbour. What do they think about him?
A He's lonely. **B** He's selfish. **C** He's arrogant.

7 You hear two young people talking on a bus. What did their friend not do?
A invite someone to a party
B get permission for a party
C arrange music for a party

8 You hear a man talking about a childhood friend. What does he think?
A His friend wasted her opportunities.
B His friend had problems with schoolwork.
C His friend had problems making friends with people.

3 **What helped you choose your answers? Why were the other options wrong? Discuss your answers with the rest of the class.**

Have your say!

- How sociable are you?
- Do you make friends easily?

Speaking

Starting point

What's happening in the picture? How do you think the people feel?

1 1.04 **Listen to a candidate answering personal questions in an English exam. As you listen, match each question to the candidate's answer.**

1 Where are you from? ___
2 Do you like living there? ___
3 What kind of things do you like doing in your free time? ___
4 Are you still at school? ___
5 What do you want to do when you leave school? ___
6 How long have you been learning English? ___

2 1.05 **Listen to the questions and answers and answer these questions as you listen.**

1 Does the candidate always answer with complete sentences? Yes / No
2 Does the candidate say 'Well, …', 'Oh, …', and 'Umm …'? Yes / No
3 Does it sound like the candidate has carefully rehearsed these answers? Yes / No
4 Does the candidate use contractions like 'I'm', 'we've', etc? Yes / No
5 Are the candidate's answers too long? Yes / No
6 Are the candidate's answers too short? Yes / No
7 Do you think the candidate will get a good mark? Yes / No

EXAM EXPERT

How should you do the exam practice task?

a Give complete answers, but don't make a speech.
b Give one-word answers where possible.

See *Speaking database* on page 193.

3 exam practice

Imagine you are Candidate A. Make quick notes.

Now work in groups of four. Two of you are candidates, one is the interviewer and one person will give you a mark out of five.

Interlocutor: Candidate A, where are you from?
Candidate A: …
↓
Interlocutor: What's it like living there?
Candidate A: …
↓
Interlocutor: And, Candidate B, where are you from?
Candidate B: …
↓
Interlocutor: Do you like living there?
Candidate B: …
↓
Interlocutor: How do you usually spend your free time?
Candidate A: …
Interlocutor: And you, Candidate B?
Candidate B: …
↓
Interlocutor: How long have you been learning English?
Candidate B: …
Interlocutor: And you, Candidate A?
Candidate A: …
↓
Interlocutor: Are you both still in full-time education?
Candidate A: …
Candidate B: …
↓
Interlocutor: So, Candidate B, what are your plans for the future?
Candidate B: …
Interlocutor: And have you decided yet what you want to do, Candidate A?
Candidate A: …

MARK SCHEME

5 Excellent – gave complete answers, didn't sound like a speech
4 Very good – mainly complete answers, sounded a little rehearsed
3 Good – some hesitation, some answers too short
2 Not very good – answers too short, didn't sound natural
1 Weak – most answers too short, some answers not clear

Reading 2 1.06

Wordpower!

argument • depressed • incompatible
miserable • nothing in common • upset

Starting point

Look at the pictures. How do you think the people are feeling?

- What do friends quarrel about?
- What advice would you give to a teenager in these situations?

1 **Look at the title of the article you are going to read. What do you think the article is about? Who is it aimed at? Where might you find an article like this?**

2 **The article gives some advice. Quickly read paragraphs 2, 3 and 4 and make a list of Dos and Don'ts that the writer mentions.**

EXAM EXPERT

How should you do the exam practice task?

a Only ask yourself which answer is right, and why.

b Ask yourself which answers are wrong, and why, and which answer is right, and why.

Are you a heartbroken teenager?

If you've been let down by a boyfriend or girlfriend, you're probably hurting. It's not stupid or childish to feel like this.

Your boyfriend or girlfriend has told you they don't want to go out with you anymore. You feel rejected, alone, unwanted and miserable. You had thought that this relationship would last forever and now it's over. Let's be honest – it's a horrible feeling. Maybe the worst feeling you've ever felt. Perhaps you feel that life's not worth living and you'll never get over it. You probably feel that no-one has ever felt this way before.

It may sound impossible now, but you will get over it. It just takes time. And you're not alone – almost everyone goes through this at some point in their life. It's an important part of growing up and actually makes us stronger. What you mustn't do is think that you have failed. Remember: relationships aren't like exams.

If a friend came between you and your boyfriend or girlfriend and helped cause the relationship to end, you'll be dealing with feelings of betrayal as well. If your parents or friends disapproved of your relationship, you might also feel humiliated and embarrassed about discussing how you feel. These

3 exam practice

Read the text. For questions 1–7, choose the answer (A–D) which you think fits best according to the text.

1 According to the writer, heartbroken teenagers often feel that they
- **A** have wasted their time being in the relationship.
- **B** do not understand why the relationship came to an end.
- **C** are the only person who has experienced this situation.
- **D** should have been more honest about their feelings.

2 What does the writer say about a relationship ending?
- **A** It helps us develop emotionally.
- **B** It helps us understand that we can all fail.
- **C** It forces us to stop being childish.
- **D** It reminds us that relationships are not like tests.

3 A heartbroken teenager might have 'feelings of betrayal' (line 16) when
- **A** their parents did not want the relationship to succeed.
- **B** they don't feel able to talk about their feelings.
- **C** their partner was responsible for the relationship ending.
- **D** someone they trusted got involved in the relationship.

feelings are normal, but it does help to talk. Try talking to your parents and friends – they may be more sympathetic than you think. Ask your parents about their first relationships. The chances are they went through similar experiences.

Don't do anything impulsive. It might seem a good idea to go out and get a tattoo or your nose pierced, but you'll probably regret it in a few days. That doesn't mean you shouldn't treat yourself: how about buying some new clothes or getting a new hairstyle? Is there a film you've been wanting to see at the cinema for ages? Not sure whether to go to that party you'd been invited to? Go! And if you're worried that your ex-boyfriend or girlfriend might be there, let them see you can have a good time without them. That'll make you feel a lot better!

Sometimes couples who split up get back together and sometimes they don't. Don't sit around waiting for your ex to call to say they've made a big mistake and think you should start going out with each other again. The chances are that won't happen, but it's actually more likely to come about if you just get on with your life rather than sit at home waiting for the phone to ring. It may sound corny, but there are plenty more fish in the sea. You will – in time – find someone new. But don't be tempted to rush into another relationship. This is called going out with someone 'on the rebound'. This kind of relationship rarely works, as you're not together for the right reasons. Give it a little time before you start your next relationship.

Here's one other thing to remember. You've just experienced one of the most traumatic things that people experience. From now on, things can only get better. Each day, you'll feel slightly less unhappy. In a week, it will be bearable. In a month, you'll be able to laugh about it. In a year, it will all seem ancient history. You've got a lot of life ahead of you – look to the future and go out and enjoy yourself!

WORK IT OUT!

Find these words in the text and underline them. Can you work out what they mean from the context?

childish • sympathetic • traumatic • bearable • impulsive • miserable

4 What does the word 'That' (line 30) refer to?
- **A** regretting the impulsive behaviour
- **B** the advice not to do anything impulsive
- **C** the idea of doing something impulsive
- **D** treating yourself to something you want

5 How should heartbroken teenagers react if they see their former partner at a party?
- **A** They should be concerned about their former partner.
- **B** They should show that they are better off now.
- **C** They should make it clear that they can survive on their own.
- **D** They should see what their former partner is doing.

6 A relationship 'on the rebound' (line 58) is one
- **A** in which you fall in love very quickly.
- **B** which is never successful.
- **C** in which both partners have just finished a relationship.
- **D** which starts too soon after a previous relationship.

7 What point is the writer making in the final paragraph?
- **A** Humans are survivors.
- **B** We benefit from painful experiences.
- **C** We forget unpleasant experiences quickly.
- **D** Time will heal the pain.

4 Circle all the different feelings mentioned in the text.

5 Find words or phrases in the article which are similar in meaning to these words and phrases.

1 recover from (paragraph 1)
2 experiences (verb) (paragraph 2)
3 caused a disagreement or argument between (paragraph 3)
4 do something special for (paragraph 4)
5 happen (paragraph 5)

Have your say!

- Is there any advice you would give that is not in the article?
- Do you disagree with any of the advice in the article?
- Can an article like this help a heartbroken teenager?

G Grammar 2

Present perfect simple and past perfect simple

Your boyfriend or girlfriend ***has told*** *you …* (paragraph 1 line 1)

Did that happen in the past? Is it still relevant now? Do we know exactly when he or she told you?

You ***had thought*** *that this relationship would last forever …* (paragraph 1 line 3)

Why is it *had thought* and not *thought*?

We use	Present perfect simple	Past perfect simple
for actions and situations continuing …	… up to now. *I've been best friends with Julie for four years.*	… up to a moment in the past. *Julie and I had been best friends for four years when she moved to another town.*
for completed actions …	… at a time in the past which is not mentioned. *Has anyone ever broken your heart?*	… before a moment in the past. *I'd had an argument with Jake when I last saw you.*
for completed actions …	… where the important thing is the present result. *Moira and I have split up.*	… where the important thing is the result at a moment in the past. *I'd just split up with Moira so I was really upset.*

See *Grammar database 2* on pages 174–175 for more information.

1 **Make sentences saying what has happened.**

1 Tim's got a suntan.
2 There's a letter for you.
3 Hello! We're your new neighbours.

2 **Complete the second sentence so that it has a similar meaning to the first sentence, using the word given. You must use between two and five words, including the word given.**

1 I think they moved here six years ago. **lived**
I think ______________ six years.
2 We bought her birthday present a few days ago. **already**
We ______________ her birthday present.
3 The Taylors are on holiday in Australia at the moment. **have**
The Taylors ______________ Australia on holiday.
4 This will be Stacy's first trip to France. **never**
Stacy ______________ France before.
5 Eleni and Alan got engaged in April. **since**
Eleni and Alan ______________ April.
6 I haven't received a reply from Andy yet. **still**
Andy ______________ a reply.

3 **Make sentences using the past perfect simple. Use the words or phrases in bold.**

1 I moved to Canberra. Before that, I lived in Brisbane and Sydney. **before**
2 Charlotte heard the news. She immediately called Phil. **as soon as**
3 First I went to the supermarket. Then I went to the post office. **after**
4 We finished eating. Diane arrived. **when / already**
5 Diane arrived. Then Rick turned up. **when / only just**

4 **Make sentences using the past perfect simple to answer these questions.**

1 Why were Grant and Dave so happy?
2 Why was Tonya annoyed with Justine?
3 Why was Adam so tired?
4 Why did Frank do so badly in the exam?

! Be careful!

It's the first time **I've been** to Italy.
It was the first time **I'd been** to Italy.

Have your say!

- What have you always wanted to do but haven't done yet?
- Is there anything you've always wanted to buy?
- Think of one thing you've done recently for the very first time. Why hadn't you done it before?

Use of English

1 Read the text in exercise 2 quickly and answer these questions.

1 Apart from his acting, what is James Dean famous for?
2 How many films did he star in?
3 How old was he when he died?

2 exam practice

Read the text below and decide which answer (A, B, C or D) best fits each gap.

EXAM EXPERT

How should you do the exam practice task?

a Quickly read the text first to get a general idea of what it is about.
b Go straight to the questions to save time.

James Dean

If you ask anyone to (1) ____ a famous rebel, the chances are they will say James Dean. But who was James Dean, and was he really as rebellious as we believe?

James Dean was born in 1931 in Indiana, USA. His father was a dental technician. The family (2) ____ to Los Angeles in 1936, but Dean returned to Indiana after his mother died, where he was (3) ____ by his uncle and aunt. Dean was a bright and hard-working student, and was not particularly rebellious at school.

After returning to California, Dean joined an acting workshop, and was given minor roles in films, on stage and in TV commercials. In 1951 he went to New York to further his acting (4) ____ . Dean's acting (5) ____ was soon recognised, and he was asked to join the Actors Studio. As he wrote in a letter to his family in 1952: 'It is the best thing that can (6) ____ to an actor.' Television and theatre work followed, and Dean became highly (7) ____ within the industry.

James Dean starred in only three films, and had only been world-famous for just over a year when he was killed in a car (8) ____ in September 1955. It was his death at such a young (9) ____ , and the rebellious roles he played in the films *Rebel Without a Cause* and *East of Eden*, rather than his off-screen (10) ____ ,that have made him a legend. Like Marilyn Monroe, Elvis Presley and Frank Sinatra, James Dean is an icon of the 20th century.

EXAM EXPERT

How should you do the exam practice task?

a Don't think of it as a text, but as separate lines, with no connection to each other.
b Read the text through first and then look at it sentence by sentence.

	A	B	C	D
1	call	tell	name	repeat
2	located	removed	lived	moved
3	brought up	grown up	taken over	taken off
4	job	career	work	employment
5	qualification	talent	knowledge	recommendation
6	become	take place	occur	happen
7	loved	adored	respected	worshipped
8	accident	misfortune	disaster	hit
9	era	period	age	time
10	condition	behaviour	quality	performance

3 Look at each gap in the text in exercise 4. What kind of word is required for each gap?

4 exam practice

Read the text on the right. Use the word given in capitals at the end of some of the lines to form a word that fits in the gap in the same line. Write your answers IN CAPITAL LETTERS.

The Perfect Friend

Because (1) ____ is one of the few kinds of relationship we have **FRIEND**
control over, it is an (2) ____ area of research for sociologists. **INTEREST**
Many studies have been done into this kind of relationship.
Although we can't usually choose our (3) ____ or bosses or **RELATE**
(4) ____ , we can choose our friends. But how do we choose **TEACH**
them? Out of all the people we meet in our lives, why do some
become our friends, and why do we find some people's (5) ____ **PERSON**
more (6) ____ than others? It's not an easy question to answer, **ATTRACT**
because we are all looking for similar qualities in our friends,
such as (7) ____ , a good sense of humour, trustworthiness and **HONEST**
(8) ____ . However, what each of us means by 'a good sense of **KIND**
humour', for example, or what each of us thinks of as 'kind',
is (9) ____ . We are all unique in many ways, and so the **DIFFER**
perfect friend for one person may seem a little (10) ____ to **BORE**
someone else!

Writing: informal letter/email

Starting point

Imagine someone your age from another country was coming to stay with your family for a couple of weeks. What would you want to know about them before they arrived?

1 **Read this email and answer the questions below.**

write reply send

From: Sophie Needham
Sent: 3rd September
Subject: Re: Hi there!

Dear Angela,

Thanks for your email. I can't wait to meet you and your parents in August!

Well, we've obviously got a lot in common. I love tennis, too, although I'm probably not such a good player as you are. And I'm very glad you like pop music. I'm crazy about The Screamers! I also love swimming. Do you?

You asked if there was anything I wanted to do while I'm staying with you. As we both like tennis, we should definitely have a game and I'd love to go swimming. Will your parents let us go to a club? We're both 15, so it shouldn't be a problem, should it?

I've attached a picture so you can see what I look like. It was taken last summer on holiday.

Please write back soon. Can't wait to meet you!!!

Bye for now!
Sophie

1 Is the language formal or informal? Give examples.
2 What is the purpose of each paragraph?
3 What information did Angela give Sophie in her email?
4 What did Angela ask in her email?
5 What questions does Sophie ask in her email?
6 Which phrases and expressions in the letter are often used in informal emails?
7 What other ways are there of saying 'Bye for now!' at the end of the email?
8 Do you think Sophie and Angela will like each other when they meet? Why?

2 **Choose true (T) or false (F).**

1 We usually start letters/emails with *Dear* …, . T/F
2 In an email, you don't need to worry about correct grammar. T/F
3 Spelling is more important in an informal letter than an email. T/F
4 An informal email is the same as an informal letter. T/F

3 **It's often possible to say the same thing in different ways. Look at these sentences from the email in exercise 1, and write them in a different way.**

1 Thanks for your email.
Thanks a lot for your email!

2 I can't wait to meet you and your parents in August!
I'm really looking forward to meeting you and your mum and dad in August!

3 Well, we've obviously got a lot in common.
____

4 And I'm very glad you like pop music.
____

5 I'm crazy about The Screamers!
____

6 You asked if there was anything I wanted to do while I'm staying with you.
____

7 As we both like tennis, we should definitely have a game and I'd love to go swimming.
____

8 Please write back soon.
____

Plan ahead

1 exam practice: informal email

You are going to the UK for two weeks in the summer to study at a language school. While you are there, you will be staying with an English family called the Wilsons. Below is an email which Adam Wilson, who is 15 years old, has sent you.

Read Adam's email and the notes you have made. Then write a suitable reply.

never done it – would love to try!

write | reply | send

From: Adam Wilson
Sent: 6th September

Subject: Your visit

Hi, there! I'm Adam. I'm looking forward to your visit, and I wanted to say hello and ask you a couple of things.

First of all, a bit about me. I'm crazy about skateboarding and I love rock and pop music. I think my favourite band at the moment is the Kaiser Chiefs. Do you know them? What kind of things do you like doing and what music do you like?

My mum asked me to ask you if there's anything you particularly want to do while you're here. I guess you'll be busy at the language school during the day, but we can do things in the evenings and at weekends if you like. Let me know!

Bye for now!
Adam

basketball, cinema, computer games

same as you!

love to go to a castle. Any near???

EXAM EXPERT

How should you write an informal email?

a Don't use paragraphs and don't worry about grammar, spelling and punctuation because they are important in letters, not emails.

b Write your email in exactly the same way you write a letter, with paragraphs and correct grammar, spelling and punctuation.

See *Writing database* on page 199 for further information.

2 Before you write, answer these questions.

1. Will your email to Adam be formal or informal?
2. What questions did Adam ask you?
3. How many pieces of information do you have to include in your email?
4. What are they?
5. What other information about yourself could you include?
6. What other questions could you ask Adam?

3 For each of the notes next to Adam's email in the question in exercise 1, write one or two sentences which could be included in your email.

4 Complete *Writing Planner 1* on page 206.

5 Write your email in 120–150 words. You must use grammatically correct sentences with accurate spelling and punctuation in a style appropriate for the situation.

6 When you have written your email, make sure that you have:

- used informal language ☐
- referred to all the notes ☐
- added some other relevant information ☐
- at least four main paragraphs ☐
- referred to Adam's email in paragraph 1. ☐

2

Travelling

Wordpower!

adventure • enjoy yourself • excitement
freedom • get bored • keep you busy

Starting point

What do people look for in a holiday? Discuss the advantages and disadvantages of these different holidays.

- an activity holiday
- a beach holiday
- a camping holiday
- a family holiday
- a holiday with friends
- a package holiday
- a sightseeing tour

1 **Look at the text without reading it in detail. What kind of holiday did the writer go on?**

2 **Read the questions in exercise 3 and decide which of these statements is probably true. Explain why.**

1 The writer and his daughter met several different people and had a variety of things to do on holiday.
2 The holiday had limited activities and the writer met very few people there.

Reading 1 1.07

Cowboy fantasies on a ranch in Montana

Ian Henderson and his daughter try living on a working ranch in the Montana mountains.

Imagine you're a 12-year-old girl. Ponies and clothes are your favourite things. You're wearing your new cowboy boots, new jeans, a blue checked shirt and a real cowboy hat when a tall cowboy asks if you'd care to help him round up the ponies. If you're imagining it properly, you're about as happy as a 12-year-old girl can be.

I'd taken my daughter to The Ranch at Rock Creek, a 6,000-acre spread in Montana which opened to guests last year and may well be the ultimate place to live out your cowboy dreams, whatever your age.

I settled in to a proper Western-style saddle and rode out beside my daughter across Rock Creek. We followed a trail along the river before heading uphill towards the high forests. We were glad of our wide-brimmed hats until we reached the shade of the pine woods.

This is big, empty country where much of the American cultural identity was forged by tough explorers such as Lewis and Clark, the first white men through Montana. Tom McCombs told us tales of grizzly bears by a mountain stream as we ate our sandwiches. Together we'd tracked elk, found where a brown bear had been hunting for food and trailed a bobcat away from a kill.

These are people who know an awful lot about rodeo, fishing, shooting and the history of where they live, and are itching to share. On my first attempt at fly fishing, I managed to catch a trout, thanks to the help of Alex the fisherman. At the shooting range, Max coaxed my daughter from being gun-shy to shattering eight clay targets in a row.

It's hard to know what those early explorers would have made of the ranch's well-appointed spa, the swimming pool or the 'Mercantile', full of upmarket clothes where my daughter bought her cowboy boots. But they would have recognised most of the ingredients in chef Josh Drage's cooking – he spends a couple of days a week on the long Montana dirt roads, buying fresh meat and vegetables from the farms farther down the valley.

The ranch house is new but feels just like a home built of logs ought to. Downstairs there are crackling log fires, leather-covered sofas, guns and animal skins on the walls, baskets of homemade cookies and books about the history of the place. Everyone has their own mountain bike for their stay with

EXAM EXPERT

How should you do the exam practice task?

So that you can check your answers easily at the end of the exam, you should

a leave enough time to do the exercise again completely.

b underline the part of the text which you think gives you the answer.

the name of their room hung on it, and you're invited to borrow hats, coats and cowboy boots whenever you need them. Someone's paid attention to almost every detail.

There are other places to stay on the property that offer fewer people and more of the silent outdoors. Along the river are cabins with underfloor heating in the stone-built bathroom, furs on the bed and the soothing soundtrack of the creek outside. There are a couple of secluded family-sized ranch houses, and for real isolation there's Trapper Cabin, which comes with its own jeep to get you to breakfast.

When you're standing on the porch, coffee in hand, looking across the early mist on the river to mountains touched gold by the sun, the sheer beauty of Montana that struck Lewis and Clark stays with you. And somehow Rock Creek makes you feel as if you belong there. My daughter swears she will be back. As soon as she's old enough she's going to join Big Tom as an apprentice cowgirl.

3 exam practice

You are going to read a description of an unusual holiday. For questions 1–6, choose the answer (A–D) which you think fits best according to the text.

1 In the first paragraph, the writer wants to emphasise
- **A** that we need imagination when choosing a holiday.
- **B** the importance of taking the correct clothes on holiday.
- **C** how suitable the holiday was for his daughter.
- **D** his concern that his daughter is not very happy.

2 From the passage we understand that Lewis and Clark were
- **A** important historical figures.
- **B** friends of Tom McCombs.
- **C** bear hunters.
- **D** criminals.

3 What does the writer say about the staff at The Ranch?
- **A** They have been there all their lives.
- **B** They are better at fishing than shooting.
- **C** They are all learning new skills.
- **D** They are keen to pass on their knowledge.

4 What are the spa, the swimming pool and the 'Mercantile' examples of?
- **A** places to buy clothes
- **B** places where you can find Josh Drage's cooking
- **C** more modern additions to the area
- **D** things that have been there for years

5 People staying at The Ranch at Rock Creek
- **A** have a choice of accommodation.
- **B** always have the free use of a jeep.
- **C** have to follow a lot of rules.
- **D** sometimes have to sleep outside.

6 From the passage we can tell that the writer
- **A** enjoyed his stay more than his daughter did.
- **B** and his daughter both enjoyed their stay.
- **C** didn't enjoy himself as much as his daughter did.
- **D** and his daughter were a little disappointed with their stay.

WORK IT OUT!

Find these words in the text and underline them. Can you work out what they mean from the context?

checked • ultimate • saddle • itching to
crackling • isolation • swears • apprentice

4 Find words in the text which have a similar meaning to these words and phrases.

1 path or narrow road (paragraph 2)
2 small river (paragraph 3)
3 followed (paragraph 3)
4 low land between hills, often with rivers (paragraph 5)
5 simply constructed houses, usually made of wood (paragraph 7)
6 alone; with no other buildings or people near it (paragraph 7)
7 the part of a building outside the door (paragraph 8)
8 absolute; total (paragraph 8)

Have your say!

- Would you like to go on a holiday similar to the one in the passage? Why? / Why not?
- Some companies offer holidays where you can learn to do something, such as fishing, skiing, painting, etc. Is there anything you would like to learn while on holiday?
- Is it better to go on holiday with family or with friends? Why?

G Grammar 1

Continuous tenses

Is this sentence correct or incorrect? Explain why / why not.

We are going on holiday to a nearby island every summer.

The present continuous and past continuous tenses refer to:

- events happening at a particular moment.
  I can't come now. I'm doing my homework.
  When you called, I was having a bath.
- temporary situations or events.
  We're staying in a wonderful hotel.
  We were living in London for a few months last summer.
- changing and developing situations.
  This area is developing quickly because of tourism.
  By the late 60s, many Spanish resorts were growing very quickly.
- the future (or the future in the past).
  John and Matt are going to France this summer.
  I was worried because we were having a test the next day.

The present perfect continuous and past perfect continuous tenses refer to:

- events continuing up to a particular moment or stopping just before it.
  I'm tired because I've been running.
  We were annoyed because the hotel manager had been lying to us.

See *Grammar database 3* on page 175 for more information.

1 Find this sentence in the text on page 18 and underline it. Underline other examples of verbs used in a continuous tense. Why has the writer used a continuous tense in each case?

You're wearing your new cowboy boots, new jeans, a blue checked shirt and a real cowboy hat …

2 Use the verbs in brackets in the correct form to complete this text.

Dear Jack,

We (1) ____________ (**travel**) for five days now – 21 left to go! Interrailing is great fun – you must try it sometime. We (2) ____________ (**get**) the train down through France to Italy, which is where we are now. We (3) ____________ (**stay**) in youth hostels and (4) ____________ (**meet**) some really cool people so far. Italian boys are very friendly! At the moment, we (5) ____________ (**sit**) in a café in Florence and Kate (6) ____________ (**practise**) her Italian on the waiter. I don't think he's impressed!
We (7) ____________ (**walk**) around the town last night when we (8) ____________ (**see**) a great seafood restaurant. We (9) ____________ (**go**) there tonight for dinner. Should be fun!

Wish you were here,

Jill

3 Correct these sentences.

1 I had been learning English for about seven years now.
2 When we were on holiday, I was swimming every day.
3 We go on holiday tomorrow.
4 Have you ever been visiting any countries outside Europe?
5 I had a shower when the hotel manager rang so I couldn't answer the phone.

4 Use these verbs in the correct form to complete the text. Some of the verbs may be used more than once.

get • help • offer • meet • seem • take • ring • be
go • work • see • enjoy • arrive • stay • show

Last summer, I (1) ____________ as a waitress in a holiday resort when I (2) ____________ a great opportunity. I (3) ____________ for about a month when I (4) ____________ an ad for holiday reps. The interviews (5) ____________ place the next day, so I (6) ____________ the number in the ad to ask where I had to go. They (7) ____________ to like me when they (8) ____________ me and they (9) ____________ me a job. A group of tourists (10) ____________ that weekend so I had to learn lots of things about the resort very quickly. When the group (11) ____________, I was ready. None of them (12) ____________ there before so I (13) ____________ them all find the hotels they (14) ____________ in and then (15) ____________ them the sights. I really (16) ____________ meeting people from different countries and helping them. I (17) ____________ back again this summer. It's a great job!

Vocabulary

Travel and tourism

1 **Put these words and phrases into the following categories: Ship, Plane and Train.**

express • carriage • ferry • platform • cruise
departure lounge • cabin • ticket inspector • flight
delayed • sail • runway • voyage • land • rails

Now use some of these words and phrases to talk about the pictures.

2 Word formation

Complete each sentence using a form of the word in bold.

1 My family runs a hotel, so I'm thinking of studying ______________ at college. **tour**
2 I find travelling backwards on trains really ______________ , so I always sit facing forward. **comfort**
3 We regret to announce that the ______________ of flight SA 121 has been delayed. **arrive**
4 Teenagers seem to prefer places like Australia to ______________ countries when they go on holiday. **Europe**
5 They made an ______________ at the airport saying that our flight had been delayed. **announce**
6 In these days of mass travel, the ______________ between Europe and America seems to be much shorter. **distant**
7 There are a number of reasons for the ______________ in the popularity of Iceland as a holiday destination. **grow**
8 I've always believed that travel ______________ the mind. **broad**
9 It's interesting to see what ______________ differences exist in different parts of the world. **culture**
10 The ______________ of many Pacific islands rely on the money that visitors spend. **inhabit**

3 **Note down as many other forms of the words in exercise 2 as you can. Don't forget to include any negative forms.**

4 Phrasal verbs

Complete each phrasal verb to do with travel and tourism using the words in the box. One of the words will be used more than once.

back • in • down • off • up

1 As the plane took ______________ , I looked out of the window and saw the city getting smaller.
2 We're leaving for Spain on the 3rd May and we get ______________ on the 10th.
3 We all went to the airport to see Grandma ______________ .
4 The train started to speed ______________ as we left the station.
5 Have you got the tickets and passports? We need to check ______________ at the desk before we look round the airport shops.
6 The ferry slowed ______________ as we got closer to the shore.

5 **Now match each phrasal verb from exercise 4 to the correct definition. There is one definition you do not need to use.**

a go to an airport, station, etc, to watch someone leave
b return from holiday
c decrease your speed
d leave the ground
e present your ticket, passport and luggage at an airport
f go on holiday
g increase speed

6 Collocations

Choose the correct word or phrase to complete these collocations.

1 a school **excursion** / **trip**
2 a business **trip** / **journey**
3 time **off** / **out** work
4 a **round-the-world** / **round-the-earth** trip
5 the holiday of a **life** / **lifetime**
6 a **five-star** / **five-mark** hotel
7 **holidaymakers** / **holidaydoers**

Listening

Wordpower!

harbour • quay • attractions • Opera House

Starting point

What place is shown in the photograph?
What do you know about this city?

1 **Look at the first question from exercise 4. Write a phrase that could be used to complete the sentence.**

To see the harbour, you should ...

2 **1.08 Listen to this extract and check your answer to exercise 1.**

3 **Look at the other sentences and try to complete them. Write your guesses here.**

2 ______
3 ______
4 ______
5 ______
6 ______
7 ______
8 ______
9 ______
10 ______

4 1.09 exam practice

You will hear part of a radio talk about Sydney, Australia. For questions 1–10, complete the sentences.

To see the harbour, you should **1** ______

The bridge connects North Sydney and **2** ______

You get the best view from the bridge by crossing **3** ______

Some people say that the Opera House was designed to look like a **4** ______

You can get in for less if you are **5** ______

The Botanical Gardens have plants from all over **6** ______

In Sydney there are people who come from **7** ______

From Sydney, Bondi Beach is located **8** ______

Swimmers on Bondi Beach are watched by **9** ______

Because of the view, Taronga Zoo is a good place for **10** ______

EXAM EXPERT

How should you do the exam practice task?

a Try to write as much as you can to fill each gap.

b Write a word or short phrase to fill each gap.

5 **Look at the correct answers to exercise 4 and your guesses in exercise 3. Choose the sentence that is true for you and compare with a partner.**

All my guesses were very close. ☐
Most of my guesses were close. ☐
Some of my guesses were close. ☐
A few of my guesses were fairly close. ☐
None of my guesses were close at all. ☐

Have your say!

- Would you like to visit Australia?
- Would you like to visit an English-speaking country?
- Which place in the world would you most like to visit?

Speaking

Starting point

A photograph captures a moment in time. What tense do we use to describe the things happening in the photograph at that moment?

A photograph often shows an example of something. What tense do we use to talk about it in general?

1 **Look at photos A and B in exercise 6 and decide which photo each comment refers to. Some comments may refer to both photos.**

On this holiday …

- you might need an experienced tour guide.
- you might get bored with doing the same thing.
- the crowds might get on your nerves.
- you can get away from your everyday life.
- good weather is important.

2 **Make a note of one other point you can make about each photo.**

3 **Choose the correct words to complete these sentences.**

1 A safari is **more** / **very** exciting than a beach holiday.
2 A beach holiday is **little** / **less** expensive than a safari.
3 On **the** / **this** one hand, a beach holiday is relaxing.
4 On the **next** / **other** hand, it can be quite boring.
5 I like beach holidays, **however** / **although** I would prefer to go on safari.
6 A safari is exciting, **whereas** / **despite** a beach holiday isn't.

4 🎧 **1.10** **Listen to this extract from an interview. Which of these things does Candidate A (Katherine) do?**

a She describes the first photograph in detail and then the second photograph. Then she talks about her ideal holiday.

b She briefly describes the photos and then talks about what similar or different ideas they both show. Then she talks about her own preferences.

5 🎧 **1.11** **Now listen to another extract. What does Candidate B (Nick) do?**

a He gives a brief response to the question, showing that he was listening to what Katherine said.

b He does the same thing as Katherine, comparing the photographs before talking about his preferences.

EXAM EXPERT

How should you do the exam practice task?

When you are asked to compare photographs you should

a talk about the main similarities and differences between the photographs.

b describe each photograph in as much detail as you can, making sure you mention everything you can see.

See *Speaking database* on page 193.

6 **exam practice**

Here are two photographs showing different kinds of holiday. I'd like you to compare them and tell us which holiday you would prefer to go on. You have about one minute to do this, so don't worry if I interrupt you.

Which holiday would you prefer to go on?

A

B

Candidate B, would you like to go camping?

Reading 2 1.12

Wordpower!

hiking • mountains • skiing • winter resort

Starting point

Do you ever go on holiday at times of the year other than the summer?

1 **Read the article about holidays quickly and match each place to the correct activity.**

1	Australia	a	dog sledding
2	Chamonix	b	cross-country skiing
3	Jukkasjärvi	c	sunbathing
4	Alaska	d	staying in an ice hotel

2 **Read the fifth paragraph of the text and decide if these statements are true (T) or false (F).**

1 The hotel is very comfortable. T/F
2 You can visit the hotel at any time of year. T/F
3 The temperature at the hotel is usually below freezing. T/F
4 Guests often complain about the extreme cold. T/F

EXAM EXPERT

How should you do the exam practice task?

a Ignore little words like *this*, *it* and *that* and concentrate on other key words.

b Look carefully at words like *this*, *it* and *that* and try to decide what they refer to.

3 **exam practice**

You are going to read an article about winter holidays. Seven sentences have been removed from the article. Choose from sentences A–H the one which fits each gap (1–7). There is one extra sentence which you do not need to use.

A There, you can watch concerts, reindeer races and even a winter fashion show.
B From Europe to America, there are some great breaks if you like your fun served cold.
C These demand a little more than your average downhill run, so you need to be physically fit.
D There's nothing like the feeling of freedom as you are pulled along the ground through spectacular frozen scenery.
E It has become world-famous and attracts guests from all four corners of the globe.
F Increasingly, though, people are looking for an extra challenge.
G He or she has more choice of winter destinations than ever before.
H This means that a winter break can often be much cheaper than getting away in the summer.

4 **Find words in the text to match these definitions.**

1 sides of mountains
2 form of mountain transport
3 comfort and quality
4 area
5 large, slow-moving mass of ice
6 putting clothes, etc, in suitcases

WORK IT OUT!

Find these words in the text and underline them. Can you work out what they mean from the context?

bound to • flock • appeal • constructed
thermal • carved • rink • huskies • vow

Have your say!

- Which of these winter resorts would you prefer to visit?
- What other kinds of winter holiday can you think of?

Winter Wonderland

Carol Whitely looks at what's available if you're planning on going away this winter.

Holidays are a summer thing, right? Sun, sand and sea? Perhaps, but the traditional view of a holiday as a time to lounge by the pool and work on your tan is rapidly changing.

More and more of us are getting away from it all in the winter. And we're not just disappearing to find distant sun, although places like Australia are very popular winter destinations. **1** ____ Whether it's action or relaxation you need, you're bound to find something to suit you.

Traditionally, a winter holiday has meant skiing, and we still flock in our thousands to the slopes. **2** ____ One of the more popular places to find it is in Chamonix, in the French Alps, at the foot of Mont Blanc. The 1924 Winter Olympics® were held there, and each year visitors from all over the world come to enjoy the spectacular scenery and winter sports.

Chamonix caters for beginners, but the real appeal of this resort is the cross-country ski trails and ski mountaineering. **3** ____ One of the highest cable cars in Europe will take you far above the town and you can spend a few hours getting back down at breakneck speed!

If you prefer a quieter life, treat yourself to a bit of luxury at Jukkasjarvi, a village in northern Swedish Lapland. Here, every November, 100 tons of ice and 300 tons of snow become the Ice Hotel. It is constructed in November and lasts until the end of April, when the spring sun finally wins the battle and the hotel melts. **4** ____ There are around 300 rooms with beds of ice covered with reindeer skins and thermal sleeping bags. They'll keep you warm in temperatures between -4°C and -9°C, although it has been known to drop to -25°. Just don't ask the management to turn up the heating or you might find yourself without a room!
The hotel includes an ice-art exhibition, an ice sauna and a cinema with a huge screen carved out of, you've guessed it, ice. If that's not enough for you, there's lots to do in the surrounding region, including skating at the local rink, and it's a short trip to the town of Kiruna for the Snow Festival. **5** ____ Learn something about the local Sami culture and find out what it's really like to spend your life in the snow.

When you've had enough relaxation, take the daredevil in you on a winter wilderness adventure. Fly into Anchorage, Alaska, for the start of your dog sledding tour. You'll travel out of town by car and by snowmobile to where your adventure begins. You'll be shown how to handle your huskies by an experienced guide and then you'll set off together into the great unknown. **6** ____ Spending the night in comfortable log cabins and the day exploring the vast icy glaciers with your team of dogs, you'll vow never to waste a week lying on a beach again!

Today's winter wanderer has so many options that there's no excuse for just sitting at home staring at grey skies. **7** ____ More and more companies are realising that we don't all want to spend Christmas eating turkey and sitting watching the TV. Find out more from your local travel agent and get packing!

G Grammar 2

so, such, too, enough

Which of these words completes the sentence?

so/such/too/enough

It was ________ a wonderful holiday that I can't wait to go back there.

… so …	adjective adverb *many/much* + noun	… that …
… such …	a(n) + adjective + singular noun adjective + plural noun *a lot of* + noun	… that …
… too …	adjective adverb *many/much* + noun	+ for and/or full infinitive
… (not) enough …	noun	+ for and/or full infinitive
… (not) …	adjective adverb	enough + for and/or full infinitive

See *Grammar database 4* on page 176 for more information.

used to, would, be/get used to G

Does this sentence refer to the past, the present or the future?

I am used to staying in hotels.

used to

- past states
  We used to own a holiday home around here.
- past habits
  We used to come here on holiday every year when I was a child.

would

- past habits
  We would come here on holiday every year when I was a child.

be/get used to

- situations that are now familiar or no longer strange
  It was strange staying in a hotel at first, but I soon got used to it.

See *Grammar database 5* on page 176 for more information.

1 Complete these sentences using *so, such, too* or *enough*.

1 The resort was ___ busy that I didn't really enjoy our holiday.
2 It was a bit ___ hot for us to spend the day on the beach.
3 We got to the hotel ___ early that our room hadn't been cleaned.
4 There wasn't ___ time for us to see all the sights.
5 It's ___ a nice day that we should go to the beach.
6 The neighbours were ___ friendly people that we went out for dinner with them.

2 Rewrite each pair of sentences as one sentence using the word given in bold.

1 The resort was very big. We got lost a few times. **so**
2 The hotel was very expensive. We couldn't stay there. **too**
3 Australia is a long way away. It takes a day to get there. **such**
4 The weather's quite bad. We aren't going to the beach. **enough**
5 The hotel was very dirty. We decided to stay somewhere else. **such**
6 The hotel was very dirty. We decided to stay somewhere else. **so**
7 I'm young. My mum won't let me go on holiday with my friends. **too**

! Be careful!

⊠ Our holiday was too enjoyable.

⊠ Our holiday was really/very enjoyable.

3 Choose the correct word or phrase.

1 When I was younger, we ___ have a tent and we went camping a lot.
a used to **b** would **c** were used to
2 Our neighbours ___ sometimes come with us on holiday.
a were used to **b** would **c** got used to
3 My mum ___ going away on business trips.
a is used to **b** used to **c** would
4 I ___ like beach holidays, but now I find them a little boring.
a am used to **b** would **c** used to
5 ___ you use to go to summer camp when you were a boy, Dad?
a Did **b** Would **c** Were

4 Make sentences about you and your family using *used to* and *would*.

Use of English

1 **Read the text in exercise 2. Decide whether these statements are true (T) or false (F).**

1 Ellen MacArthur started sailing when she was eight. T/F
2 She bought her first boat when she was 18. T/F
3 She was the first woman to sail alone around Britain. T/F
4 She communicates with people while she is at sea. T/F

2 exam practice

Read the text below and think of the word which best fits each gap. Use only one word in each gap. Write your answers IN CAPITAL LETTERS.

EXAM EXPERT

How should you do the exam practice task?

When you have chosen words to fill all the gaps, you should

a read the whole text again quickly to see if it makes sense.

b go straight on to the next task.

ELLEN MACARTHUR

Imagine you're sailing at night with a hurricane blowing, thousands of miles from the nearest dry land. Suddenly, there is (1) __________ loud noise and your sail breaks free. Your only chance (2) __________ survival is to climb the mast in the darkness and fix (3) __________, even though you haven't slept for two days. It's all just part of a typical working day for Ellen MacArthur, the first woman to sail alone (4) __________ the world.

Ellen (5) __________ to go on sailing trips (6) __________ holiday with her aunt when she was eight years old and she fell in love with it. She (7) __________ go sailing whenever she could and she saved all her pocket money until finally she (8) __________ able to buy her first boat, an 8ft dinghy. When she was 18, Ellen sailed alone around the coast of Britain, (9) __________ was a great achievement. Now, as well as (10) __________ a famous sailor, she is an author and her stories of her adventures at sea are very popular. She likes (11) __________ keep in touch with people while she's in the middle of the ocean, (12) __________ search for her online and you might be able to send her an email!

3 exam practice

Complete the second sentence so that it has a similar meaning to the first sentence using the word given. Do not change the word given. You must use between two and five words, including the word given. Write the missing words IN CAPITAL LETTERS.

EXAM EXPERT

How should you do the exam practice task?

When you do the sentence transformations, you should

a change the word you are given to the correct grammatical form.

b never change the word you are given.

1 We began visiting this resort 10 years ago.
been
We ________________ this resort for 10 years.

2 My dad didn't go abroad until he was 30.
when
My dad ________________ first went abroad.

3 Our holiday was so terrible that we came back early.
such
We ________________ that we came back early.

4 We finally succeeded in finding a hotel with a pool.
managed
We finally ________________ a hotel with a pool.

5 We would go to the mountains every summer when I was a child.
used
We ________________ to the mountains every summer when I was a child.

6 The sea was too cold to go swimming.
enough
The sea ________________ to go swimming.

7 I don't find it strange to stay in luxury hotels.
staying
I ________________ in luxury hotels.

8 They announced that our flight had been delayed.
made
They ________________ saying that our flight had been delayed.

Writing: review

Starting point

Compare the hotels in these photos.
Have you ever stayed in a hotel? What was it like?
What facilities and services do hotels often provide? Make a list.

1 **Look at this exam question and read the review. Then read the statements 1–6 and choose true (T) or false (F).**

Your school produces a monthly English-language magazine. You have been asked to visit a local hotel and to write a review for the magazine.

Write your review in 120–180 words in an appropriate style.

The Seaview Hotel

The Seaview Hotel is a large building in the centre of town. From the outside, it looks impressive, but the atmosphere inside is warm and friendly. The owners have recently modernised the hotel, but I was pleased that they'd managed to keep some of the traditional character of this lovely old building.

The hotel has 120 rooms, all of which have bathrooms. The room I stayed in was very clean and bright. There are also three luxury suites for guests who can afford a little more comfort. Other facilities include a gym and a sauna. The gym is well equipped and is free for guests to use. Unfortunately, the sauna was closed when I visited.

The level of service was very high. A problem I had with the lights in my room was soon solved. In fact, all the staff seemed very happy to deal with any request – even when I asked for hot chocolate at four in the morning!

In conclusion, the Seaview is a lovely hotel which is perfect for anyone who wants to visit the town.

1 A review is a description of your experience of a hotel, a restaurant, a film, etc. T/F
2 You should never give your own opinion in a review. T/F
3 A review is a very informal piece of writing. T/F
4 A review is a very formal piece of writing. T/F
5 This review tries to say everything possible about the hotel. T/F
6 This review chooses a few key areas to talk about (appearance, facilities, service). T/F

2 **Tick (☒) what else the writer could have written about in this review.**

- the cost of staying at the hotel ☐
- the meals provided at the hotel ☐
- the car he/she drove to the hotel in ☐
- how close the hotel is to other places ☐
- why they should change the name ☐

3 **Imagine the writer wants to add a paragraph to the review about prices at the hotel. Look at this table. What is the cheapest option and what is the most expensive option?**

THE SEAVIEW HOTEL

All prices given are per room per night, breakfast included.

	Mar 1st–May 31st	June 1st–Aug 31st	Sept 1st–Feb 28th
single room	€90	€110	€80
double room	€105	€120	€100
suite	€135	€150	€120

4 **Imagine the writer of the review in exercise 1 wants to add a paragraph about the cost of staying at the Seaview Hotel. Using the information in exercise 3, write a paragraph (40–50 words) to go between the second and third paragraphs of the review.**

Plan ahead

1 exam practice: review

You recently saw this notice in an English-language magazine called *World Traveller*.

> **Hotel Reviews**
>
> We'd like to invite all our readers to write a review of a hotel. It might be a hotel you've stayed in, or one near where you live. It might be the best hotel you know – or it might be the worst! Send us your reviews. The best review each month wins a prize of a two-night stay at a hotel of your choice.

Write your review.

EXAM EXPERT

How should you write a review?

a Try to describe every feature of the thing you are reviewing, without missing anything out.

b Describe the key features that you think your readers will be most interested in.

See *Writing database* on page 198 for further information.

2 Use your imagination to answer these questions.

1 Are you going to write about a real hotel or an imaginary one? What's it called?
2 Is it a hotel you have stayed at or one near where you live?
3 What three adjectives best describe this hotel?
4 What does the hotel look like?
5 Where is the hotel?
6 What are the two best things about the hotel?
7 What are the two worst things about the hotel?
8 Which of the following are you going to talk about?
- ☐ location
- ☐ service
- ☐ facilities
- ☐ cost
- ☐ meals

9 Is your review going to be generally positive, generally negative or balanced?
10 Who would enjoy staying at this hotel?

3 Put these adjectives you might use in a review into the correct category.

awful • disappointing • dreadful • fantastic
great • impressive • lovely • marvellous
shocking • terrible • wonderful

Positive	Negative

4 Complete *Writing Planner 2* on page 206.

5 Write your review in 120–180 words in an appropriate style.

6 When you have written your review, make sure that you have:

- checked your spelling and grammar ☐
- used paragraphs ☐
- written about a few key features of the hotel ☐
- used some good adjectives ☐
- written a review of the right length. ☐

Check your progress! Units 1–2

1 Use a word from the box to complete each sentence.

carriage • resort • destination • arrival
cruise • brochure • cabin • platform

1 We were very disappointed when we got there. The hotel had looked so much nicer in the ______________ .
2 Bella and Derek are going on a(n) ______________ round the Indian Ocean in the summer.
3 The train leaves at half past three, so I'll meet you on the ______________ at about quarter past.
4 We are pleased to announce the ______________ of flight BA 635 from Barcelona.
5 The coach stops in Tamworth, but its final ______________ is Birmingham.
6 We had a tiny ______________ right at the bottom of the ship.
7 Blackpool is a well-known holiday ______________ in the north-west of England.
8 I had to walk up the train with my heavy suitcase because I'd got into the wrong ______________ .

8 marks

2 Write one word in each gap to complete the sentences.

1 Could you ______________ me up outside the supermarket at half past four?
2 I love watching planes speed down the runway, ______________ off and disappear into the distance.
3 We have to ______________ in before we can go through to the departure lounge.
4 Adrian and Kelly have been ______________ out with each other for over a year.
5 I don't know how Kelly ______________ up with Adrian – he's so selfish!
6 Could you ______________ after my hamster while I'm away next weekend?
7 Denise was ______________ up on a farm, so she knows a lot about tractors.
8 Tim and Ed are going on holiday next Tuesday. Shall we go to the airport to ______________ them off?
9 If we leave here at six, we won't ______________ back home before midnight.
10 I can't believe Doug ______________ you down. He's usually so trustworthy.

10 marks

3 Complete the second sentence so that it has a similar meaning to the first sentence, using the word given. Do not change the word given. You must use between two and five words, including the word given.

1 I'd moved there in 2009.
living
I ______________ three years in 2012.
2 There were so many people on the train that we had to stand.
such
There were ______________ on the train that we had to stand.
3 You're too young to have a girlfriend!
enough
You're ______________ to have a girlfriend!
4 I last had a holiday in June.
since
I have ______________ June.
5 Were you naughty when you were a child?
use
When you were a child, ______________ naughty?
6 I still find sharing a flat strange.
got
I still ______________ sharing a flat.
7 We finally managed to persuade them to put us on a later flight.
succeeded
We finally ______________ them to put us on a later flight.
8 I was so bored in the lesson that I fell asleep!
such
It ______________ that I fell asleep!
9 I wouldn't tolerate her treating you like that!
put
I don't know how ______________ her treating you like that!

18 marks

4 Read the text below. Use the word given in capitals at the end of each line to form a word that fits in the space in the same line.

Jerry

Jerry is a bully and has one of the most (1) ____________ personalities	ATTRACT
of anyone I know. He's totally (2) ____________ – he never does what	OBEY
his parents or teachers tell him to do, he's (3) ____________ (he's always	HONEST
telling lies), and I try to keep my (4) ____________ from him as much as	DISTANT
possible. (5) ____________ , he's my brother, so that's not always easy!	FORTUNE
It's strange having a (6) ____________ whom everyone dislikes. It makes	RELATE
me feel (7) ____________ at school, because sometimes people think I	COMFORT
must be just like him, but in fact I'm completely (8) ____________ .	DIFFER
I hope as Jerry grows older he'll realise how important (9) ____________	FRIEND
is and he'll stop being so (10) ____________ to everyone. One thing is	KIND
sure – he'll never get a girlfriend until he changes his ways!	

10 marks

5 Match. There is one letter you do not need to use.

1 holidaymaker ___
2 acquaintance ___
3 colleague ___
4 stranger ___
5 rep ___
6 adolescent ___

a someone you know, but not very well
b someone you do not know at all
c someone on vacation
d someone who is almost an adult
e someone who works for a holiday company
f someone from another country
g someone you work with

6 marks

6 Write one word in each gap to complete the sentences.

1 Why don't you borrow some money ____________ your brother?
2 My mum's never approved ____________ me having an earring.
3 I don't believe ____________ ghosts.
4 Can you help me ____________ this exercise? I don't really understand it.
5 The room's not very clean. Do you think we should complain to the manager ____________ it?
6 Carl offered to drive us, so that saved us ____________ having to take the train.
7 A technical fault prevented the bus ____________ leaving on time.
8 I'm responsible ____________ dealing with any complaints our guests have.

8 marks

Total: 60 marks

3

Technology

Wordpower!

app • domestic appliance • download
gaming • mobile device • search engine

Starting point

In which areas of your life is technology important?
How long do you spend online each week?
Which computer programs or services do you use most?

1 **Say which of the two statements below you agree with most, giving reasons. Consider the use of technology in some of these tasks:**

shopping • solving mathematical problems
writing essays • doing housework
learning languages • making music
finding information • communication

1 I'm totally in favour of technology. Computers and labour-saving devices can help us do things more quickly – leaving us free to do more important things. Intelligent devices and things like smartphones are the future.
2 The more we let technology interfere in our lives, the more we move away from a natural existence. Technology and computers can help us do nearly everything but it is not always a good thing. We need to learn to do things, and to think, for ourselves.

2 **Read the text quickly and answer the following questions.**

1 Which aspects of technology are talked about?
2 In which area has technology been unsuccessful up to now?
3 Is the writer for or against technology? How do we know?

Reading 1 1.13

www.teenblog.co.uk/3000-blog

Home | On the move

Looking Forward 3000

The future is here already, they say, and in the field of technology it's certainly true that events are unfolding fast. Here at Looking Forward 3000, we take pride in our ability to bring you the best articles and the most up-to-date information about technological developments. In fact, next month, we will have been predicting the future with great accuracy for exactly a decade. Happy Birthday to us, then, and to celebrate, we're offering some fantastic prizes in our competition (click here, or on the link below to enter). On this website, you'll be able to find the latest developments in technology, as well as our predictions for what is going to happen in the near (and not so near) future.
In our feature article you can find out why computers cannot yet translate successfully from one language to another. We've grown used to being able to have what we want at the touch of a button or the click of a mouse. We have online dictionaries with huge databases, so why can't we use them to translate perfectly into other languages? As *Paul McIntyre* explains, English has many words with similar meanings. Consider *chair* and *seat* – how would a piece of software know which one is best suited to the context? And how would a machine know how to translate *Take a seat!* as *Sit down!* rather than *Pick up a seat!*, for instance, or, in American English, *He got the chair*, meaning *He was sentenced to death in the electric chair*? Of course, we can also use these two words as verbs (as in *to chair a meeting*, or *The restaurant seats 200 people*). For all the millions of pounds and many years spent on development, we still need people to translate for us if we don't want to end up with mistakes in the text because a machine does it literally, word for word. Yet we will have better machine translation in the future, and experts are making progress using a similar method to predictive text on mobile phones.
Read more …
There's also a new article on technology in the home. *Jeremy Fletcher* looks into intelligent labour-saving devices, including the Smart Manager fridge, made by LG. For around €2,000, you can take a step into the future with this home appliance. What

Ladies and gentlemen | Greenery

3 exam practice

Read the text and decide if each statement is true (T), false (F) or not stated (NS).

1 The website is just over 10 years old.
2 English is more difficult than other languages for computers to translate.
3 Text message software is helping improve machine translation.
4 One way to communicate with the Smart Manager fridge is to talk to it.

In the home | Eye in the sky

you do is scan the bar codes of your shopping (or your receipt) before you put the items in the fridge. There's a handy scanner on the door to help you to do this. Alternatively, you can describe the item using the fridge's built-in voice-recognition technology or scan the receipt with a smartphone and send the information to the fridge that way. The computer in the fridge will then monitor your food and add things to an online shopping list before you run out. If you prefer to do your shopping the old-fashioned way, you can communicate with your fridge using a smartphone app while you're in the supermarket, so you can find out exactly what you need. By the way, the Smart Manager will also notify you on your smartphone if you've accidentally left the fridge door open. It even suggests recipes for you, based on the ingredients inside and any other information you provide it with, such as if you are on a diet or you have food allergies. The LCD screen on the door tells you exactly what to do to follow the recipe. The fridge can also switch the oven on for you (as long as it's an LG Smart Oven). Think these modern devices might suit your lifestyle? Want to get information on your TV screen about what your washing machine is doing at this very moment? Like the idea of a vacuum cleaner that cleans the house ready for you when you come home? There's probably a smart device just for you.
Read more…
And, of course, in the gadgets section, you can find out what we'll all be buying next year, as well as what's hot in the market right now. There's plenty to choose from, including the latest generation of tablets and readers, robust helmet-mounted cameras for extreme sports enthusiasts, internet radios and TVs, incredible mobile devices and other must-have items.
Read more…

Browse our archives

SUBSCRIBE TO THE MAGAZINE VERSION – CLICK HERE

Click here for details of our LF3000 Birthday Competition. Hurry, the competition closes in 12 days

i-learn

5 The Smart Manager can tell you when your fridge needs cleaning.
6 Recipes produced by the Smart Manager take into account what you can and can't eat.
7 The Smart Manager fridge is able to communicate with other kitchen appliances.
8 None of the gadgets mentioned are available to buy yet.

4 Find words and phrases in the text to replace the words and phrases in italics in these sentences.

1 We expect lots of interesting *changes* in the next few years.
2 If you *press the mouse button* on this word, it takes you to the main article.
3 This is the *program* that I use most.
4 When sending text messages, I use *the program that guesses the word you are writing.*
5 In the supermarket, they *pass a special machine over* items to find the price.
6 In the future, all computers might work with *a program that allows you to speak directly to them.*
7 The cameras outside help you *watch* what is happening in the garden.
8 I spend all my money on *small electronic devices.*

WORK IT OUT!

Find these words in the text and underline them. Can you work out what they mean from the context?

handy • notify • robust • take pride in • unfolding

Have your say!

- Do you think a machine will ever be able to translate languages as well as a person? Why? / Why not?
- Do you like the idea of an intelligent fridge? Why? / Why not?
- Are you interested in gadgets? Which ones do you own? What would you like to own?

EXAM EXPERT

How should you do the exam practice task?

a Remember that 'false' means that contradictory information is given in the text, whereas 'not stated' means that we don't know from the text if it's true or not.

b Remember that 'false' means that contradictory information is given in the text, whereas 'not stated' means that it's true, but not mentioned.

G Grammar 1

The future

Which different forms of the verb *open* can be used to fill this gap?

The Museum of Technology ______________ next week.

There are a number of different ways of expressing the future in English.

will: *No-one will use cash in a hundred years' time.*

be going to: *We're all going to have implants in our teeth in the future.*

present continuous: *We're getting our new computer next week.*

present simple: *My physics exam is next Tuesday.*

modals: *Do you think humans might live on other planets in the future?*

shall: *Shall we download and watch a film tonight?*

Remember that *will* is often more formal than *be going to*.
Remember that there is often more than one way of expressing the same idea.

See *Grammar database 6* on pages 176–177 for more information.

1 What difference do these phrases make to the meaning of the sentence?

What sources of energy ______________ to power cars in the future?

1 will we use
2 are we going to use
3 are we using
4 could we use
5 might we use
6 shall we use

2 Complete the sentences using *will*, *shall*, *be going to*, present continuous or present simple.

1 Hurry up! ______________ (**the bus / leave**) in a few minutes.
2 One day, ______________ (**everyone / have**) solar-powered cars which can fly.
3 I know! ______________ (**I / buy**) Tim some rechargeable batteries for his birthday.
4 When I grow up, ______________ (**I / be**) an inventor.
5 ______________ (**we / help**) you set up your new computer?
6 I'm sorry, but ______________ (**I / lend**) you any more CDs.

3 Use the words in brackets and the verbs in the box in an appropriate tense to complete this text. You can use the verbs more than once.

be • do • drive • find • implant
get • introduce • leave • live

I wonder what (1) ______________ (**the world**) like in 10 years' time. (2) ______________ (**I**) 24 years old. (3) ______________ (**I**) school by then, of course, and (4) ______________ (**I / probably**) my degree. (5) ______________ (**I / still**) in the same town? I've no idea! Maybe. If I am, (6) ______________ (**I**) here for 20 years. That's a long time! (7) ______________ (**I**) a job? I hope so! I don't think (8) ______________ (**robots**) everything. (9) ______________ (**there / still**) jobs, won't there? A lot of new technology (10) ______________ between now and then, of course. Perhaps (11) ______________ (**we / all**) around in electric cars, and (12) ______________ (**there / not**) so much pollution. I don't think (13) ______________ (**doctors**) mobile phones in everyone's teeth by then. That sounds like a silly idea to me.

Future perfect simple and future continuous G

Circle the correct form of the verb to complete this sentence.

*By the end of today, **I'll send / I'll have sent / I'll have been sending / I'll be sending over** 25 emails.*

We use the future perfect simple to show that something is completed at some time between now and a point in the future.

We'll have stopped using notes and coins by the year 2030.

We use the future perfect continuous to show that an action is in progress up to a point in the future.

By the year 2032, we'll have been doing our shopping with digital money for about two years.

We use the future continuous to talk about an action in progress at a point in the future or habits or repeated actions at a point in the future.

This time next week, we'll be visiting Phil's laboratory again.

In a hundred years' time, we'll all be flying around in flying cars.

See *Grammar database 6* on page 177 for more information.

V Vocabulary

Technology

1 Match each of the words or phrases with an item in the picture.

bulb ___	microwave ___
clock ___	plug ___
cooker ___	socket ___
dishwasher ___	toasted sandwich maker ___
freezer ___	vacuum cleaner ___
fridge ___	washing machine ___
kettle ___	

2 Phrasal verbs

Use the correct form of these phrasal verbs about technology to complete the sentences.

break down • come on • come up with
cut off • get through • look into • put in

1 If you ____________ an appliance like a washing machine, you install it.
2 If you ____________ a new idea for a product, you have an idea.
3 If you ____________ a new development, you investigate it.
4 If a car ____________, it stops working.
5 If your electricity is ____________, it is disconnected.
6 If you can't ____________ to someone on the phone, you can't connect to them.
7 If something has ____________, it has developed or improved.

3 Word formation

Complete each phrase using a form of the word in bold.

1 a great ____________ **achieve**
2 highly ____________ **benefit**
3 a ____________ person **create**
4 a recent ____________ **develop**
5 an important ____________ **discover**
6 a major ____________ in something **improve**
7 a useful ____________ **invent**
8 bring out a new ____________ **produce**
9 a ____________ fact **science**
10 a ____________ to a problem **solve**

4 Find other forms of the words in exercise 3. Put them into four categories: Verb, Person, Other nouns and Adjectives.

5 Confusable words

Choose the correct word to complete each sentence.

1 Do you know who **discovered / invented** the biro?
2 The company is currently **developing / inventing** a more powerful microchip.
3 Scientists do **investigation / research**.
4 The car **engine / machine** caught fire and we had to call the fire brigade!
5 We've bought a small **mobile / portable** TV to take on holiday with us.
6 Kitchen **tools / appliances**, such as fridges and washing machines, have become much cheaper recently.
7 Tents and rucksacks are examples of camping **equipment / tools**.

! Be careful!

invent = create something that didn't exist before

discover = find or find out something for the first time

6 Word patterns

Use these words to complete the sentences. You will use one of the words twice.

with • in • to • on • for • of

1 Dana's not very interested ___ computer games.
2 I'm really looking forward ___ starting our science project next week.
3 Al's involved ___ making sure our equipment is safe to use.
4 Our whole way of life depends ___ us having electricity and oil.
5 Are you going to apply ___ a job in a factory?
6 Let me know when you've finished ___ the newspaper.
7 The article was full ___ useful advice on how to take good photos.

Listening

Wordpower!

digital camera • electric typewriter • wheel
obsolete • old-fashioned • groundbreaking

Starting point

Do the things in the pictures have anything in common? In what ways are they different?

1 **Match each word or phrase with its definition.**

1 agriculture	a not wasting time, money or energy
2 catalogue	b completely changing the way something is done
3 efficient	c the work or study of farming
4 handy	d situations, images and sounds that seem real but are in fact produced by computers
5 revolutionary	e a book or magazine which advertises products you can buy
6 virtual reality	f a small tool or piece of equipment
7 gadget	g useful

2 **Read the opinions in exercise 3 and choose one. Try to express that opinion in your own words. Ask your partner to guess which it is. Now guess which opinion your partner is expressing. Which words helped you and your partner guess correctly?**

3 1.14 exam practice

You will hear five people talking about technology. For questions 1–5, choose which of the opinions (A–F) each speaker expresses. Use the letters only once. There is one extra letter which you do not need to use.

A Some modern technology is unnecessary.
B It is impossible to survive without technology.
C Technology is nothing new.
D Expect major technological advances in the near future.
E Don't expect major technological advances in the near future.
F It's amazing what you can buy these days.

Speaker 1 ______
Speaker 2 ______
Speaker 3 ______
Speaker 4 ______
Speaker 5 ______

EXAM EXPERT

How should you do the exam practice task?

a Note down key words and phrases you hear as you listen the first time.
b Do not make any notes because this is listening and not writing.

4 **Did you note down any key words and phrases? What were they? Compare your notes with the rest of the class.**

Have your say!

- Look back at the different opinions in exercise 3.
- Which do you agree/disagree with?

Speaking

Wordpower!

air conditioner • drinks machine
MP3 player • laptop

Starting point

Choose one of the items in the pictures in exercise 4. Do not say what it is, but describe what it looks like and what we use it for. Ask your partner to guess which item you are describing.

1 **Look at the pictures again. Make notes about how each item could be used by a youth club.**

2 **Tick (☒) the phrases that are correct. Use the correct phrases to suggest an item. Say how it could be used by the youth club.**

1 … would be useful as it's …
2 … would be useful because it's …
3 … would be useful since it's …
4 What do you think about getting the … ?
5 What are you thinking about getting the … ?
6 What about getting … ?
7 How about getting … ?
8 I'm liking to suggest getting …
9 I'd like to suggest getting …
10 I'd like to suggest to get …
11 Wouldn't it be better to get … ?

3 **1.15** **Listen to two candidates doing exercise 4. Is there anything they could have done better?**

4 exam practice

I'd like you to imagine that your local youth club has been awarded some money by the local council. Here are some of the things that you are considering buying.

Talk to each other about how useful these things would be for the youth club. Then, decide on the two items that you should definitely buy. You have about three minutes for this.

- How useful would these things be for the youth club?
- Which two should you definitely buy?

5 exam practice

Does technology make our lives easier?

Do we rely too much on technology?

What technological advances can you see happening in your lifetime?

Would you like to be an inventor? What kind of things would you invent?

How do you think the world will change over the next 50 years?

EXAM EXPERT

How should you do the exam practice task?

a Always wait for the other candidate to speak first, and always agree with him/her.
b Try to have a natural conversation with the other candidate.

EXAM EXPERT

How should you do the exam practice task?

a Remember that it's fine to say you're not sure about something.
b Never say you're not sure about something because it makes you sound stupid.

See *Speaking database* on page 193.

Reading 2 1.16

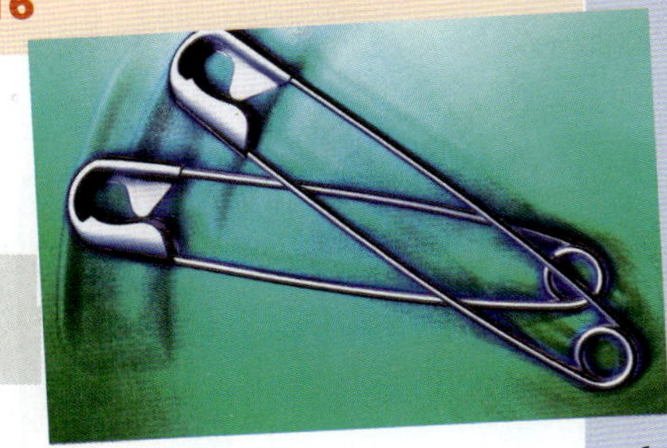

Wordpower!

ice-cream cone • safety pin
tin opener • correction fluid

Starting point

What do we use each of the items in the Wordpower! box for? When do you think they were invented?

1 **Read the article quickly and find information to complete the table. If the information is not given in the article, put a cross in the box.**

	Inventor(s)	Date(s) invented	Place(s) invented
Safety pin			
Ice-cream cone			
Correction fluid			
Tin opener			

2 exam practice

You are going to read a magazine article about some inventions. For questions 1–15, choose from the inventions (A–D). The inventions may be chosen more than once.

In which of the paragraphs does the writer state the following?

1 The inventor had a famous son. ___
2 The inventor had not been in the country long. ___
3 Someone else became rich because of the invention. ___
4 Not everyone was interested in the invention at first. ___
5 The inventor made and sold this product in his/her spare time. ___
6 This was not the inventor's first invention. ___
7 Members of the public never used the first version. ___
8 The inventor was not very skilled at his/her job. ___
9 Two people came up with the idea separately. ___
10 A change in production resulted in the creation of a new product. ___
11 He/She quickly adapted an existing product. ___
12 It's surprising that this wasn't invented earlier. ___
13 The inventor had borrowed some money. ___
14 The invention eventually led to great wealth for the inventor. ___
15 The inventor got an idea from another culture. ___

A The Safety Pin

Walter Hunt had come up with numerous other inventions before he created the safety pin in 1849. None of them, however, had made him any money! Owing 15 dollars to a friend, he decided to invent something new to make enough to pay back the debt. He took a piece of wire, coiled it in the centre, shielded one end and – hey presto – he'd created the world's first safety pin. He took out a patent on his invention, sold the rights to it for 400 dollars, paid his friend back and had 385 dollars to spare. Then he watched his latest brainwave go on to become a million dollar earner for someone else!

B The Ice-Cream Cone

The first ice-cream cone was produced in New York in 1896 by Italo Marchiony, who had emigrated from Italy only a few years before. He was granted a patent in December 1903. As with many great inventions, a similar creation was independently introduced – in 1904 by Charles Menches. He was selling ice cream – in dishes, like all ice-cream sellers at the time – at the St Louis World Fair. So many people were ordering ice cream that he ran out of dishes. He looked

EXAM EXPERT

How should you do the exam practice task?

a Read the text very slowly and carefully from start to finish before you look at the questions.

b Skim read the text first. Then, for each question, scan the text from the beginning until you find the answer.

Where did they come from?

Angela Stewart looks at four everyday items we take for granted and asks 'Where did they come from?'

around, and saw a Syrian man selling a Middle Eastern dessert called 'Zalabia', a wafer-like pastry sold with syrup. 'Give me Zalabia,' cried Menches. He rolled up the Zalabia into a cone, scooped his ice cream onto the top and the second ice-cream cone was born!

C Correction Fluid

You know that white stuff you paint on paper to cover mistakes? It was originally called 'Mistake Out' and was the invention of Bette Nesmith Graham. After her divorce, she realised she would have to find a job to support herself and her son, so in 1951 she became a typist. Unfortunately, she was not a particularly good one, and soon recognised the need for a white paint which could be used to cover all her mistakes. Using her kitchen and garage as a laboratory and factory, she gradually developed a product that other secretaries and office workers began to buy. While continuing to work as a secretary, she educated herself in business methods and promotion. Bette offered 'Mistake Out' to IBM, who turned it down. Undeterred, she changed the name to 'Liquid Paper' and continued to sell it from home for the next 17 years. In 1979, 'Liquid Paper' was bought by Gillette for $47.5 million plus royalties! Incidentally, Bette was also the mother of Mike Nesmith, a member of the well-known sixties pop group *The Monkees*.

D The Tin Opener

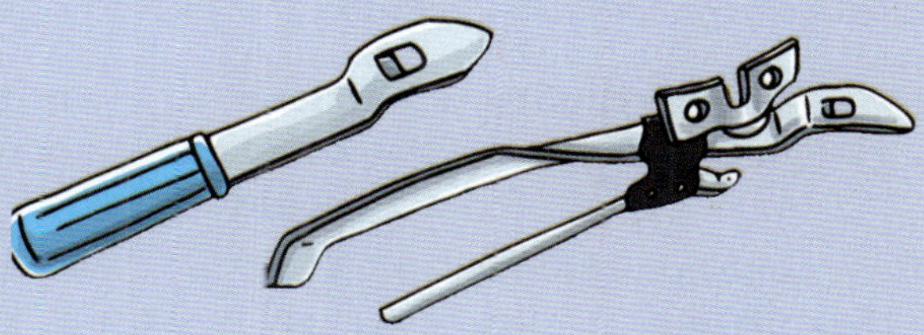

Strangely enough, the first practical tin opener was developed more than 40 years after the metal tin was introduced. Tinned food was developed for the British Navy in 1813. Made of solid iron, the tins usually weighed more than the food they held! Although the inventor, Peter Durand, successfully figured out how to seal food into tins, he gave little thought as to how to get it out again. The instructions read: 'Cut round the top with a chisel and hammer.' It was only when steel tins were brought out that the tin opener was invented. The first was devised by Ezra Warner in 1858. This type never left the shop, as a shop assistant opened all tins before they were taken away! The more modern tin opener, with a cutting wheel, was invented by William Lyman in 1870. Pull-open tins, which do not need a tin opener at all, were introduced in 1966.

3 Find words or phrases in the article which are similar in meaning to these words and phrases.

1 don't think about (subtitle)
2 lots of (paragraph A)
3 suddenly (paragraph A)
4 given, allowed to have (paragraph B)
5 slowly, step by step (paragraph C)
6 unrelated to the subject (paragraph C)
7 solved the problem (paragraph D)
8 close (so the air can't get in or out) (paragraph D)

WORK IT OUT!

Find these words in the text and underline them. Can you work out what they mean from the context?

debt • brainwave • emigrated
undeterred • chisel • ran out of

Have your say!

- How important were each of these inventions?
- How different would the modern world be if they hadn't been invented?

Grammar 2

Articles

Which box in the table below should each of these sentences be put into?

The digital camera I bought is great!
I'm going to get a digital camera.
The digital camera has changed the nature of photography.
Digital cameras are still quite expensive.

	singular countable nouns	plural countable nouns	uncountable nouns
a(n)	**one non-specific thing:** *I haven't got **a** computer.* If the next word begins with a vowel sound, use ***an***: *I haven't got **an** umbrella.*	☒	☒
the	**one specific thing:** *This is **the** computer which I told you about.* **general group or category:** ***The** tin opener is a great invention.*	**several specific things:** *These are **the** CDs I told you about.*	**specific:** ***The** technology in this equipment is very advanced.*
no article		**generally:** *Cars cause pollution.*	**generally:** *Technology is nothing new.*

See *Grammar database 7* on pages 177–178 for more information.

1 **Look at these phrases from the article on pages 38–39 and answer the questions.**

… more than 40 years after the metal tin was introduced.
1 Is this one specific tin or metal tins generally?
… a member of the … pop group …
2 Is this one specific pop group or pop groups generally?

2 **There are 10 mistakes with articles in this paragraph. Find them and correct them.**

The Jason Tarbuck, a inventor from UK, has come up with an unique way to prevent the people from locking themselves out of their houses. Invention, called the LockSafe, uses the small electronic sensor on a door lock to check that key is outside the door before it locks. A sensor detects an infrared light beam from the key or key chain.

! Be careful!

She's at school. (as a student or teacher)
She's at the school. (as a visitor)

Time clauses

Choose the correct form of the verb to complete this sentence.

I want to be an astronaut when I will grow / grow up.

After certain time words and phrases, we use a present tense (present simple, present continuous, present perfect) even though we are referring to the future.

when: *I'll buy a computer when I have enough money.*

as soon as: *Send me a text message as soon as you arrive.*

before: *I'll turn off the lights before I leave.*

after: *Can you lend me that DVD after you've watched it?*

until/till: *I'll wait until you get online.*

while: *I'll think of you while you're doing your science exam.*

See *Grammar database 8* on page 178 for more information.

3 **Join these sentences using the word or phrase in bold.**

1 The price of smartphones will come down soon. Then my brother will buy one. **when**
2 I'll finish the science report. Then I'll hand it in immediately. **as soon as**
3 You'll fall asleep. After that, the doctors will start the operation. **before**
4 You can't use your bank card at the moment. The bank will send you a PIN, and then you can use it. **until**
5 I'm going to watch that movie tonight on TV. I'll record it for you at the same time. **while**

4 **Complete these sentences about you.**

1 As soon as I … later today, …
2 Before I … tonight, …
3 I won't … until I …
4 When I … tomorrow, …
5 While I … this evening, …

Use of English

1 **Read the text in exercise 2 quickly and decide if these statements are true (T) or false (F).**

1. The text mentions how we use power today. T/F
2. The text describes a new way of getting power. T/F
3. The text says some people already have wireless electricity. T/F

EXAM EXPERT

How should you do the exam practice task?

- **a** Only look at two words on each side of each gap because they always tell you what the missing word is.
- **b** Look carefully at all the words in a sentence because clues to the missing word could appear anywhere.

2 exam practice

Read the text below and think of the word which best fits each gap. Use only one word in each gap. Write your answers IN CAPITAL LETTERS.

Wireless electricity

All of us in the developed world use electricity every day in many different ways. As (1) ____________ as we walk into a room we turn on lights without even thinking about it. We expect that when we flick a switch, the power (2) ____________ be there any time of the night or day and if for any reason our power is cut (3) ____________ , it creates major problems. Today's homes are full (4) ____________ electrical sockets and every day millions of us plug our mobile phones, laptops and PDAs in to charge (5) ____________ batteries. This could become a thing of the past, though, if scientists succeed (6) ____________ developing wireless electricity. Think of Wi-fi. Until quite recently, all computers connected to (7) ____________ internet had to be connected to a phone line. Today, many computers are capable of using (8) ____________ wireless connection, giving the computer user much (9) ____________ freedom. Researchers want to do the same with electricity. In the future, instead of plugging your mobile into the wall, you'll be able to charge it simply (10) ____________ leaving it near the power supply in your home. We can all (11) ____________ forward to a day when the idea of connecting a TV to a hole in the wall will seem very old-fashioned. (12) ____________ then, we'll all just have to keep plugging things in.

3 **Look at the gaps in exercise 4 and decide what kind of word (noun, adjective, etc) is required for each gap.**

4 exam practice

Read the text below. Use the word given in capitals at the end of some of the lines to form a word that fits in the gap in the same line. Write your answers IN CAPITAL LETTERS.

EXAM EXPERT

How should you do the exam practice task?

- **a** Don't worry too much about spelling because you get a mark if it's nearly right.
- **b** Be very careful with your spelling because if you make one spelling mistake, it's wrong.

The Modern Kitchen

Thomas Edison knew his new (1) ___ , the light bulb, **INVENT**
would be (2) ___ , but it's unlikely that he realised quite **REVOLUTION**
how much we would come to rely on this new source
of power. For example, the (3) ___ of electricity has **INTRODUCE**
completely changed the kitchen. The modern kitchen is
overflowing with electrical (4) ___ . We boil our water with **APPLY**
electric kettles, cook on electric cookers and put our dirty
dishes in the (5) ___ . It's hard to imagine how we would **DISH**
survive without all this (6) ___ . Before electricity, people **EQUIP**
spent much longer preparing food. These days, for a busy
parent whose kids are hungry, the simplest (7) ___ is to **SOLVE**
take some (8) ___ food out of the freezer and pop it in **FREEZE**
the microwave. It might not always be the healthiest option, but at least it's quick. That's
rather an (9) ___ on having to cook a meal from scratch. It's been particularly **IMPROVE**
(10) ___ for women – no longer do they have to stay all day chained to the cooker. **BENEFIT**

Writing: article

Starting point

Look at the pictures. How much do we depend on the technology shown?
What are some of the drawbacks of relying on technology?

1 **Read this article and underline any of the drawbacks you mentioned.**

Why I'm not a fan of modern technology

Are you worried about how much we rely on technology? I am, and the situation's getting worse every year.

Technology makes us lazy. I've got friends in my class who can't do simple maths – they have to use a calculator just to work out six times seven! And many teenagers I know would rather spend their free time in front of their computer than meet their friends. That's not healthy! What's more, ____ .

What will life be like in a hundred years? Will everyone be unemployed because robots will be doing all the jobs? Will the environment be completely polluted? Will ____? I think that's a possibility, and it's frightening.

Technology is here to stay, and some of it is very beneficial, but we have to be careful. We should use technology to make our lives easier, not let it destroy our way of life.

2 **Read the article again and answer these questions.**

1 Does the writer use
- contractions (*I've*, *I'll*, etc)?
- formal expressions like *Moreover*, *Furthermore*, etc?
- very formal, semi-formal, or very informal language?

2 Find two examples that the writer gives to illustrate a point.

3 Find an expression that means the same as *Moreover*.

4 Why does the writer ask questions in the article?

5 Where do you think you would find an article like this?
   a) in a scientific journal
   b) in a magazine for teenagers
   c) in a physics textbook

6 If the article appeared in either of the other two options, how would it be different?

3 **Complete the unfinished sentences in paragraphs 2 and 3 using your own words and ideas. Make sure you use the right style.**

Have your say!

- Do you agree with the opinions of the writer in the article?

Plan ahead

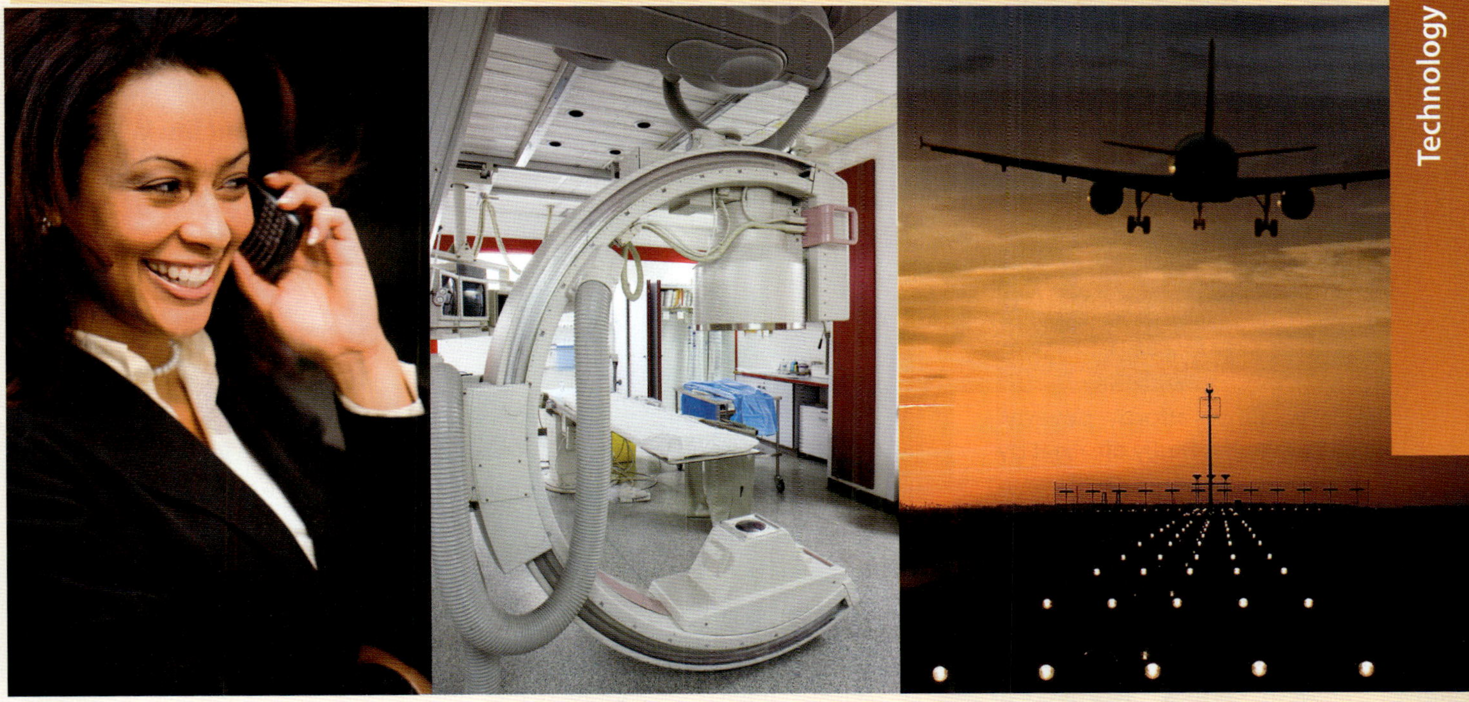

1 exam practice: article

Your school magazine is running a series of articles under the title 'Why I'm a fan of modern technology'. Write an article to appear in the series expressing your opinion.

> **EXAM EXPERT**
>
> **How should you write an article?**
>
> **a** Look at who the readers of your article will be, and choose the appropriate level of formality.
>
> **b** Be as formal as you can to impress the person marking your paper.
>
> See *Writing database* on page 194 for further information.

2 Answer these questions.

1 Who is going to read your article?
2 Should it be very formal?
3 Should you have an introductory paragraph?
4 Should you give some examples to support your opinion?
5 Should you come to a conclusion at the end?

3 Make a list in note form of general benefits of modern technology. Next to each point in your list, note down an example. Discuss these with the class.

General benefit	Example
helps us communicate	*if stuck in traffic – can call on your mobile*

4 Complete *Writing Planner 3* on page 207.

5 Write your article in 120–180 words in an appropriate style.

6 When you have written your article, make sure that you have:

- written the title of the article at the top ☐
- used semi-formal language ☐
- followed your paragraph plan ☐
- given some examples ☐
- tried to interest the reader ☐
- checked your spelling and grammar. ☐

4

Money

Wordpower!

wealthy • afford • poverty
well off • badly off • get by

Starting point

Compare these two photographs of different people. Describe what you think their lives are like.

1 **Read the title and subtitle of the article on page 45. What is it about?**

2 **Read the article quickly and find what kind of business each person runs.**

1 Marc Maiffret
2 Mike Becker
3 Andy Wolf
4 Robert Tuchman
5 John Christakos

Reading 1 1.17

3 exam practice

You are going to read an article from a magazine about business. For questions 1–15, choose from the people (A–E). The people may be chosen more than once. When more than one answer is required, these may be given in any order.

A MARC MAIFFRET
B MIKE BECKER
C ANDY WOLF
D ROBERT TUCHMAN
E JOHN CHRISTAKOS

Which of the people mention the following?

I like making money out of something I love doing.	1 ___	2 ___	
You should learn from how other companies do things.	3 ___		
Most people don't try to benefit from their ideas.	4 ___		
You may have to learn new skills.	5 ___		
You shouldn't follow all the advice you are given.	6 ___	7 ___	
I didn't get the right experience before I started.	8 ___		
Young people have to work harder to be successful.	9 ___		
It's important to have a clear idea of your aims.	10 ___	11 ___	12 ___
You need to allow time for enjoying yourself.	13 ___		
I found a new way to do something.	14 ___		
You shouldn't give up if you fail.	15 ___		

EXAM EXPERT

How should you do the exam practice task?

When you find words or phrases in the text which have a similar meaning to words or phrases in the questions you should

a choose that paragraph/person as the correct answer.
b read the relevant sentences very carefully before choosing your answer.

4 **Find these words in the text. Match them to the correct definitions.**

1 fortune	**a** put money into a business
2 set up	**b** customers
3 invested	**c** businessmen/women
4 company	**d** start (a business)
5 product	**e** a business
6 clients	**f** large amount of money
7 cheap	**g** what a business sells
8 entrepreneurs	**h** inexpensive

Making a million

Ready to take your first steps down the road to independence? Then take the advice of these young millionaires all under 30. They know what it takes to succeed.

Marc Maiffret was once a 17 year old who hated going to school and turned to hacking out of boredom. Now 21, he has made a fortune out of computer security. 'The thing I'm happy about is that my biggest passion in life is something that actually makes a good business,' says Maiffret. So what advice does Marc have for young people? 'Be ready to work a lot. If you're younger, it is harder to impress people. You'd better be ready to make work your only focus and know what you want to achieve. You've still got to have fun and make time for that, but it takes a lot of hard work and a lot of dedication,' he says.

Rather than going high tech, **Mike Becker** went in the opposite direction. As a teenager, he collected toys and items from his childhood. 'I knew there were people like me out there so I set up a cool little business based on what I love,' he says. Becker decided to bring back the bobblehead (a plastic toy that you wear on your head) and invested his savings of $35,000 in his business. His company now makes around $2 million a year. 'Be very clear about what it is you're selling. Ask yourself whether there is a market for it. Be prepared to extend your range of abilities,' Becker advises. 'Everyone comes across a good idea in their life, but they seldom do anything about it. It's really about putting things into practice.'

The good idea that **Andy Wolf** came up with was the snowskate. 'If you snowboard,' he says, 'you are surrounded by snow and you can't do skateboard tricks. I wanted to do both, so I came up with the snowskate. It's like a snowboard you don't tie to your feet.' His product is becoming so popular that mountain resorts are starting to build snowskate parks. His advice? 'There are definitely set ideas on how you should run a business. Not all those things are right. Believe in yourself and don't give up. You have to have a plan and stick to it.'

Sport has made **Robert Tuchman** well off, but he started with nothing. After university, he couldn't find a job in television, so he worked in advertising. 'What companies really wanted was to take their clients to sporting events. I established a business to do that. We now make around $10 million a year. If you want to be successful, you've got to go for it. Don't ever let anyone say it can't be done. If it doesn't work the first time, give it another try and another try, until you find a way to make it work.'

John Christakos and his business partners couldn't afford designer furniture when they were students so they decided to produce their own. They all studied business and knew that there was a large market for cheap but stylish furniture. Their business is now worth about $3 million a year. When asked for his advice to young entrepreneurs, John says: 'Work for other small companies in other fields. I never did that, so we discovered problems and solutions for the first time. If you were thinking of going into business on your own, you'd learn a lot from the right kind of experience.'

So, whatever your interests are, if you want to make a million, the opportunities are there. Every billionaire has to start somewhere!

WORK IT OUT!

Find these words and phrases in the text and underline them. Can you work out what they mean from the context?

hacking • dedication • savings • seldom
give up • go for it • billionaire

Have your say!

- What are the possible problems of being very wealthy?
- Would you like to be extremely rich?

G Grammar 1

Conditionals (1): zero, first, second

Does this sentence refer to the past or the present?

If I had more money, I would buy another CD.

zero conditional

if + a present tense + a present tense

used for general or scientific truths

If you have your own business, you work very hard.

first conditional

if + present tense + *will* (or other modal) + bare infinitive

if + present tense + imperative

used for real or likely situations

If you are having problems, your bank manager will try to help.

If you are having problems, speak to your bank manager.

second conditional

if + past (simple or continuous) + *would* (or other modal) + bare infinitive

used for impossible, unlikely or hypothetical situations

If I were you, I would set up my own business.

See *Grammar database 9* on pages 178–179 for more information.

1 Find this sentence in the article on page 45 and underline it.

If you're younger, it is harder to impress people.

Find another five conditional sentences and underline them. Decide whether each one is a zero, first or second conditional.

2 Choose the correct word or phrase to complete each sentence.

1 If I had enough money, I **will** / **would** buy a new computer.
2 **We'll** / **We'd** get there before the shops close if we hurry up.
3 I always buy clothes in the latest style, if I **can** / **could** afford it.
4 If you don't have the receipt, they **won't** / **wouldn't** give you your money back.
5 I always **spend** / **would spend** too much money if I **went** / **go** shopping.

3 Use these prompts to write sentences using *if*.

1 I/be/you/I/ask my parents for more pocket money
2 you/win/the lottery/what/you/do with the money?
3 the shops/ busy this afternoon/we/drive to the new supermarket
4 charities/have more money/people/be/more generous
5 you/go/to the police/you/find/someone's wallet?

4 Complete these sentences for yourself.

1 If charities ask me for money, …
2 If I go shopping, …
3 If I have a little extra money, …
4 If I needed more money, …

unless, in case, as long as, provided that G

Take some money ________ you see something you want to buy.

Which of these words and phrases completes the sentence above?

unless, in case, as long as, provided that

unless = except if

I'll get you some new trainers, unless they're too expensive.

in case = because … might

Let's leave now in case the shops close early.

as long as/provided that = only if

I'll lend you some money as long as/provided that you pay me back tomorrow.

See *Grammar database 10* on page 179 for more information.

5 Use the words in the box to complete the text. You can use the words more than once.

unless • in case • as long as

WINNING THE LOTTERY

Claire Owen had never won anything, (1) ________ you count a spelling contest when she was seven. Then, one day, she won 20 million euros on the national lottery. 'I asked my husband to pinch me (2) ________ I was dreaming!' laughs Claire. 'Then I started to panic (3) ________ I'd lost the ticket, but I had it safely in my purse. I knew the win could affect my life badly (4) ________ I was careful, but I thought I would be okay (5) ________ I used the money wisely. I invested some, (6) ________ I needed it in the future, and I gave some to friends and family. Being rich is okay, (7) ________ you remember who you are and who your true friends are.'

Vocabulary

Money

1 Each of the nouns in bold is in the wrong sentence. Write a word or phrase in bold from another sentence to replace the incorrect one.

1 If you don't have the **discount**, I'm afraid we can't give you your money back.
2 This computer game I bought from here doesn't work so I'd like a **receipt**, please.
3 Only €20 for such a nice dress? That's a real **checkout**!
4 Buy two boxes of washing powder and we'll give you a **cashpoint** of 20%!
5 I went back to the newsagent's because the assistant had given me too much **credit card**.
6 You can pay for your flight over the phone if you have a **currency**.
7 Just a second. I need to go to the **change** to get some money.
8 I was at the supermarket and I got to the **bargain** and suddenly realised I didn't have any money!
9 To order your copy of *TeenScene*, send a **refund** for €5 to the address below.
10 The **cheque** in Italy used to be the lira, until they started using the euro.

2 Phrasal verbs

Match each phrasal verb to do with business and money to the correct meaning.

1 Tom doesn't have much money so he often has to do without expensive holidays.
2 I'm saving up to get a new skateboard.
3 They don't have much money, but they get by.
4 Sarah was shocked to hear that she had come into a large amount of money.
5 I'm thinking of setting up a company to sell jewellery.
6 If your new watch doesn't work, take it back.
7 Lots of local businesses have closed down recently.

a avoid spending money, often for a specific purpose
b stop doing business completely
c live without having something you can't afford
d return something to the shop you bought it from
e manage to survive on a small amount of money
f start (a business, etc)
g inherit

! Be careful!

☒ It isn't worth it. ☒ It doesn't worth it.

3 Word formation

Complete this table. Include all possible forms you can think of, including negative forms.

Noun	Verb	Adjective	Adverb
economy economist			
	☒	poor	
style stylist	style		
fashion	☒		
	advertise	☒	☒
finance	finance		
commerce commercial	commercialise		
expense expenses	☒		
	invest	☒	☒
	pay		☒

4 Confusable words

Choose the correct word to complete each sentence.

1 The country is facing serious **economic** / **economical** problems.
2 It would be more **economic** / **economical** if we all went in one car instead of two.
3 Do you think you could **lend** / **borrow** me 10 euros until tomorrow?
4 I don't like **lending** / **borrowing** money from my friends.
5 My dad has decided to go into **business** / **company** as an accountant.
6 My family has a dry-cleaning **industry** / **company**, so I help out at weekends.

Listening

Wordpower!

allowance • chores
pocket money

Starting point

Do your parents give you an amount of money every week?
Do you have to do anything for the money they give you?

1 **Decide whether you agree (A) or disagree (D) with these statements. Explain your choices.**

1 Teenagers today have more money than teenagers in the past. A/D
2 There is more to spend your money on today than in the past. A/D
3 Teenagers are more likely to work for money than in the past. A/D

2 **Read the questions in exercise 3 and decide whether the following statements are probably true (T) or false (F).**

1 The person being interviewed works for an organisation called Moneyspot. T/F
2 Alison is the name of the person asking the questions in the interview. T/F
3 Alison talks about how parents today give money to their children. T/F
4 Alison talks about how teenagers today spend their money. T/F
5 Alison mentions how teenagers use the internet to spend money. T/F
6 Alison only talks about what teenagers do, not their parents. T/F
7 Alison thinks getting a part-time job is a bad idea for teenagers. T/F

EXAM EXPERT

How should you do the exam practice task?

a The questions don't come in the same order as the information in the listening so remember that the answers to earlier questions could come at the end.
b The questions come in the same order as the information in the listening so the answer to earlier questions is always near the beginning.

3 **1.18 exam practice**

You will hear an interview with a financial expert. For questions 1–7, choose the best answer (A, B or C).

1 What is the main purpose of Moneyspot?
A to advise young people on saving money
B to persuade people to save more money
C to provide information about economic conditions

2 What does Alison say about teenagers in the past?
A They got less money than teenagers today.
B They got their money from different sources than teenagers today.
C They got more money from working than teenagers today.

3 Alison says that many parents today
A don't like giving their teenage children money.
B put money into a bank account for their teenagers.
C are too busy to remember to give their children money.

4 Most teenagers' money today is spent on
A things that weren't available to buy in the past.
B things that teenagers in the past weren't interested in.
C the same things teenagers in the past spent their money on.

5 What difference does Alison say the internet has made?
A Teenagers can buy things they couldn't find in the shops in the past.
B Teenagers are less likely to want to learn how to drive than in the past.
C Teenagers can find things much cheaper than they are in the shops.

6 Alison suggests that parents generally
A don't understand how good teenagers are with money.
B don't give their teenage children enough money.
C don't encourage their teenage children to save properly.

7 Alison suggests teenagers work part-time even though
A it's unlikely to help them in their future careers.
B nobody really wants to employ young people.
C the law limits the amount of work they can do.

Have your say!

- What is the right amount of pocket money for someone your age?
- What do young people learn from having their own money?

Speaking

Wordpower!

corner shop
convenient range of products

Starting point

Which of the places in the pictures do you prefer to shop at? Why?

1 **Do you agree or disagree with these statements? Explain why.**

Shopping on the internet can be dangerous because you never know who to trust.

Small corner shops have more character than large department stores.

We should just have huge supermarkets that sell everything.

2 **1.19** **Listen to this candidate comparing two photographs. What do you think the photographs he is talking about might show?**

3 **Listen again. The candidate uses five different words and phrases for giving examples. Make a note of them.**

EXAM EXPERT

How should you do the exam practice task?

While the other candidate is speaking, you should

a try to plan what you are going to say in Part 2.

b listen to what they are saying.

See *Speaking database* on page 193.

4 **Make notes to complete this table.**

	at a street market	on the internet
Have you ever bought anything …?		
What kinds of things do people buy …?		
What are two advantages of shopping …?		
What are two disadvantages of shopping …?		
How do you feel about shopping …?		

5 **Compare your answers. Make a note of good ideas you hear.**

6 exam practice

Here are two photographs showing different ways of shopping. I'd like you to compare them and tell us how you feel about these ways of shopping. You have about one minute to do this, so don't worry if I interrupt you.

How do you feel about these ways of shopping?

Candidate B, which kind of shopping do you prefer?

Reading 2 1.20

Wordpower!

ad • aimed at • brand • marketing

Starting point

What does this picture show?
Do you think there are too many ads on TV?

1 **Read the first two paragraphs of the article and match each country to the statement that describes that country.**

1 Sweden
2 France
3 the UK
4 Greece

a people think children learn something useful from advertisements
b advertisements for toys are not allowed at certain times
c all advertising aimed at young children is banned
d advertising food to children is controlled

Views concerning advertising aimed at children differ widely in Europe. In Sweden, it is considered unacceptable and is banned for children under 12 with the approval of the majority of the population. In France, advertisements are seen as part of preparing children for future life in a consumer society.

There seems to be agreement that certain regulations at least are necessary. However, the degree to which advertising to children is regulated again varies widely from country to country. In the UK, there are rules on food advertising, health, hygiene, safety and decency and there are restrictions on broadcast time (for alcohol, medicines and slimming products). Greece has a ban on advertisements for children's toys between 7am and 10pm and a total ban on advertisements for war toys.

Children's reactions to advertisements can be very different from grown-ups. If adults see a product advertised and don't find it when they go shopping,

2 exam practice

You are going to read a newspaper article about children and advertising. For questions 1–8, choose the answer (A–D) which you think fits best according to the text.

1 Most people in Sweden
- **A** agree with the ban on advertising to children.
- **B** would prefer children to learn about advertising.
- **C** think children have a right to view advertisements.
- **D** would like to introduce a ban on advertising to children.

2 According to the text, which of these ads would be allowed in Greece?
- **A** an ad for toy soldiers at 11pm
- **B** an ad for a new game at 1pm
- **C** an ad for a doll at 6am
- **D** an ad for a remote-controlled car at 9pm

3 When adults don't find something they have seen in an advertisement,
- **A** they can often be quite childish about it.
- **B** it becomes irrelevant to them.
- **C** they don't understand why it was advertised.
- **D** they continue looking until they find it.

4 According to the text, why do companies spend a lot on advertising?
- **A** It is successful at persuading people to buy their products.
- **B** It means they are able to influence the content of TV programmes.
- **C** It teaches people how advertising works.
- **D** They know that people prefer the ads to the programmes.

5 Ads aimed at children are more powerful when they are
- **A** connected to schoolwork.
- **B** shown during children's programmes.
- **C** shown at breakfast time.
- **D** shown on a weekday.

6 The text implies that advertisements in the past
- **A** presented a different lifestyle.
- **B** were more attractive to children.
- **C** focused more on the product.
- **D** showed toys children didn't want.

7 What do children learn from advertising?
- **A** how to live in a modern economy
- **B** how to have a successful career
- **C** which TV characters are popular
- **D** what to do to work in advertising

8 Why is the writer worried about the power of companies?
- **A** They often sell products which are unsafe.
- **B** They often use children in their advertisements.
- **C** They don't understand how children react to ads.
- **D** They just want to make a lot of money out of children.

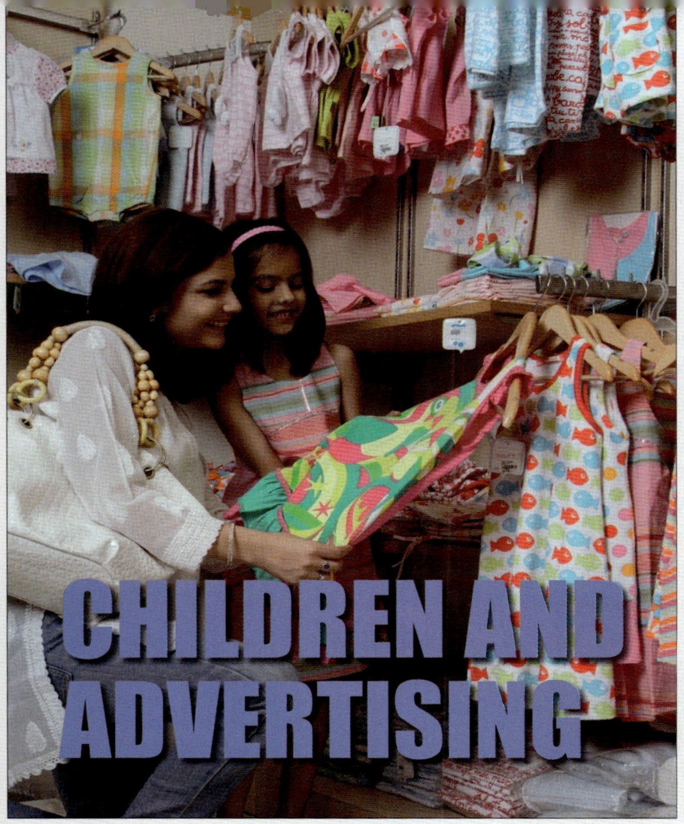

CHILDREN AND ADVERTISING

they forget about it. As children develop the ability to recognise and understand ads and their purpose, they start making demands. If these demands are not fulfilled, they might start screaming or throwing themselves to the floor. It is difficult to explain to young children the reasons why they cannot have everything which – according to advertising – is 'for them'.

Research by advertising agencies has confirmed that children's personal preferences can be targeted and changed by TV advertising. If adults, who have had years of practice in seeing through and being able to deal with ads, could not be influenced in their decisions to choose or buy products, then no company would spend millions on advertising. Research has also confirmed the influence of the media upon the close match between children's tastes and the content of the programmes they watch. Teachers say they know what has been on TV the night before by the games the children play the next day. The effectiveness of advertising increases when the ads are shown in between or around programmes aimed at children, or when children perceive an advertisement to be made 'for them' as, for example, with toys or breakfast cereals.

Advertisements today are not so much about the products but rather about the character of the consumers and how they should feel when they use or possess the advertised product. Messages to children are all about the happiness, social status or success which accompany the possession or consumption of a certain toy or type of food.

Advertisement research found that the media can shape children's preferences for different toys, TV characters, lifestyles, etc at different ages. Children's preferences are formed by the media and presented to them again in advertising. Children who are exposed to a lot of advertising are thus educated about a particular lifestyle: they are educated about living in a consumer society. They learn certain attitudes – the importance of money, what products are needed, how they are used and how products are supposed to make them feel.

Allowing business interests and economic criteria to determine what children are exposed to when watching ads will undoubtedly have some effect on their future view of society. After all, the companies certainly do not have the children's moral or social well-being in mind; they are only concerned about profits.

3 **Find words or phrases in the text to match these definitions.**

1 shopper (paragraph 1)
2 rules (paragraph 2)
3 rule saying something is not allowed (paragraph 2)
4 companies that produce ads (paragraph 4)
5 how high up you are in society (paragraph 5)
6 way of living your life (paragraph 6)

EXAM EXPERT

How should you do the exam practice task?

a Read the text from start to finish and think about the first question. Then read it all again and think about the next question. Continue like this.

b Find the paragraph that each question refers to and study that paragraph carefully while you think about that question.

WORK IT OUT!

Find these words in the text and underline them. Can you work out what they mean from the context?

hygiene • demands • seeing through
influenced • possess • well-being

Have your say!

Do you agree with these statements?

- Advertising aimed at young children should be controlled.
- Parents should let young children watch anything they want on TV.

G Grammar 2

Countable and uncountable nouns

Is this sentence correct or incorrect? Explain why / why not.

Your money are on your desk where you left them.

Some nouns are countable. We can use *a* or *an* with these words.
a dog, two dogs, many dogs

Some nouns are uncountable. We can't use *a* or *an* with these words. Most of these are singular and take a singular verb (*is*, not *are*).
money, some money, not much money, The money is …

Some of them are plural and take a plural verb.
jeans, some jeans, My jeans are …

Quantifiers

much: uncountable nouns, usually in negative sentences and questions
I don't have much money.

many: countable nouns, usually in negative sentences and questions
I don't have many CDs.

a lot of, lots of: both countable and uncountable nouns
I have lots of friends.
Mr Jones has a lot of money.

few: countable nouns = 'not many'
I have few friends in my neighbourhood.

a few: countable nouns = 'some, not none'
I am happy if I have a few close friends.

little: uncountable nouns = 'not much'
I have little money, so I can't afford to come.

a little: uncountable nouns = 'some, not none'
I have a little money, so I can afford to come.

See *Grammar databases 11* and *12* on pages 179–180 for more information.

1 Choose the correct word or phrase to complete this text.

LAKSHMI MITTAL

Lakshmi Mittal is the richest man in Britain, but not (1) **many / much** people outside the world of business know his name. He was born in India in 1950, where his father ran (2) **a / –** steel company. Lakshmi went into the family business and after (3) **few / a few** years started his own company, Mittal Steel. There is so (4) **many / much** demand for steel that he made a huge amount of money from it. He is worth over $20 billion! However, his money (5) **is / are** invested in his companies around the world, and a drop in the price of steel can mean the value of his wealth (6) **fall / falls**. Lakshmi gives (7) **an / –** advice to many organisations, and helps people with (8) **little / a little** money through the charities he is involved in. But he also likes to spend his money on himself and his family. His daughter's wedding in 2004 cost $78 million!

2 Explain the difference in meaning between each of these pairs of words.

wood / a wood
coffee / a coffee
chicken / a chicken
glass / a glass
paper / a paper
iron / an iron
chocolate / a chocolate

3 Complete these phrases using the words in the box. Find all the possible answers.

advice • bread • clothing • fruit • information • jeans
knowledge • luggage • news • paper • scissors

1 a bit of ____________
2 a piece of ____________
3 a slice of ____________
4 a pair of ____________
5 a sheet of ____________
6 an item of ____________

! Be careful!

☒ I need some new clothes.
☒ I need a new clothes.

4 Choose the correct word or phrase to complete each sentence.

1 I have **little / a little** free time, so why don't we go shopping?
2 The boss is a very private man and has **few / a few** contacts with the press.
3 I have so **little / a little** money that I don't know how I'm going to pay the rent.
4 Can I give you back the money I owe you in **few / a few** days?
5 I've only been to this shop **few / a few** times before.
6 You might succeed in business if you make **little / a little** effort.

Use of English

1 **Read the text in exercise 2 quickly to answer this question.**

How do German teenagers differ from French and British teenagers?

2 exam practice

Read the text on the right and decide which answer (A, B, C or D) best fits each gap.

EXAM EXPERT

How should you do the exam practice task?

If you don't know what one of the answers means, you should

a choose it if you think the other words are wrong.

b never choose it because it might be wrong.

Teen spending

A large-scale (1) ___ has been done by advertisers on the spending (2) ___ of today's teenagers. It has (3) ___ with some fascinating results. Girls across Europe ranging in age from 15 to 18 were interviewed. The researchers (4) ___ that these girls want to be successful and sophisticated and are willing to spend to (5) ___ the look they want – when they have the money, that is!

Feeling confident is the most important factor when it (6) ___ to buying clothes. Another interesting (7) ___ of information coming out of the study is that German teenagers (8) ___ clothes that are practical and comfortable, while British and French teenagers are more (9) ___ about appearance, although they all agreed that the clothes should (10) ___ them properly.

All the girls who were interviewed (11) ___ for clothes regularly, half of them buying something from a department store or a large clothes shop at least once a month. They also see it as a (12) ___ activity and going round the shops with their friends is the main way they learn what the latest trends are.

1	**A** research	**B** study	**C** question	**D** search
2	**A** customs	**B** actions	**C** habits	**D** methods
3	**A** turned out	**B** come up	**C** gone down	**D** brought out
4	**A** created	**B** invented	**C** discovered	**D** portrayed
5	**A** reach	**B** succeed	**C** manage	**D** achieve
6	**A** goes	**B** makes	**C** comes	**D** brings
7	**A** amount	**B** lot	**C** piece	**D** unit
8	**A** go for	**B** wear out	**C** take back	**D** make up
9	**A** concerned	**B** interested	**C** keen	**D** focused
10	**A** dress	**B** match	**C** wear	**D** fit
11	**A** shop	**B** buy	**C** purchase	**D** pay
12	**A** friendly	**B** team	**C** linked	**D** social

3 exam practice

Complete the second sentence so that it has a similar meaning to the first sentence using the word given. Do not change the word given. You must use between two and five words, including the word given. Write the missing words IN CAPITAL LETTERS.

EXAM EXPERT

How should you do the exam practice task?

When you have completed the second sentence, you should

a read both sentences again to check the meaning.

b immediately write your answer on the answer sheet.

1 You'll never have enough money for a new mobile if you don't save a little each week.
unless
You'll never have enough money for a new mobile ______________ a little each week.

2 I'll get you a book for your birthday, provided that I've got enough money.
long
I'll get you a book for your birthday, ______________ I've got enough money.

3 There isn't much money left in my bank account.
only
There ______________ money left in my bank account.

4 A great deal has changed in this area since the new shopping centre opened.
many
There ______________ in this area since the new shopping centre opened.

5 I lent Frances 50 euros last month and she still hasn't given it back.
from
Frances ______________ last month and she still hasn't given it back.

6 I started work at nine o'clock this morning and I still haven't finished!
been
I ______________ nine this morning and I still haven t finished!

Writing: essay

Starting point

What do these photographs show?
Do you do any of these chores at home? Who does these jobs?

- washing-up
- taking out the rubbish
- tidying up your room
- cleaning the car

1 **Read this writing task and these extracts from two essays. Do the extracts come from the beginning or the end of the essays?**

You have had a class discussion on money and your teacher has asked you to write an essay giving your opinion on the following question:

Should teenagers earn their pocket money?

Write your essay in 120–180 words in an appropriate style.

2 **Decide how good you think the two extracts are. Consider the following points. Compare your answers.**

- formality
- use of grammar
- vocabulary
- relevance to topic
- use of discursive phrases
- sentence length/complexity

A

... and parents and teenagers just argue about work all the time, anyway.

And kids today also work hard. It's not fair to make them work at home as well. We have to do a lot of schoolwork. Most of the kids in my class work 10 hours a week, so why should they do the washing-up? We are tired because of exams in English, maths, chemistry, etc. So, please, just listen to your teenage children and give them the money they need.

That's all. My opinion is ...

B

... which may cause tension and disagreements within the family.

In addition to that, adolescents today are under a lot of pressure. Parents should understand that things have changed since they were young. While they had time to help with chores, modern teenagers are busy doing homework and revising for exams. It doesn't seem fair to add to their difficulties by making them earn their pocket money.

In conclusion, I would argue that ...

Plan ahead

1 exam practice: essay

You have had a class discussion on money and your teacher has asked you to write an essay giving your opinion on the following question:

Should teenagers work part-time to earn money?

EXAM EXPERT

How should you write an essay?

a Try to present a clear argument using formal language.

b Try to entertain your reader with interesting descriptions.

See *Writing database* on page 195 for further information.

2 Do you think teenagers should work part-time to earn money? Try to find three main reasons. Compare your ideas. Make a note of any good ideas you hear.

3 Complete *Writing Planner 4* on page 207.

4 Write your essay in 120–180 words in an appropriate style.

5 When you have written your essay, make sure that you have:

- checked your spelling and grammar ☐
- used paragraphs ☐
- used formal language ☐
- used good discursive phrases ☐
- presented a clear argument. ☐

3 Complete the final paragraph from extract B using your imagination. Compare your ideas.

In conclusion, I would argue that teenagers should not be asked to do chores to earn their allowance because …

4 Find words or phrases in extract B to answer these questions.

1 Which words are used to introduce the point of the paragraph?
2 Which word means 'whereas'?
3 Which phrase introduces the final paragraph of the essay?

5 Choose the odd one out.

1	**a** for example	**b** in contrast	**c** for instance
2	**a** in addition	**b** furthermore	**c** on the other hand
3	**a** but	**b** yet	**c** so
4	**a** in my opinion	**b** moreover	**c** as far as I'm concerned
5	**a** to begin with	**b** firstly	**c** as a result
6	**a** in conclusion	**b** to sum up	**c** despite this

Check your progress! Units 3–4

1 Match. There is one letter you do not need to use.

1 kettle ___
2 freezer ___
3 socket ___
4 bulb ___
5 cashpoint ___
6 plug ___
7 laptop ___

a a portable computer
b the glass part of a light
c a device for storing frozen food
d a machine for getting money
e a device for boiling water
f what connects a device to the electricity supply
g a machine that washes cups, plates, etc
h a place in a wall that provides electricity

7 marks

2 Choose the correct preposition to complete each sentence.

1 My dad has been involved **on** / **in** / **for** computer programming all his life.
2 I've decided to apply **in** / **on** / **for** a job in a software company.
3 When you've finished **with** / **for** / **at** the computer, turn it off.
4 This article is full **with** / **of** / **for** scientific words I don't understand.
5 Are you looking forward **to** / **on** / **at** your first day at work?
6 How successful you are in business depends **for** / **on** / **to** how hard you work.
7 My sister isn't as interested **on** / **of** / **in** high-tech gadgets as I am.

7 marks

3 Complete the second sentence so that it has a similar meaning to the first sentence, using the word given. Do not change the word given. You must use between two and five words, including the word given.

1 If you don't have any money, why not borrow some from a friend?
lend
Why don't you ask a friend ______________ money, if you don't have any?

2 There aren't many successful businesses in this area.
only
There are ______________ succeed in this area.

3 You might need to get a taxi home, so take some more money.
case
Take some more money ______________ to get a taxi home.

4 I want to study computing, but my grades aren't good enough.
would
If my grades ______________ study computing.

5 I started working here in 2001.
been
I ______________ 2001.

6 If I can afford it, I'll get you a CD for your birthday.
unless
I'll get you a CD for your birthday, ______________ enough money.

7 Henry Ford thought of the assembly line, with each factory worker doing one small job.
came
Henry Ford ______________ idea of the assembly line, with each factory worker doing one small job.

8 Pay me back on Tuesday and I'll lend you €50.
long
I'll lend you €50, ______________ me back on Tuesday.

9 I have to go to the launderette because our washing machine has stopped working.
down
Our washing machine ______________, so I have to go to the launderette.

10 I can't install this game because there isn't much space in my computer's memory.
only
There ______________ space in my computer's memory, so I can't install this game.

20 marks

4 Read the text below. Use the word given in capitals at the end of some of the lines to form a word that fits in the space in the same line.

Career File: Working in Science

Many people are attracted to a career as a (1) ___ and	SCIENCE
it can certainly be very rewarding. Finding (2) ___ to	SOLVE
problems that affect people's lives can be very (3) ___	CREATE
and give you a real sense of (4) ___ . If you are one of the	ACHIEVE
lucky ones, you might even come up with something that	
is (5) ___ to large numbers of people around the world.	BENEFIT
At the same time, though, it's important to realise that	
success in science demands (6) ___ and a lot of hard work.	DEDICATE
Behind every great (7) ___ lie long hours of work in the	DISCOVER
laboratory, not to mention years of (8) ___ education.	EXPENSE
It's a big (9) ___ of time and money, but the chance	INVEST
to be involved in the latest (10) ___ makes it worthwhile.	DEVELOP

10 marks

5 Choose the correct phrasal verb to fill the gap in each sentence.

1 The computer has ___ a long way over the last 30 years.
A taken on **B** come on **C** broken down **D** put in

2 I heard that they are ___ a new software company in town.
A putting in **B** getting through **C** taking back **D** setting up

3 I don't want to go out tonight because I'm ___ for my holidays.
A saving up **B** keeping up **C** getting by **D** making out

4 I ___ quite a lot of money when my grandfather died.
A came into **B** looked into **C** took off **D** let down

5 Did you manage to ___ to Dennis on the phone yesterday?
A put in **B** get through **C** take back **D** check in

6 The Carters don't have a lot of money, but they seem to ___ .
A get by **B** break down **C** give up **D** close down

7 My dad's decided to ___ a new washing machine.
A cut off **B** take after **C** put in **D** come on

8 Scientists are ___ the possibility of life on other planets.
A doing without **B** taking back **C** seeing off **D** looking into

8 marks

6 Write a word from the box in each gap to complete the sentences.

obsolete • revolutionary • wealthy • mature • gullible • numerous • convenient • sceptical

1 It's much more important to be happy than it is to be ________ .

2 I'm quite ________ about claims that computers can think like humans. I don't think it's really possible.

3 Your father and I have decided that you're probably old enough and ________ enough to be left on your own for the evening.

4 The company is bringing out a(n) ________ new design for a car that runs off hydrogen.

5 I know that large supermarkets have a broader range, but the old corner shop used to be so ________ when all I needed was a pint of milk.

6 Things change so fast that a computer that is new today will be ________ in a few years' time.

7 We have had ________ complaints about this video game and we shall be investigating it very carefully.

8 I just told John that they've invented a robot that does your English homework and he believed me! He's so ________ !

8 marks

Total: 60 marks

5

Leisure

Wordpower!

essential • keep up to date • texting
social networking • stay in touch

Starting point

Calculate your 'screen time' (ie hours per day in front of a screen, eg *TV*, *mobile device*, *computer*, etc) and tick (☒) one of the boxes below. Compare with a partner and discuss these questions:

- Look at the pictures. Why do young people enjoy using these things?
- Which of them do you use?
- Do they do any harm?
- Is your 'screen time' healthy?

My screen time	
0–1	
1–2	
3–4	
4–5	
over 5	

Reading 1 🎧 2.01

Turn off the Wii™, kids, and we'll go on a bear hunt

As family life suffers, what can parents do to fight the lure of the screen, asks Margarette Driscoll

When Mark Wright told his son Joe, 15, he was taking him on a trip – but that he had to leave his computer behind for a week – Joe was horrified, 1 ______ Like many parents, Wright, who runs an adventure travel company, Families Worldwide, had become exasperated by his son's 'addiction' to computer games and decided it was time to do some father-son bonding, away from Xbox®, Wii™ and DS™.

The trip last May achieved its goal, at least for as long as it lasted. Joe admits that he forgot about the internet after a couple of days. 'You can't really compare it with seeing bears up close. That was amazing,' he says. But when they got home, Joe was back on the laptop 2 ______ 'It drives me berserk,' says Melanie, his mother. As a parent of teenagers, I can understand how she feels. My two girls (aged 16 and 19) tell me they and their friends are kept glued to Facebook by what they call 'fomo' – fear of missing out. Friends with teenage sons report, like the Wrights, an endless war against games sneakily being played instead of homework done.

Barnaby Lenon, former headmaster of Harrow school, shone a spotlight on the problem. He said that many teenagers – especially boys – had become 'addicted' to computers and that this was affecting their development: 'Children spend far too long on computers and as a result they are not doing the two things that we want them to do, which are reading and talking.' Lenon, now chairman of the Independent Schools

1 Read the text quickly, ignoring the gaps for now, and decide which of the statements below best sums up the passage.

1 Too much time in front of a TV screen or computer damages our eyes and makes us unhealthy because we don't get enough fresh air and exercise.
2 Using computers and other electronic devices can cause relationship problems and stop us from developing important skills.

2 Read the text again, ignoring the gaps, and match the people to the things they believe.

1 Mark Wright ___
2 Melanie Wright ___
3 The writer of the article ___
4 Barnaby Lenon, and probably Dr Sigman ___
5 Dr Sigman, but probably not Mr Lenon ___
6 The French government and Dr Sigman ___

a We must not make TV programmes for children under three.
b The government should suggest how many hours of screen time is safe.
c My son needed time away from the computer.
d My daughters are scared they might miss something important.
e Children are not learning to read and talk properly.
f I get very annoyed.

Council, says it is not only educational attainment but family relationships that are being damaged **3** ______ It seems that Lenon is not the only one who believes this. 'The amount of time families spend together is dropping rapidly and we ought to be worried about that, as children need conversation to learn to interpret facial expressions as part of their development,' says Dr Aric Sigman, a psychologist who has written a report for the European Parliament on the impact of computer use on children. Lenon suggests that parents limit computer use to about an hour or two a day. He also says they should not buy smartphones or other hand-held devices for children **4** ______

He would like to see schools setting guidelines for computer use above and beyond that needed for homework. 'It may still be a question of persuasion and negotiation, but having guidelines from school gives authority to what parents are saying,' he says.

Sigman goes further and suggests the government should issue advice on time spent using computers or watching television. 'Screen time needs to be regarded as just another form of consumption that we measure in units per day,' he says. 'It seems odd to me that the government gives guidance on our eating patterns yet there is nothing on our children's main leisure activity **5** ______ '

The French government has already outlawed broadcasting to children under three years old **6** ______ Sigman agrees with a total ban on screen time before the age of three. Then he recommends time limits of half an hour a day for 3 to 7 year olds, one hour for 7–12s, one and a half hours for 12–15s and two hours (over and above work) for adults.

The bear-hunting trip inspired Wright to devise other trips to take parent and child out of their normal environment and encourage communication, **7** ______ But for those who can't afford or can't face a trip to the wilderness as an antidote to Facebook, Xbox® and the rest, there seems to be no alternative to that old parental standby – nagging.

EXAM EXPERT

How should you do the exam practice task?

- **a** If a sentence ending fits grammatically, it must be the correct answer.
- **b** A sentence ending must fit grammatically and must make logical sense for it to be the correct answer.

WORK IT OUT!

Find these words in the text and the missing sentence endings and underline them. Can you work out what they mean from the context?

antidote • berserk • bonding • exasperated
hamper • negotiation • outlawed

3 exam practice

You are going to read a newspaper article about how young people spend their free time. Seven sentence endings have been removed from the text. Choose from sentence endings A–H the one which fits each gap (1–7). There is one extra sentence ending which you do not need to use.

A until they are at least 15 years old.
B even if only for a short time.
C and the family arguments over computer use continued.
D even though the week involved trekking and bear-hunting in the Tatra Mountains of Slovakia.
E because of fears that watching television might hamper language development and attention.
F even though it may be harmful.
G unless they are carefully monitored by caregivers.
H by allowing children too much time on computers.

4 Write a word or phrase from the article in each gap to complete the sentences.

1 Jimmy plays games all day and all night – it's like an ______ with him. (paragraph 1)
2 Sue always thinks she's ______ on something so she phones her friends every night. (paragraph 2)
3 I told him he couldn't use my laptop, but he ______ came into my room and took it when I was out. (paragraph 2)
4 You ______ too much time playing games and not enough on your schoolwork. (paragraph 3)
5 Our teacher gave us some useful ______ for how to use the internet safely. (paragraph 4)
6 My parents think mobiles are ______ to our health so I haven't got one. (paragraph 5)
7 James has got an ______ problem – he never really listens to his teacher. (paragraph 6)
8 Joni's mum thinks ______ her is the only way to get her to do her homework. (paragraph 7)

Have your say!

- Do you agree with Dr Sigman's screen time limits?
- How do your parents feel about your daily screen time?
- Who in the article do you relate to or agree with most?

G Grammar 1

Modals (1): ability, permission, advice/criticism, obligation

Which of these sentences offer advice? What does the other one do?

a *You must phone us as soon as the concert finishes.*

b *You should get there early as there'll be a big queue.*

We can use modals and semi-modals to express permission, ability, obligation, advice and criticism.

Permission

Can/Could/May I stay at Pauline's house tonight?

Ability

Nate can play the guitar really well.
I couldn't swim until I was five years old.
She could have gone to the party, but she didn't want to.

Obligation

You must be home by 11 o'clock.
Do I have to be home by 11 o'clock?

Advice/criticism

You ought to/should take a break. You've been working too hard.
You ought to/should have booked tickets beforehand.

See *Grammar database 13* on pages 180–181 for more information.

1 **Find these phrases from the article on pages 58–59 and use the correct modal or semi-modal in the gap. Then choose the function of the modal or semi-modal.**

1 … but that he ________ leave his computer behind for a week …
obligation / ability

2 … I ________ understand how she feels.
permission / ability

3 … we ________ be worried about that …
advice and criticism / obligation

4 He also says they ________ buy smartphones …
advice / obligation

2 **Choose the correct word or phrase to complete this text.**

I still can't **believe / to believe** it's true, but my parents finally said I **mustn't / didn't have to** go with them to visit my aunt and uncle, and that I **can / could** go with Billy and Angela to the Lady Gaga concert! We **had to / must** queue up for over an hour to get tickets, but it was definitely worth it. The concert was fantastic! She sang all the songs from her new album. You **ought / should** get it – it's great! We should **have taken / take** some water with us, though, as the drinks at the venue were really expensive. I couldn't even **afford / have afforded** a can of lemonade, so I had **borrow / to borrow** some money from Angela. (I **must / ought to** remember to pay her back!) Anyway, it was one of the best days of my life. I wish you could **have come / come** too!

3 **Choose a word or phrase from the box to complete each sentence.**

don't have to • should have • can't • had to
mustn't • could • shouldn't • be able to

1 You ________ sit in front of the computer all day. Why don't you go out and get some fresh air?
2 I'd love to ________ take a day off, but I ________ .
3 We ________ got Christine a ticket too.
4 Do you think I ________ invite a few people round next Saturday night?
5 You can go to the party, but you ________ stay out too late.
6 You ________ come with us, but you can if you like.
7 Lizzie ________ beg her dad for ages before he agreed to take her to the fair.

4 **Talk about yourself.**

1 What can you do really well?
2 What should you do every day?
3 What do you have to do this evening?
4 What could you have done last weekend but didn't do? Why not?

V Vocabulary

People associated with leisure time activities

1 Match the people with their definitions.

1 cast
2 audience
3 spectator
4 lifeguard
5 host
6 guest
7 viewer
8 sightseer
9 crowd

a a person watching a sporting event
b a large group of people
c the actors in a play
d a person who organises a party, etc
e a person watching TV
f the people watching a play, attending a concert, etc
g a person looking at a tourist attraction
h a person who is invited to a party
i a person who saves swimmers who are in trouble

2 Phrasal verbs

Use a phrasal verb to do with leisure in the correct form to complete each sentence.

catch on • come across • come round
flick through • get away • take to • take up

1 I saw the ad for the water park as I was ____________ a magazine.
2 I ____________ some really old comics as I was looking round the second-hand bookshop.
3 My dad's decided to ____________ hang-gliding. I hope he doesn't hurt himself!
4 A few of my friends ____________ last night and we watched some DVDs.
5 Hip hop has really ____________ in the last few years – it's more popular than pop these days.
6 She said she'd meet me for a coffee if she could ____________ from work for an hour or two.
7 Sean and I have ____________ going for a walk every Sunday afternoon. It's so relaxing!

! Be careful!

☒ Thanks for the party. I really enjoyed myself!
☒ Thanks for the party. I really entertained myself!

3 Word formation

Complete this table. Include all possible forms you can think of, including negative forms.

Noun	Verb	Adjective
		active
	amuse	
	appreciate	
	attend	
day	☒	
	enjoy	
	enter	☒
	entertain	
	excite	
	☒	happy
humour	humour	
	☒	popular

4 Word patterns

Choose the correct word or phrase to complete each sentence.

1 I finally succeeded **to get** / **in getting** a couple of tickets for the concert.
2 How did you manage **to organise** / **in organising** the party in such a short time?
3 I hope you're able **to come** / **coming** bowling with us on Tuesday.
4 I wish I was capable **to take** / **of taking** such great photos.
5 We've arranged **to meet** / **meeting** in the park at half past eight.
6 I've never enjoyed **to go** / **going** to the circus.
7 My parents don't allow me **stay** / **to stay** out after midnight.
8 My mum lets me **buy** / **to buy** my own clothes.

Listening

Starting point

Look at the picture. What do you think has happened here? What would you do in this situation?

1 2.02 **Read the questions in exercise 2. Listen to the beginnings of the six extracts. Match each extract to one of the questions 1–6 and write down a word or phrase which gave you the answer.**

Extract A ____________

Extract B ____________

Extract C ____________

Extract D ____________

Extract E ____________

Extract F ____________

EXAM EXPERT

How should you do the exam practice task?

- a If you're not absolutely sure of the answer, don't write anything on the answer sheet.
- b If you're not absolutely sure of the answer, make an educated guess based on what you understood.

2 2.03 exam practice

You will hear people talking in six different situations. For questions 1–6, choose the best answer (A, B or C).

1 You hear two teenagers playing a computer game. How do they think the game could be improved?

A by making it more competitive
B by making it easier to enter the castle
C by giving the players more information

2 You hear a woman talking about a trip to a funfair. How did she feel on the ride she describes?

A She enjoyed it more than her son.
B She was more scared than her son.
C She regretted taking her son on it.

3 You hear two people deciding what to do for the evening. What do they finally decide to do?

A go to the cinema
B play pool
C stay at home

4 You hear this woman talking on her mobile phone in a café. What probably happened to the person she is speaking to?

A She got stuck in traffic.
B She had an accident.
C She got held up at work.

5 You hear a man talking about camping. What does he say about it?

A The campers get on well with each other in the campsite.
B It's nice to live without electrical appliances for a few days.
C He takes the whole family camping every year.

6 You hear a telephone information service. What kind of show can you see at the theatre next Saturday?

A a musical
B a comedy
C a science fiction play

Have your say!

- Have you been in any situations similar to the ones you've just listened to? In what ways were they the same and in what ways were they different?

Speaking

Wordpower!

basics • campfire • open air
penknife • put up (a tent) • torch

Starting point

What do people usually do when they go camping?
How do they cope without electricity and other things we take for granted at home?

1 **Match to make phrases connected with camping. Then match each phrase with a picture in exercise 3.**

1	Swiss army	**a**	bag
2	inflatable	**b**	rod
3	sleeping	**c**	knife
4	MP3	**d**	cooker
5	fishing	**e**	player
6	gas	**f**	boat

2 🎧 **2.04 Look at the exam task in exercise 3 and listen to these students doing the task. For each extract, write a word in the gap to complete the useful phrase.**

1 I think X would be ____________ because/since …
2 X would ____________ be ____________ useful …
3 I'm not ____________ we'd (really) ____________ X …
4 What do you ____________ about ____________ X?
5 I think X is a good ____________ …
6 X would/might/could ____________ ____________ useful …
7 Let's ____________ …
8 I'd ____________ to ____________ …

EXAM EXPERT

How should you do the exam practice task?

a Don't disagree with the interviewer because your opinions affect your marks.

b Don't worry about the opinions you express, as long as they are logical, because you are being marked on your ability to speak English.

3 exam practice

I'd like you to imagine that you are both going camping for a week in the summer with some friends. Here are some things you might take with you. Talk to each other about how useful these things would be and then decide which two things you would definitely not take with you. You have about three minutes.

- How useful would these things be?
- Which two would you definitely not take with you?

4 **Do exercise 3 with two students as the candidates. The rest of the class is going to provide feedback. When you have finished, swap roles.**

EXAM EXPERT

How should you do the exam practice task?

a Remember there are two parts to the task and try to do both of them within the three minutes.

b Don't even try to do the second part of the task as you probably won't have time for it.

See *Speaking database* on page 193.

5 exam practice

Would you like to go on a camping trip like this with your friends?

Why does camping appeal to so many people?

Does what someone likes doing in their spare time change as they get older?

In what ways are leisure facilities different in small towns and villages compared to large towns and cities?

What are the leisure facilities like in the area where you live?

Reading 2 2.05

Wordpower!

slide • diving board
rubber ring • rapids

Starting point

Have you ever done any of the activities in the photos? Which do you think are the most enjoyable / exciting / frightening?

1 **What different activities can you do (a) at the beach, (b) at a water park, (c) at a traditional swimming pool? Make a list.**

2 **Quickly read the first paragraph of the article. What were leisure centres like in the 1970s?**

EXAM EXPERT

How should you do the exam practice task?

a Try to answer the questions without looking back at the text.

b Where possible, read the question, find the answer in the text and then match it to the best option.

3 exam practice

You are going to read an article about water parks. For questions 1–8, choose the answer (A–D) which you think fits best according to the text.

1 What does the word 'that' (line 17) refer to?
- **A** the drinks machine
- **B** a day out in the 1970s
- **C** the leisure centre's facilities
- **D** what you did after leaving the centre

2 The idea behind water parks is that people
- **A** want more than just a simple swimming pool.
- **B** felt leisure centres were too expensive.
- **C** need to be entertained 24 hours a day.
- **D** don't enjoy swimming.

3 How do water parks in Britain differ from those in Mediterranean countries?
- **A** Pools in British water parks are always inside.
- **B** Pools in Mediterranean water parks are always in the open air.
- **C** Mediterranean water parks are sometimes connected to a holiday resort.
- **D** British water parks have indoor and outdoor facilities.

4 What point is the writer making in the fourth paragraph?
- **A** Water parks do not have an entrance fee, whereas leisure centres do.
- **B** Water parks provide value for money if you stay long enough.
- **C** People rarely spend more than a couple of hours at a leisure centre.
- **D** Despite their benefits, water parks are too expensive.

5 How do water park slides differ from leisure centre slides?
- **A** Water park slides are much faster.
- **B** Water park slides are connected to a water supply.
- **C** Water park slides are more frightening.
- **D** Water park slides are much wider.

6 What do the rapids and the lazy pool have in common?
- **A** The water is moving.
- **B** They both take you round in a circle.
- **C** They are designed for children.
- **D** They are both very exciting.

7 What is the effect of the word 'boast' in line 87?
- **A** It emphasises that what follow are positive attractions.
- **B** It shows that water parks advertise heavily.
- **C** It demonstrates that water parks are always expanding.
- **D** It reminds us that water parks are very modern.

8 What is the purpose of this article?
- **A** to persuade towns to build more water parks
- **B** to inform people about their local water park
- **C** to describe how leisure facilities have changed
- **D** to advertise a particular service

Let's Get Wet

Fun in the swimming pool has come a long way in the last 25 years. Dawn Davis looks at the latest generation of water parks.

Back in the 1970s, a typical family day out was a trip to the local leisure centre. Every town had one and they were basically all the same, with a large rectangular swimming pool (shallow at one end, deep at the other), a separate deep-water area with several diving boards, and a kiddie-pool for babies or those who couldn't swim. If you were lucky, there was a short, straight slide that had to be kept wet with a bucket of water. And after your leisure centre experience, there was a drinks machine selling hot chocolate for mum and cans of fizzy drinks for the kids. And that was it.

How things change! Now – thankfully – we have the water park, based on the notion that swimming on its own is not the most interesting activity in the world. People get bored easily, and demand a lot more entertainment for their money.

In Britain, most water parks are a combination of pools in an enclosed area and in the open air. In Mediterranean countries, because of the warmer and drier climate, they are more often than not completely outdoors. Some are dedicated water parks, and others are part of a larger leisure or holiday complex. All, however, provide much more than the chance to swim a few lengths.

Unlike the leisure centre, there's little point just turning up for an hour or two. This is partly because there's so much to do, and partly because there's usually an entrance fee which, although quite reasonable if you make the most of what's on offer, is not cheap.

So what is there to do? All water parks have a number of slides. These are not the old-fashioned straight slides of the 1970s, though. They come in all shapes and sizes – some are open, some are totally enclosed tunnels, some are steep, some are bumpy, some twist sharply, some you can go down in pairs or on rubber rings. All of them have water flowing down them. You can often choose how you want to go down – head first, feet first, on your front or back, sitting up, lying down. Your position affects your speed – and how much water will splash into your face!

Other attractions often include the rapids – in which you make your way through a man-made river, surviving the obstacles such as backwards flowing currents, waterfalls and rapids. It's exhilarating and – at times – a little scary, and for some reason kids are much better at getting round than adults. The baby-brother of the rapids is the lazy pool, where the current gently takes you round a circular channel of water. It's relaxing more than exciting, and some lazy pools even have a jacuzzi halfway round.

Some larger water parks have a wave machine in the main pool which makes waves up to a metre high. That makes the whole swimming experience rather more thrilling than in the old leisure centre days. Some have a 'death slide', where you hold onto a bar which slides down a cable over the pool. When it hits the end, you drop into the water! There's also a lot more on offer than a drinks
machine. Many water parks boast 87
shops, cafés, bars and restaurants, and a bar actually in the middle of the pool is not uncommon in many Mediterranean water parks. Just remember to keep your money dry!

4 Find a word from the article to complete these phrases.

1 day ____________
2 drinks ____________
3 fizzy ____________
4 leisure/holiday ____________
5 ____________ fee
6 all ____________ and sizes
7 wave ____________

WORK IT OUT!

Find these words in the text and underline them. Can you work out what they mean from the context?

notion • combination • obstacles • steep • twist
cable • current • reasonable • splash • thrilling

Have your say!

- Which would you prefer to the beach, a water park or a traditional swimming pool?

Grammar 2

Comparatives and superlatives

Circle the correct words to complete these sentences.

That was ***a / the more/the most*** *exciting ride I've ever been on.*

This ride was ***more / most*** *exciting* ***than/from*** *the others.*

Do you think this ride is as exciting ***than / as*** *the other one we went on?*

We use the comparative to compare things and people that are different and separate from each other.
Coldplay *are better than any other band.*

We use the superlative to compare one member of a group with the whole group.
Our town's got the best water park in the area!

Be careful! The number of syllables in the original adjective and the way it is spelled determine how we form the comparative and superlative, eg *nicer* and *bigger* but *more interesting*.

Be careful! There are a number of irregular comparatives and superlatives, eg *bad / worse / worst*.

We use *as … as* to compare two things that are similar or the same.
The film is just as good as the book.

See *Grammar database 14* on page 181 for more information.

1 **Find these extracts in the article on page 65 and write the correct word or phrase in each gap.**

1 … the ____________ generation of water parks.
2 … swimming on its own is not ____________ activity in the world.
3 … because of the ____________ climate, …
4 All, however, provide ____________ the chance to swim a few lengths.

2 **Complete each sentence using the correct form of the word in brackets.**

1 That was the __________ (**funny**) programme I've seen for a very long time.
2 The Justin Bieber concert was great, but I wish it had gone on __________ (**long**).
3 The trip to Disneyland Paris ended up being __________ (**expensive**) than we'd thought.
4 Going on that roller coaster was one of the __________ (**bad**) experiences of my life!
5 The entrance fee cost __________ (**little**) this year than it did last year.
6 I only knew a few people at the party, as Jason had invited __________ (**many**) of them.

! Be careful!

☒ Most people/things/etc = generally
☒ Most of the people/things/etc = one specific group
☒ The most of the people/things/etc

3 **Complete the second sentence so that it has a similar meaning to the first sentence, using the word given. You must use between two and five words, including the word given.**

1 The play wasn't nearly as boring as I'd expected it to be.
more
The play ____________ I'd expected it to be.

2 Don't worry! It's the safest ride in the whole theme park.
dangerous
Don't worry! It's ____________ ride in the whole theme park.

3 Sara said it was the best party she'd ever been to.
never
Sara said she'd ____________ party.

4 The museum was further than we'd been told.
as
The museum ____________ we'd been told.

Questions

With the verb *to be* (as a main verb or an auxiliary verb), we form questions by inverting the subject and verb.
Were you scared when you went down the rapids?
Are you going to go down again?

With the verb *to have* as an auxiliary verb, we form questions by inverting the subject and verb.
Have you seen the new Meryl Streep movie?

With all other verbs (including *to have* as a main verb) we form questions using the verb *to do*.
Do you have a DVD player? Did you go to the fair?

Be careful! With question words, whether we use *to do* or not depends on whether the question word refers to the subject or object of the verb. Compare:

What *went wrong?* **(subject)** ***What*** *did you do yesterday?* **(object)**

Who *bought the tickets?* **(subject)** ***Who*** *did you buy tickets for?* **(object)**

See *Grammar database 15* on page 182 for more information.

4 **Ask your partner four questions about a game or free-time activity he/she enjoys. When you have finished, swap roles.**

Use of English

1 **Quickly read the text in exercise 2 and answer these questions.**

1 When was the first Goosey Fair held?
2 Why is it called Goosey Fair?
3 What happens to the town in the evening?

2 exam practice

Read the text below and think of the word which best fits each gap. Use one word in each gap. Write your answers IN CAPITAL LETTERS.

> **EXAM EXPERT**
>
> **How should you do the exam practice task?**
>
> **a** Remember that most of the words tested here are lexical words like nouns and main verbs.
>
> **b** Remember that most of the words tested here are grammatical words like pronouns, articles, prepositions, etc.

Tavistock Goosey Fair

Although many towns and cities in Britain have an annual fair, few are (1) ____________ famous than Tavistock Goosey Fair, held on the second Wednesday of October. Dating back to the 12th century, Goosey Fair is one of (2) ____________ oldest fairs in the UK, and is still as popular (3) ____________ ever.

Hundreds of years (4) ____________ , farmers (5) ____________ to bring their geese for sale and drove them through the streets (6) ____________ Tavistock to the market. That's (7) ____________ the name 'goosey' comes from. These days, there are (8) ____________ many geese to be found at Goosey Fair, but it is (9) ____________ fact still possible to have a goose lunch at the various hotels and restaurants in the town on the day of the fair.

Goosey Fair attracts visitors from all over the country. The streets are closed (10) ____________ traffic and (11) ____________ are hundreds of stalls selling everything from fruit and vegetables to the (12) ____________ up-to-date electronic equipment. In the evening, the town becomes a large funfair, with lots of different rides and attractions.

3 **Quickly read the text in exercise 4. How does a music festival differ from a concert?**

4 exam practice

Read the text below. Use the word given in capitals at the end of some of the lines to form a word that fits in the gap in the same line. Write your answers IN CAPITAL LETTERS.

> **EXAM EXPERT**
>
> **How should you do the exam practice task?**
>
> **a** This kind of task never tests plural forms, so you don't need to ask yourself whether the missing word should be singular or plural.
>
> **b** This kind of task often tests plural forms, so you need to ask yourself whether the missing word is singular or plural.

Music Festivals

People have always gone to concerts to hear their favourite musicians
perform. Since the 1960s, a related form of (1) ___ has grown in — ENTERTAIN
(2) ___ : the music festival. A music festival is usually organised over a — POPULAR
couple of days and is like a series of mini-concerts from a number of artists.
The (3) ___ get to see different acts and usually have to pay an — SPECTATE
(4) ___ fee to get into the festival. At larger festivals, such as Glastonbury in — ENTER
the UK, they can then choose which stage to visit. It can be very (5) ___ — EXCITE
and the crowd shows their (6) ___ of the musicians by dancing and — APPRECIATE
cheering. At many festivals, other (7) ___ are also organised, such as — ACTIVE
juggling or fire-eating displays.
The first major festival took place in America at a place called Woodstock.
It was free, and the (8) ___ was very high – many thousands of people got — ATTEND
together at this very (9) ___ event. Many of the musicians who performed — ENJOY
there went on to become very (10) ___ . — FAME

Writing: formal letter/email

Starting point

Imagine you attended the music festival in the photo. What positive things might you say about the experience? What criticisms could you make?

1 Read the letter below and answer these questions.

1 Does Leslie know the name of the person he is writing to?
2 Is the letter formal or informal?
3 Does Leslie use contractions (*I'll*, *I'd*, etc)?
4 Why is Leslie writing the letter? (two reasons)
5 What positive aspects of the festival does he mention?
6 How many suggestions does he make in his letter?
7 Why didn't he write 'Yours sincerely,' above his name?
8 Why did he write his surname as well as his first name?

Dear Sir / Madam,

I am writing with regard to the Dankhurst Music Festival, which I attended for the first time this year.

First of all, I would like to congratulate you on a very successful event. I thought that having different stages for different music styles was a particularly good idea. The festival was thoroughly enjoyable and I am planning to attend next year. However, there are several suggestions I would like to make regarding next year's festival.

I believe that the entrance fee of €40 is too expensive for students. I would like to suggest you introduce a cheaper student rate. Secondly, although the campsite was large enough, there were not enough toilets. I think it is important that more of these are provided. Finally, ______

I do hope you take my suggestions into account when organising next year's event.

Yours faithfully,

Leslie Parker

2 Find these words and phrases in the letter and choose their correct meaning.

1 with regard to
about / in support of
2 attended
went to / heard about
3 a particularly good
the only good / a very good
4 thoroughly
fairly / extremely
5 regarding
about / watching
6 take … into account
obey / consider

3 Use these notes to complete Leslie's final suggestion in the third paragraph. Remember that the letter is polite and formal.

food in snack bars (almost all) – with meat!

not much choice for us vegetarians!

vegetarian food too?

Plan ahead

1 exam practice: formal letter

You are staying in Britain and have recently been to a music festival. You enjoyed the festival, but you have some suggestions to make so that the next one will be better organised.

Read the advertisement for the festival and the notes you have made beside it. Then write a letter to the organiser giving your opinion of this year's festival and making your suggestions for next year.

> **EXAM EXPERT**
>
> **How should you write a formal letter/email?**
>
> **a** Always use the actual words in the notes in your letter/email.
>
> **b** Use the ideas in the notes, but use more formal grammar and vocabulary.
>
> See *Writing database* on pages 196–197 for further information.

14th ANNUAL CALLINGTON

MUSIC FESTIVAL — *excellent! especially: friendly atmosphere*

Three days of the latest rock, pop, reggae and rap in the beautiful setting of Callington Castle — *only one rapper – should be more – rap very popular!*

Free camping site — *too small – also use field next to it?*

Toilet and washing facilities

Cheap food and beverages

Entrance fee: £25 — *maybe make it a bit more? Could get more/better bands*

2 Before you write, answer these questions.

1 Why are you writing the letter?
2 Do you know the name of the organiser?
3 What will you mention as being particularly good?
4 What does 'beverages' mean in the advertisement?
5 Do you have to mention beverages in your letter? Why? / Why not?
6 How many suggestions will you make in your letter?
7 What are they?
8 Will you write 'Yours sincerely,' or 'Yours faithfully,' above your name?

3 For each suggestion, write a sentence or group of sentences to include in your letter.

4 Complete *Writing Planner 5* on page 208.

5 Write your letter in 120–150 words. You must use grammatically correct sentences with accurate spelling and punctuation in a style appropriate for the situation. Do not write any addresses.

6 When you have written your letter, make sure that you have:

- followed your paragraph plan ☐
- referred to all the notes ☐
- used formal, polite English ☐
- used some of the words and phrases from exercise 2 and the model letter on page 68 ☐
- started and finished your letter in an appropriate way. ☐

6

Nature

Wordpower!

bottle bank • demonstration • collect
litter • protest • recycle • dump • sort

Starting point

Compare the two photographs. What can we do to help protect our environment?

1 **Look at the title of the article you are going to read. Which of these things do you expect to be mentioned in the article?**

- how to use less water
- the chemistry of water
- weather conditions at sea
- how water is wasted

2 **Read the article quickly and check your answers to exercise 1.**

EXAM EXPERT

How should you do the exam practice task?

When a question asks why the writer mentions something, you should

a read the options (A, B, C, D) and choose one which is factually true.

b read the text carefully to find the reason and then choose the option that best expresses it.

Reading 1 2.06

Making every drop count

Lisa Campbell looks at the challenge of conserving water

Drip, trickle, splash. Do you ever think about the water we use every day for cleaning, drinking, cooking and growing plants? Water is essential to life. It is one of the most common substances in the universe, and our planet, with its vast oceans, is lucky to have a generous share of it. Unfortunately, 97 per cent of that share is salty, and much of the rest is in the form of ice at the North and South Poles. Getting an adequate supply of fresh water is not always easy, especially in the developing world, where drought is a constant threat in some areas.

Half of the world's population still suffer from water services inferior to those available to the ancient Greeks and Romans. More than a billion people don't even have access to clean drinking water and face problems caused by pollution and disease. As the world's population grows, there is increasing pressure on agriculture, which demands large amounts of water. Changing the course of rivers and building dams threaten fish, with rare species of fish becoming extinct in some seas and lakes.

Throughout the first three quarters of the 20th century, the quantity of fresh water used by each person doubled. The emphasis was

3 exam practice

You are going to read an article from a magazine. For questions 1–7, choose the answer (A–D) which you think fits best according to the text.

1 Why does the writer mention the North and South Poles?
  A They are badly affected by pollution.
  B Most of the Earth's water is frozen there.
  C They affect the amount of drinking water available.
  D They provide many people with a water supply.

2 The water services in ancient Greece and Rome were
  A more efficient than most people think.
  B designed to provide water for half the world's population.
  C badly polluted and carried disease.
  D better than those in many parts of the world today.

3 Why are some fish in danger, according to the writer?
  A An increasing population means more fish are eaten.
  B Lakes are becoming increasingly polluted.
  C Humans alter the direction that some rivers take.
  D They are forced into areas with salty water.

on using more and more water. Large-scale facilities were built for water treatment and recycling and large numbers of reservoirs were constructed to store water. However, many people have now realised that basic human and environmental needs are the top priority. The building of new water facilities is now less important than using what we already have efficiently and wisely. Repairing the existing system could have huge benefits. Through leaking pipes and faulty equipment, Mexico City, for example, loses enough water to meet the needs of a city the size of Rome.

Over the last 25 years, new technology and greater awareness of the problem have meant that water is used more efficiently. Industrial processes have been discovered that use less water; it now takes only six tons of water to make a ton of steel, compared to 60 tons 60 years ago. People around the world are also more effective at protesting against the effects of water use on their local environment.

Despite this, a lot of water is still wasted. We can all do our bit for the environment by following a few simple water conservation dos and don'ts.

Bathroom
The bathroom is a key area where you can save water. Short showers use less water than baths, especially if you have a special water-saving showerhead fitted. Toilets which use less water can be fitted, and even a plastic bottle filled with water in the cistern will save a litre with each flush. Up to 12 litres of water is lost every minute if you leave the tap running while you brush your teeth or wash your hands.

Kitchen and Laundry
Fill a sink to wash up instead of leaving the tap running and you can reduce the amount of water needed by half. Dishwashers and washing machines should only be used when they are full, and then on a short cycle when possible.

Outdoors
You can save water outside the home in a number of different ways. If you have a garden, rainwater can be recycled to water plants, which should be done in the evening or early morning so that less water is lost through evaporation. Pavements and balconies should be swept instead of being washed. It can also help to save water if any leaks or waste in your neighbourhood are reported to your local council.

So, next time you have a shower or open a bottle of drinking water, think about where the water comes from and where it's going.

4 What do people now think is most important in water use?
- **A** building large treatment facilities
- **B** finding less wasteful ways to use water
- **C** moving water from one city to another
- **D** storing water so that people can use more

5 What does the writer say has happened in industry?
- **A** Most steel is now made without using water.
- **B** More efficient methods are used to create steel.
- **C** Less steel is being produced due to a lack of water.
- **D** More steel is being made than ever before.

6 The writer says that water can be saved in the bathroom by
- **A** having showers and baths less often.
- **B** brushing your teeth in running water.
- **C** using bottled water instead of tap water.
- **D** replacing bathroom fittings with more efficient ones.

7 Which of these water-saving measures is not mentioned in the text?
- **A** informing the right people about waste
- **B** using rainwater to wash your balcony
- **C** turning the tap off when washing up
- **D** making sure the dishwasher is full when used

WORK IT OUT!

Find these words in the text and underline them. Can you work out what they mean from the context?

trickle • the developing world • dams • reservoirs
conservation • sink • evaporation • leaks

Have your say!

- What other ways of saving water can you think of?

Grammar 1

The passive

Complete this sentence using the correct form of the verb in brackets.

Recently, industrial processes _______________ that use less water. (discover)

To form the passive, we:

- put the person/thing the action is done to before the verb
- put the person/thing doing the action after the verb (when necessary)
- use *be* in the correct form + past participle.
  Some species have been hunted to extinction.
  The river is polluted by local factories.

Apart from a tense, the form of the verb *be* used may be:

- the full infinitive
  Some people don't want the new dam to be built.
- the bare infinitive
  Companies should be prevented from polluting the water supply.
- the *-ing* form
  Most people don't like being told to pick up their litter.

We use the passive:

- when we don't know who does/did/etc the action
- when we aren't interested in who does/did/etc the action
- when it's obvious who does/did/etc the action
- for emphasis, formality and impersonal style.

See *Grammar database 16* on pages 182–183 for more information.

1 **Find all examples of the passive you can in the text on pages 70–71.**

2 **Rewrite these sentences correctly.**

1 The theory of evolution has suggested by Charles Darwin.
2 The elephants in this area should protect by a ban on hunting.
3 I'm really looking forward to be taken to the zoo tomorrow.
4 A new species of bird was been discovered by scientists.
5 People should being encourage to recycle their waste.
6 The government being put under pressure to change the law on fishing.
7 Many dolphins kill accidentally by tuna nets.
8 Global warming has predicted for a long time now.

3 **Look at the photograph. What do you think could be done with old appliances like this?**

4 **Read this text about recycling electrical appliances. Complete the text using the words in the box in the correct form.**

criticise • use • buy • make
smash • sort • take apart • dump
require • collect • introduce

RECYCLING ELECTRONIC WASTE

Millions of new TVs, fridges, air-conditioning units and washing machines (1) _______________ every day around the world. So what happens to the old ones? In Japan, where around 20 million electrical appliances (2) _______________ by the side of the road or in rivers every year, new legislation (3) _______________ in 2001 which means that all electrical goods must be 50–60% recyclable.

Recycling these high tech machines isn't easy. They can't just (4) _______________ into small pieces that can (5) _______________ again. Special plants, like the Matsushita Eco-Technology Centre (6) _______________ for the process. Each appliance (7) _______________ very carefully and the components (8) _______________ into different categories. The plastic in these machines, for example, (9) _______________ and reused to make internal components for new appliances.

Although Matsushita, who owns Panasonic, (10) _______________ by some people for creating the problem in the first place, most people agree that progress (11) _______________ in dealing with this space age environmental challenge.

V Vocabulary

1 Choose the correct word or phrase to complete each sentence.

endangered species • rural • smog
greenhouse effect • global warming
fossil fuels • green • sewerage system
nature reserve • urban

1 ________ is the gradual rise in temperature in many parts of the world.
2 A(n) ________ is one which is under threat of extinction.
3 Something that is ________ is related to the countryside, rather than the city.
4 Something that is ________, such as a product, is not harmful to the environment.
5 ________ is an unpleasant mixture of smoke and fog hanging over a city.
6 The ________ is caused by the sun's heat being trapped by gases in the Earth's atmosphere.
7 The ________ is the pipes and facilities for taking dirty water from homes and factories, usually to be treated.
8 A(n) ________ is an area where wildlife is specially protected.
9 Something that is ________ is related to the city, rather than the countryside.
10 ________ include coal, gas and oil.

2 Phrasal verbs

Match each phrasal verb to do with the environment to the correct meaning.

1 go off
2 die out
3 run out
4 give off
5 cut down
6 bring out
7 clear up
8 throw away

a become extinct
b produce heat, a smell, a gas, etc
c produce and start to sell a new product
d stop being fresh
e use all of something and not have any left
f (of the weather) become better after cloud or rain
g get rid of (rubbish, etc)
h cut a tree, etc, so that it falls

3 Complete each sentence using a phrasal verb from exercise 2 in the correct form.

1 If we continue to use fossil fuels at the present rate, we will eventually ________ of oil.
2 *BurgerEar* is planning to ________ a new, environmentally friendly container for their fast food.
3 You'd be surprised at how much of the rainforests is ________ every single day.
4 I threw the bananas away because I thought they had ________.
5 Trees and plants ________ oxygen, which all living things need.
6 We should be very careful what we ________ and try to recycle as much as we can.
7 There will be heavy rain showers in the morning, but it should ________ by the afternoon.
8 Unless something is done, the snow leopard will ________ within the next decade.

4 Word formation

Complete this table. Include all possible forms you can think of, including negative forms.

Noun	Verb	Adjective	Adverb
environment	☒		
globe	☒		
harm			
industry	☒		
nature	☒		
poison			☒
	pollute		☒
success			
value			☒
world	☒		

5 Word patterns

Complete these sentences using the correct preposition.

1 If you see a water leak, report it ________ your local council.
2 The government should create posters to inform people ________ the danger to the environment.
3 During his speech, the politician referred ________ the new law as 'an environmental disaster'.
4 Many people have reacted ________ the situation by organising protests.
5 The company has been accused ________ dumping tons of chemicals in the river.
6 Many animals depend ________ human help for survival in the wild.
7 Unless we take better care ________ the world around us, we'll regret it.

Listening

Starting point

**What is this a photograph of?
Which is more important: economic development or preserving the environment?**

1 2.07 **Listen to an extract from an interview and decide whether the following statements are true (T) or false (F).**

1 The local council wants to stop building in the area. T/F
2 Greenwatch tries to protect the environment. T/F

2 Before you listen to the complete interview, look at the sentences in exercise 3 and try to complete them. Write your guesses here.

1 ______________________
2 ______________________
3 ______________________
4 ______________________
5 ______________________
6 ______________________
7 ______________________
8 ______________________
9 ______________________
10 ______________________

EXAM EXPERT

How should you do the exam practice task?

a Always read the complete sentence when you have filled the gap to make sure the grammar is correct.
b Don't worry about reading the complete sentence when you have filled the gap because the grammar isn't important.

3 2.08 exam practice

You will hear part of a radio interview about the environment. For questions 1–10, complete the sentences.

The local council's aim is to 1 ______
The council is planning to build 2 ______
One of the problems people in the area face is 3 ______
Greenwatch would like to see the creation of 4 ______
Many birds stop at the Eastford Downs as they go 5 ______
The Eastford Downs are also important for 6 ______
Greenwatch has organised meetings and 7 ______
Local people seem to be aware that the Downs are 8 ______
Anyone interested should call Greenwatch for 9 ______
This weekend, Greenwatch are organising a 10 ______

4 Look at the correct answers to exercise 3 and your guesses in exercise 2. Choose the sentence that is true for you and compare with a partner.

All my guesses were very close. ☐
Most of my guesses were close. ☐
Some of my guesses were close. ☐
A few of my guesses were fairly close. ☐
None of my guesses were close at all. ☐

Have your say!

- What environmental problems does your local area face?
- What solutions can you think of?

Speaking

Wordpower!

oil tanker • oil slick • deforestation • construction industry

Starting point

How do these forms of pollution affect the environment? What other forms of pollution can you think of?

1 **Rewrite these sentences correctly and underline the expressions used for introducing an opinion.**

1 From my opinion, there is no point recycling things if large businesses are allowed to pollute our natural environment.
2 As far that I'm concerned, the government is doing everything it can to protect the environment.
3 To my view, we should worry about running out of fossil fuels when it happens, not before.
4 It seems me that children should be taught how to care for the environment from a very young age.

2 **Discuss whether you agree or disagree with the statements in exercise 1.**

3 **2.09 Listen to this candidate comparing two photographs and answer these questions.**

- What do the photographs she is talking about show? Be specific.
- What phrases does she use to introduce her opinions?
- Which do you think is the bigger threat?

4 exam practice

Here are two photographs showing different things that threaten our natural environment. I'd like you to compare them and tell us which you think is the bigger threat. You have about one minute to do this, so don't worry if I interrupt you.

Candidate B, how do you feel about problems like these?

EXAM EXPERT

How should you do the exam practice task?

While the other candidate is speaking, you should

a always say how each picture makes you feel and which one you prefer.

b listen carefully to any instructions and make sure you do what you have been asked to do.

See *Speaking database* on page 193.

Reading 2 2.10

Wordpower!

beetle • grasshopper
ladybird • mosquito

Starting point

What do you know about these insects? What other insects do you know the names of in English?
Match the insects in the pictures to the following names.

- beetle
- grasshopper
- ladybird
- mosquito

1

2

3

4

1 **Look at the title of the article opposite. What is the article about?**

2 **Read the text quickly, ignoring the gaps, and decide if these statements are true (T) or false (F).**

1 Most species of ant are found in the rainforests. T/F
2 Different ants have different jobs to do. T/F
3 Some ants use their own bodies to make a nest. T/F
4 Ants only fight to protect themselves. T/F

An ant's eye view

Sam Miller tells us about his fascination with ants.

They are found all over the world. They can lift up to 50 times their own body weight. They seem to behave in complicated ways, yet each individual is typically no more than a couple of centimetres long. Ants. These social insects have fascinated me since I first bent down with a magnifying glass to watch them take sugar from a bowl. There are more than 4,500 species of ant, with most of them found in the rainforests. Unfortunately, due to deforestation in these areas, many species will never be recorded.

Ants live in a colony, which is built around the queen. She is the largest ant and her sole occupation is producing eggs, while all her physical needs are taken care of by the worker ants around her. **1** ______ They perform such functions as

3 exam practice

You are going to read an article about ants. Seven sentences have been removed from the article. Choose from sentences A–H the one which fits each gap (1–7). There is one extra sentence which you do not need to use.

A They are fed enormous quantities of honey until their bodies become so big that they cannot move.

B They destroy every living thing in their path.

C Ants follow the trail that other ants have left to locate a food source.

D These are all female and infertile.

E These ants don't have a permanent home.

F Once this critical period is over and the first workers are at work, the colony rapidly develops.

G This is generally the best way to get rid of ants from your garden.

H All ant species will fight to protect their colony and some will attack other species.

EXAM EXPERT

How should you do the exam practice task?

a In order to save time, look at each gap in turn without reading the whole text and quickly choose a sentence you think fits.

b Read the whole text before you try to match the sentences with the gaps.

foraging for food and defending the colony from attack, as well as tending to the queen and the colony's eggs.

A colony is founded when a new queen sets off in search of a possible location. Once she has chosen her spot, she begins to lay eggs, some of which are for eating during the difficult first few months. **2** ______ Each species has its own characteristic way of doing things. The leafcutter ant, for example, cuts sections from leaves which it carries back to the nest. These are used as a kind of fertiliser for fungus gardens the ants create underground. There, the leaves provide a rich source of nutrients for the fungus, which the ants eventually consume.

Then there's the honeypot ant. These ants select certain workers to act as living containers for food. **3** ______ They act as a store for the food and feed other ants by producing the honey when they receive the right chemical signals. These signals are an important part of all ants' lives and are used for, among other things, establishing identity and indicating the source of food.

They also help to explain how such simple things can display such complex behaviour. **4** ______ If an obstacle blocks the ants' path, they swarm in all directions, attempting to go around it. The ants who discover the shorter way will get there faster and leave a stronger scent trail. Gradually, as more and more ants follow this trail, it becomes even stronger, until all the ants are following the quicker route.

This kind of communication is very important in nomadic species, such as the army ant. **5** ______ Instead, they form a nest using their own bodies, with millions of them hanging from a tree. When they decide to move on, the whole colony marches through the forest, carrying the queen and the eggs.

The sight of a column of these ants on the move is one of the most frightening sights in the rainforest. **6** ______ Insects, young birds, lizards and other small animals that fail to escape in time can look forward to a rather unpleasant end.

It's not just the army ant, though, that can be a threat. **7** ______ They do this using acid produced in their bodies as a weapon. After a successful attack, some species of ant will take eggs from the losing colony and return them to their own, raising the ants to work as slaves. There's a never-ending list of things they do; ants lead intriguing lives, and tiny though they may be, I never tire of studying them!

WORK IT OUT!

Find these words in the text and the missing sentences and underline them. Can you work out what they mean from the context?

select • foraging • tending to • critical • obstacle • sole • founded • trail

4 Match these words from the text and the missing sentences to the definitions.

1	infertile	a	find the position of
2	acid	b	kind of plant, such as a mushroom
3	locate	c	unable to produce eggs or young
4	fertiliser	d	strong, harmful chemical
5	fungus	e	something put on plants to help them grow

Have your say!

- If you could study an insect, what kind of insect would you choose? Why?

Grammar 2

-ing form or infinitive

Choose the correct option.

*Ants often seem **behaving** / **behave** / **to behave** in complicated ways.*

After some verbs, nouns and adjectives, we use the full infinitive.
*I hope **to study** biology at university.*
*It's important **to save** water.*
*It is our aim **to persuade** the council to stop building.*

After modal verbs, *make* and *let*, we use the bare infinitive.
*All of us should **use** less water.*
*We make people **recycle** their rubbish here.*
*The council lets factories **pollute** the local river.*

After some verbs and after prepositions, we use the *-ing* form.
*Please avoid **dropping** litter in this area.*
*How can we prevent an environmental disaster from **happening**?*

Some verbs can be followed by both the *-ing* form or the full infinitive without a change in meaning.
*We should all start **to take/taking** responsibility.*

With other verbs, the meaning changes.
*We stopped **eating** our sandwiches.*
*We stopped **to eat** our sandwiches.*

See *Grammar database 17* on page 183 for more information.

1 Complete these sentences using the verbs in brackets in the correct form.

1 We can't afford not ____________ (**protect**) our environment.
2 Can we manage ____________ (**save**) just some species?
3 We could suggest ____________ (**introduce**) a ban on hunting in this area.
4 I'm really looking forward to ____________ (**visit**) the nature reserve.
5 Parents should let their children ____________ (**take part**) in demonstrations about the environment.

2 Choose the correct form.

1 Did you remember **to get** / **getting** the seeds I wanted?
2 I don't remember **to read** / **reading** about the greenhouse effect.
3 We should try **to stop** / **stopping** people from damaging the environment.
4 I'll never forget **to see** / **seeing** the rainforests for the first time.
5 Oh! I meant **to call** / **calling** Ralph to talk to him about our trip to the zoo.
6 For many companies, the new law will mean **to produce** / **producing** less pollution.

prefer, would rather, had better

Does this sentence refer to the past or the present?

I'd rather you didn't do that.

prefer

- expressing preferences
  *I **prefer** dogs **to/rather than** cats.*
  *I **prefer** playing with dogs **rather than** cats.*
  *I **would prefer to have** a dog **rather than** a cat.*

would rather

- expressing preferences
  ***I would rather have** a dog **than** a cat.*
  *I **would rather** you **didn't drop** litter outside my house.*

had better

- giving advice
  *You **had better tell** the council about the leak.*

See *Grammar database 18* on page 184 for more information.

! Be careful!

He'd better pick up his litter. ('d = had)
He'd rather spend time in the countryside. ('d = would)

3 Make questions using these prompts.

1 you/rather/visit a farm/a zoo?
2 you/prefer/go fishing/bird-watching?
3 what/you think/we/better/do about litter in our town/city?
4 you/rather/work outdoors/indoors?

Use of English

1 Read the text in exercise 2, ignoring the gaps, and answer the following questions.

1 What is one result of increasing world temperature?
2 Why is the sea level rising in some parts of the world?
3 What is one explanation for the increase in temperature?

EXAM EXPERT

How should you do the exam practice task?

a The words you need to write are always positive, so you don't need to think about negative forms.

b Always ask yourself whether a negative form is needed or not. Read the whole text to check.

2 exam practice

Read the text below. Use the word given in capitals at the end of some of the lines to form a word that fits in the gap in the same line. Write your answers IN CAPITAL LETTERS.

It's getting hotter!

There seems to be little doubt that (1) ___	GLOBE
warming is a real phenomenon. Temperatures	
are rising in many places (2) ___ and	WORLD
(3) ___ farmland is being lost as sea levels rise due to	VALUE
melting of the polar ice. This could cause major problems	
for mankind in the future. (4) ___ disagree, though,	SCIENCE
about whether this (5) ___ change is being caused by	ENVIRONMENT
human actions or not. Some believe that the climate	
has always changed like this and it has (6) ___ causes,	NATURE
while others think what is happening is unique. One	
explanation is the greenhouse effect. This is where	
(7) ___ in the atmosphere traps the Sun's rays, like a	POLLUTE
giant greenhouse. While nobody claims that releasing	
chemicals into the atmosphere can be (8) ___ , not	HARM
everyone is convinced that all the temperature change is	
due to (9) ___ activity. It's an important question, because	INDUSTRY
a (10) ___ can only be found once we understand exactly	SOLVE
what is causing the problem.	

3 exam practice

Complete the second sentence so that it has a similar meaning to the first sentence using the word given. Do not change the word given. You must use between two and five words, including the word given. Write the missing words IN CAPITAL LETTERS.

1 They are building a new road through the Downs.
is
A new road ____________ through the Downs.

2 I hope we manage to persuade the government to ban hunting.
succeed
I hope we ____________ the government to ban hunting.

3 I heard that the dodo became extinct because it couldn't fly.
out
I heard that the dodo ____________ because it couldn't fly.

4 They should discuss the pollution problem in tomorrow's meeting.
discussed
The pollution problem ____________ in tomorrow's meeting.

5 Please try not to waste water.
avoid
Please try ____________ water.

6 I'd prefer you not to walk on my lawn.
did
I'd ____________ walk on my lawn.

7 Eventually, there'll be no fossil fuels left.
out
Eventually, we ____________ fossil fuels.

8 We should create less rubbish.
stop
We need ____________ much rubbish.

EXAM EXPERT

How should you do the exam practice task?

a Instead of writing *do not*, write *don't* because it's only one word.

b Remember that contractions count as two words, except *can't*, which counts as one.

Writing: article

Starting point

**What are the people in the photograph doing?
How effective do you think action like this is?**

1 **Look at this exam question and read this article. What are the three main points the writer makes?**

Your school magazine has invited you to suggest ways in which ordinary people can help to protect the environment. Write an article for the magazine, giving your suggestions.

Write your article in 120–180 words in an appropriate style.

DOING YOUR BIT FOR THE ENVIRONMENT!

We all know what the problem is. Global warming's getting worse and we throw away a small mountain of rubbish every day. It can seem like there's no solution, but a few simple changes to your life can really help the environment.

First of all, ask yourself if you recycle everything you could. Paper and glass are easy, but what about plastic, or tin cans? Find out from your local council how you can recycle more of the things you use every day.

Secondly, think about how much water you use. A few simple steps could save you money and help protect the environment. For example, ______________________________

____

____

____

Finally, what if you don't have any facilities or schemes in your area? That could be your chance to start writing to your council to demand them.

So, don't just sit there! We can all do our bit, from saving water to recycling, from writing letters to joining protests. If everybody does a little, then perhaps together we can really make a difference!

2 **Underline where the writer does the following things.**

- asks the reader a question to involve them in the article
- uses a phrase to introduce the point of each paragraph
- gives specific advice to the reader
- uses contractions to give the article an informal style

3 **What other phrases could be used to introduce each paragraph?**

4 **Complete the third paragraph in an appropriate way. Look back at the text on pages 70–71 for ideas.**

Plan ahead

1 exam practice: article

Your school magazine has invited you to suggest ways in which your school could be more environmentally friendly.

Write an article for the magazine, giving your suggestions.

EXAM EXPERT

How should you write an article?

- **a** Never ask your reader questions because they aren't there to answer them.
- **b** Ask your reader rhetorical questions to involve them in the subject of the article.

See *Writing database* on page 194 for further information.

2 Read the task in exercise 1 and decide whether the following statements are true (T) or false (F).

1. Your article will appear in an international magazine for scientists. T/F
2. You should make your article as formal as possible. T/F
3. You should use a new paragraph for each main point you make. T/F
4. It's a good idea to give an article like this a title. T/F

3 Make notes to answer these questions.

1. Which of these effects might your school have on the local environment?

litter • wasting water • wasting paper
any other problems • noise

2. What solutions can you think of for each of these problems?
3. What part of your article will these problems be discussed in?

introduction • main body • conclusion

4 Complete *Writing Planner 6* on page 208.

5 Write your article in 120–180 words in an appropriate style.

6 When you have written your article, make sure that you have:

- checked your spelling and grammar ☐
- used paragraphs ☐
- used appropriate phrases to introduce each paragraph ☐
- used an appropriate style ☐
- asked your readers a rhetorical question ☐
- made suggestions. ☐

Check your progress! Units 5–6

1 Choose the correct word to fill the gap in each sentence.

1 I've lived in a city all my life, so I've never experienced life in a(n) ___ environment.
A urban **B** rural **C** global **D** local

2 I think there's a ___ in the pipe; maybe we should call a plumber.
A lack **B** lock **C** lake **D** leak

3 Dana drinks a lot of ___ drinks like lemonade and orangeade.
A frozen **B** fresh **C** fizzy **D** flat

4 They need to put more ___ bins in the town centre.
A paper **B** litter **C** waste **D** sewerage

5 My dad wears a suit to work, but he changes into ___ clothes when he gets home.
A informal **B** casual **C** relaxed **D** calm

6 There was a terrible oil ___ when the tanker hit the rocks in a storm.
A slick **B** drop **C** pool **D** spread

7 I bought a cool fishing ___ yesterday!
A pole **B** rod **C** stick **D** bar

8 We're going on a ___ to protest about the closure of the park.
A production **B** presentation **C** construction **D** demonstration

8 marks

2 Write a word from the box in each gap to complete the sentences.

catch • clear • come • die • flick • go • run • take

1 We've nearly ____________ out of milk. Could you go and get some for me?
2 Pandas are likely to ____________ out if we don't do something to protect them soon.
3 I usually ____________ through all the magazines while I'm waiting to see the dentist.
4 Richie really wants to ____________ up snowboarding, so we're going to get him a board for his birthday.
5 Put the fruit in the fridge or it'll ____________ off.
6 If you ____________ round here at about half past six, we can watch that DVD before we go out.
7 Will you help me ____________ up all this mess?
8 When Monopoly first came out, nobody thought it would ____________ on so quickly.

8 marks

3 Complete the second sentence so that it has a similar meaning to the first sentence, using the word given. Do not change the word given. You must use between two and five words, including the word given.

1 I had thought the film would be better.
as
The film ____________ I had thought it would be.

2 They don't let children under three go on this ride.
not
Children under three ____________ go on this ride.

3 Getting a professional to cut down those trees would be a good idea.
better
We ____________ a professional to cut down those trees.

4 Why didn't you ask Helen to help you?
should
You ____________ Helen to help you.

5 I'd prefer you not to smoke in here.
rather
I ____________ smoke in here.

6 This is the fastest roller coaster in the world!
goes
No other ____________ this one.

7 We don't want to damage the environment.
avoid
We want ____________ the environment.

8 Why are you always criticising me?
go
Why are you always ____________ me?

9 People don't recycle enough rubbish in this country.
away
Too much ____________ in this country.

18 marks

4 Write one word in each gap to complete the sentences.

1 Do you think humans are capable ___ saving the planet?
2 How did Caroline react ___ the news?
3 If we don't take care ___ our local environment, who will?
4 It depends ___ the weather whether we go to the water park or not.
5 I think we've succeeded ___ persuading people that global warming is a real phenomenon.
6 Are you accusing me ___ lying?
7 I don't know why you refer ___ environmental campaigners as 'crazy greens'!
8 Why don't you report your noisy neighbours ___ the local authorities?

8 marks

5 Match to make phrases. There is one letter you do not need to use.

1 bottle ___	**a** fee
2 global ___	**b** reserve
3 entrance ___	**c** effect
4 fossil ___	**d** bank
5 nature ___	**e** species
6 greenhouse ___	**f** fuel
	g warming

6 marks

6 Complete each sentence using a form of the word in brackets.

1 Although ______________ (**attend**) at the school concert wasn't compulsory, every single student turned up.
2 We showed our ______________ (**appreciate**) by sending her some flowers.
3 I don't know how anyone can get any ______________ (**enjoy**) from fishing!
4 Scientists used to think this chemical was dangerous, but now they know it's completely ______________ (**harm**).
5 My parents give me a monthly ______________ (**allow**), which I use to buy clothes and CDs.
6 Some drugs are highly ______________ (**addict**).

6 marks

7 Each of the words in bold is in the wrong sentence. Write a word or phrase in bold from another sentence to replace the incorrect one.

1 At the end of most plays, the **sightseers** comes onto the stage to bow. ______________
2 Hundreds of **spectators** rang in to complain about the TV programme. ______________
3 Everyone in the **lifeguard** started screaming when Jennifer Lopez came on stage. ______________
4 The tennis player found it hard to concentrate because one of the **audience** was coughing loudly. ______________
5 I work as a **cast** at the local swimming pool during the summer. ______________
6 Thousands of **viewers** visit the Acropolis every year. ______________

6 marks

Total: 60 marks

Revision 1

Reading

Starting point

Have you ever seen a pop-up or a flashing message on your computer saying that you have won a prize? Did you click on it? What happened?
Have you ever received an email that you thought was suspicious? Describe it. What did you do about it?

1 Read the article, ignoring the gaps for now, and complete these sentences with a word or a short phrase.

1 The writer received an email saying his friend's wife's money __________ at the airport.
2 The __________ in the email was not perfect.
3 In a lottery scam, people give hundreds because they expect to get __________ .
4 In some scams, people ask for money to open __________ so that they can move money to another country.
5 If you get close to finding out the truth, you might be __________ , according to some reports.
6 Because they feel embarrassed, some __________ don't want to get the police involved.
7 When booking a holiday, you might think you're getting a __________ but you will have to pay extra.
8 You are more likely to __________ if someone appears to be honest.

2 exam practice

You are going to read an article about ways in which people try to steal money from you online. Seven sentences have been removed from the article. Choose from sentences A–H the one which fits each gap (1–7). There is one extra sentence which you do not need to use.

A But before you book a holiday this way, think twice.
B Of course, people who send money will never see it again.
C Eventually, he explained that the email account had been taken over by hackers.
D Again, you receive an email, but this time you are told that you have won a fortune.
E I could have got my money back but it wasn't worth having.
F Most of us are honest and we want to believe that others are too.
G No-one wants to admit that he or she has been fooled.
H She was asking me to help by sending money.

Don't be fooled!

Internet scams, where people trick you out of your money, are not likely to go away any time soon, James Hallam reports.

Last summer, I received an email from the wife of an old friend. The message said that they were stuck in Italy after all their money had been stolen as they waited to check in at the airport and now they couldn't afford to get back home. 1 ____ Several things struck me as odd about the email. Firstly, why didn't my friend write? I had only exchanged

3 Find words or phrases in the text which have a similar meaning to these words and phrases.

1 show (their) tickets (paragraph 1)
2 invent; think of (paragraph 2)
3 inherit; get (money) when someone dies (paragraph 3)
4 the money a country uses, eg dollars/ pounds/euros (paragraph 3)
5 start (paragraph 3)
6 when (they) get there (paragraph 4)
7 a feeling that you've done something silly (paragraph 4)
8 the place where something is (paragraph 5
9 luxury (paragraph 5)
10 shared interests (paragraph 6)

emails once with his wife and I had never met her. Secondly, there were some odd things about the email, such as the less than perfect English and the fact that it wasn't addressed to me by name, simply beginning, 'Hello.' Despite the fact that I didn't really believe the email, I felt the need to write to my friend to sort it out. 2 ____ The email had been sent to everyone in her address book.

But what happened to me was quite a simple trick. There are people out there who have come up with all kinds of ways to cheat us. A common one is known as the lottery scam. 3 ____ In order to get this money, however, you need to send a small amount to cover 'registration fees' or something similar (the 'small' amount is usually in the hundreds, but you are assured that you will be receiving millions).

There are variations of the lottery scam – sometimes the writer pretends to be someone who has come into a large amount of money but needs to get it out of the country in a different currency and they want you to lend them some money to open a bank account. Or they want to set up a business and they invite you to invest in it, always with the promise of a much larger amount in return. 4 ____ Even if only a small percentage of people fall for it, it can still add up to a lot of money for the criminals.

And it gets worse. In some of these scams, people have travelled to foreign countries to try to get their money back. On arrival, they have often been tricked into giving yet more money. There are reports of people being attacked because they have come too close to discovering the truth. Cases like this are difficult to confirm, however. 5 ____ There is a great deal of embarrassment involved, so victims don't always go to the police.

On the subject of travelling, be very careful of any special holiday deals that you find on the internet. Often, it seems as if you are being offered an amazing bargain online. 6 ____ What seems like a great discount could actually cost you more. In many cases, for example, the price you pay includes flights but not accommodation. You could also find that your hotel is in a very different location to what the website said. And of course, it is very easy for companies to put pictures on their site that are misleading – that picture of a five-star hotel might have been taken years ago, before they built a motorway next to it! Naturally, the same risks apply to anything you buy on the internet, so beware!

Perhaps one of the cruellest ways people can trick you is when there are emotions involved. Many of us have online friendships, sometimes with people we haven't met in person. Imagine, then, if one of these people suddenly asks you to borrow money because his or her grandmother is sick and can't afford to pay for medicine. You would want to help, wouldn't you? 7 ____ That's why it is easy to be fooled by someone if they seem sincere and we have things in common with them. The story about the sick grandmother might be true, but it probably isn't. Thinking carefully before you act could save you from making a huge mistake.

Listening

1 2.11 exam practice

You will hear people talking in eight different situations. For questions 1–8, choose the best answer (A, B or C).

1 You hear this conversation at the cinema. Which film do the couple decide to see?
A *Long Goodbyes*
B *Starburst*
C *Floating Voters*

2 You hear part of a documentary on the radio. What is the speaker's job?
A scientist
B journalist
C farmer

3 You hear a woman talking to a friend on the phone. What does she want her friend to do?
A invite someone to a party
B put someone up for the night
C give someone a gift from her

4 You hear a man talking in a computer shop. What does he want to buy?
A a printer
B a monitor
C a mouse

5 You hear a guide speaking in a zoo. What does she say about this animal?
A It is unique.
B It is rare.
C It is dangerous.

6 You hear a man talking to a customer. What does he refuse to do?
A take the item back
B return the customer's money
C offer a discount

7 You hear an announcement on a plane. What is the problem?
A The airport is closed.
B There is bad weather ahead.
C The plane will arrive late.

8 You hear a girl talking about a computer game. What does she dislike about it?
A the music
B the characters
C the graphics

2 2.12 exam practice

You will hear five people talking about their hobbies. For questions 1–5, choose from the list (A–F) what each speaker says. Use the letters only once. There is one extra letter which you do not need to use.

Speaker 1 ______
Speaker 2 ______
Speaker 3 ______
Speaker 4 ______
Speaker 5 ______

A I find it relaxing.
B My collection is valuable.
C I'm losing interest in my hobby.
D My hobby has taught me a lot.
E I don't have enough time for my hobby.
F This hobby is new to me.

Have your say!

- What other things do people collect that the speaker didn't mention?
- Why do you think people like collecting things?
- What other hobbies can you think of?

Speaking

1 Answer the following questions about yourself.

- Have you always lived in this town?
- Have you travelled much?
- Have you ever been abroad?
- Where did you spend your last holiday?
- Do you have any plans for your next holiday?

2 Read the examiner's instructions and do the task.

Candidate A, here are two photographs of different places. I'd like you to compare them and say which place you would prefer to spend a week's holiday in. You only have one minute for this.

- Which place would you prefer to spend a week's holiday in?

Candidate B, which place would you prefer to visit?

Candidate B, here are two photographs of different means of transport. I'd like you to compare them and say how you feel about travelling in these ways. You only have one minute for this.

- How do you feel about travelling in these ways?

Candidate A, which means of transport would you prefer to travel on?

3 Read the examiner's instructions and do the task.

I'd like you to imagine that you are going on holiday together to Australia. Here are some things you might do on your holiday. Talk to each other about what each activity would be like and then choose three activities to do on your holiday. You only have three minutes for this.

- What would each activity be like?
- Choose three activities to do on your holiday.

4 Ask and answer the following questions.

- Do you think it's important for people to have holidays?
- What can people learn from travelling abroad?
- Do you think holidays and travel will change over the next 50 years?

Use of English

1 exam practice

Read the text below and decide which answer (A, B, C or D) best fits each gap.

Global Positioning System

GPS is a remarkable (1) ___ . You may have seen your parents using a GPS system in their car, or you might even have GPS on your smartphone. It tells you your exact position, possibly making the simple map and compass (2) ___ .

The (3) ___ of GPS was developed by the US military and the system was set (4) ___ by them. It is based on a network of 24 satellites in orbit around the Earth. Using radio signals, the hand-held receiver calculates the (5) ___ to the satellites and is then able to figure (6) ___ where the user is to (7) ___ a few metres.

There are (8) ___ practical applications of this system. For example, it was used during (9) ___ of the Channel Tunnel, connecting England to France, to (10) ___ sure that the two ends of the tunnel met in the middle. Scientists are currently (11) ___ new ways to use GPS, such as the study of earthquakes. GPS systems could track the way the ground beneath our feet moves and one day (12) ___ that an earthquake is likely could save thousands of lives.

1	**A** appliance	**B** discovery	**C** solution	**D** invention
2	**A** traditional	**B** classic	**C** obsolete	**D** old
3	**A** concept	**B** ideal	**C** image	**D** thought
4	**A** off	**B** up	**C** in	**D** over
5	**A** length	**B** line	**C** distance	**D** size
6	**A** off	**B** up	**C** on	**D** out
7	**A** within	**B** among	**C** between	**D** around
8	**A** uncountable	**B** numerous	**C** massive	**D** grand
9	**A** installation	**B** construction	**C** shaping	**D** manufacture
10	**A** do	**B** have	**C** make	**D** take
11	**A** researching	**B** experimenting	**C** estimating	**D** predicting
12	**A** declaring	**B** doubting	**C** knowing	**D** wondering

2 exam practice

Read the text below and think of the word which best fits each gap. Use only one word in each gap. Write your answers IN CAPITAL LETTERS.

Dinosaur extinction

After ruling the Earth (1) _________ 200 million years, the dinosaurs suddenly (2) _________ extinct around 65 million years ago. Scientists disagree about the precise reasons why they died (3) _________, but they agree that (4) _________ was probably the result of a dramatic change in the Earth's climate. There are two main answers (5) _________ the question of what caused the change. A huge volcanic explosion has (6) _________ suggested as one possible cause, while another popular theory claims that the change (7) _________ be explained as the result of a large meteorite crashing into the Earth. However the explosion came (8) _________, both theories agree that disaster spread over the planet. Large amounts of dust in the atmosphere blocked the Sun's heat and temperatures dropped. It (9) _________ estimated that around 25 per cent of plant life on the Earth was destroyed by fire. With the conditions they (10) _________ used to disappearing, the dinosaurs could (11) _________ survive. Only smaller animals, such as birds and mammals, could adapt (12) _________ the new situation.

Writing: email

1 Look at the task in exercise 2 and answer these questions.

1 Should your email be formal or informal?
2 Who are you writing to?
3 How should you start and end your email?
4 What information do you want?

2 exam practice: email

You and your family are considering going on a cruise around the Mediterranean. You have seen the advertisement below and would like more information.

Read the advertisement and the notes which you have made below carefully. Then write your email to the travel agent, covering the points in your notes and adding any relevant information about your family.

SEAVOYAGER CRUISES

Enjoy a relaxing cruise around the Mediterranean this summer!

Let our fast, modern ships take you on a voyage of discovery in a world of pleasure and fun you never even knew existed!
Enjoy our on-board facilities while at sea, including the swimming pools, the games rooms and a whole week of organised activities.
Stop at exotic resorts along the coasts of Southern Europe and Northern Africa, where you can shop till you drop, or take it easy over a coffee and watch the world go by!

Try food from the whole region, or stick with what you know in our many restaurants.

For more information about how you can join us on this luxury adventure of a lifetime, including cost and availability, contact:

William Faldo
Faldo Travel
P.O. Box 117
London
SE12 4RD

'organised activities' – what activities? any for young children?

which resorts?

price? discounts for groups?

available from 24th June to 8th July?

3 Write your email in 120–150 words. You must use grammatically correct sentences with accurate spelling and punctuation in a style appropriate for the situation.

4 When you have written your email, make sure that you have:

- checked your spelling and grammar ☐
- used paragraphs ☐
- used formal language, including indirect questions ☐
- asked for all the information you need ☐
- started and finished your email in an appropriate way. ☐

7

Sport

Wordpower!

stamina • teamwork • sense of balance
agility • coordination

Starting point

Choose one of the sports in the photographs and explain what skills you need to do it well.

1 Read the article quickly to find the answers to these questions.

1 When were the first Extreme Games or X Games held?
2 Which extreme sport is also an Olympic® event?
3 What are the two main forms of BMX?
4 When did the first BMX magazine come out?
5 When were roller skates invented?

Reading 1 2.13

2 exam practice

You are going to read a magazine article about sports. Seven sentences have been removed from the article. Choose from sentences A–H the one which fits each gap (1–7). There is one extra sentence which you do not need to use.

A This form of the sport is based on skateboarding competitions.
B Athletes would show off their skills for the people watching to copy.
C A number of people have objected to these dangerous sports, highlighting the risk of accident.
D Several of the sports that fall into this category have also been known as 'outlaw sports' because they were banned in many areas for being too dangerous.
E This design was easier to control and led to an increase in popularity for the sport.
F This is partly because they are often considered to be different from older, established sports.
G Fans of motocross, but too young to ride motorbikes, they named their sport 'pedal cross'.
H For example, BMX racing and mountain biking are both based on cycling.

EXAM EXPERT

How should you do the exam practice task?

When you have chosen a sentence to fit each gap

a don't bother rereading the text with the sentences replaced to check it makes sense as this takes too much time.
b quickly reread the whole text with the sentences replaced to check it makes sense.

3 Find forms of these words in the text. Match them to the correct definitions.

1 freestyle	a a sport or activity using boots with wheels
2 roller skating	b one sport that forms part of a sporting competition
3 recreational	c a sloping surface used for jumping off
4 event	d a dangerous move in certain extreme sports
5 stunt	e done for amusement or enjoyment
6 ramp	f (of a sport) using any method

Going to extremes

John Hancock reports on the history of some of your favourite extreme sports.

Whether it's a jaw-dropping move on a skateboard or the raw speed of BMX, there's no doubt that extreme sports have taken off in a big way over the last 25 years. Some need snow, some need wheels, but they all share an element of danger, usually combined with acrobatic stunts.

ESPN, the American TV sports network, organised the first Extreme Games (now the X Games) in 1995 and coined the phrase 'extreme sports'. 1 ____ However, some, older more traditional sports, such as freestyle skiing, skydiving, surfing and water-skiing, are also sometimes considered extreme sports.

Extreme sports have also been characterised as 'alternative sports'. 2 ____ Also, many of the athletes have adopted alternative fashions and have seen themselves as outside the usual sporting world.

Many extreme sports are in fact new versions of older sports, often made possible by technological changes or improvements in equipment. 3 ____ In-line skating is a form of roller skating.

For the most part, extreme sports originated as recreational activities for individuals, but often in a group context. 4 ____ As they have become competitive, extreme sports have been at least partly absorbed into the mainstream, although snowboarding is still the only extreme sport to have become an Olympic® event.

One of the most spectacular extreme sports is BMX. There are two main forms, BMX racing, which takes place on a dirt track of about 300 to 400 metres with a series of jumps, and freestyle BMX, involving stunts and tricks. The sport has come a long way since a group of kids first started organising races at Palms Park, Santa Monica, California, back in 1969. 5 ____ They couldn't have known what they were starting. Races quickly got bigger and the sport became known as BMX, which stands for 'bicycle motocross'. The first American national championship was held in 1974 and the first magazine devoted to the sport appeared in the same year. It went from strength to strength throughout the eighties and nineties and today there are over 50 national BMX organisations around the world.

Another popular extreme sport is in-line skating, with around 30 million skaters worldwide. In-line skates are generally assumed to be very new and modern, but actually all roller skates were in-line from the first known pair in 1716 until 1863. It was then that James Plimpton invented a skate with four wheels in a rectangular arrangement. 6 ____ In 1966, the original in-line skates returned, but it wasn't until 1980 that two ice hockey-playing brothers, Scott and Brennan Olson of Minneapolis, realised that in-line skates could be used for training and practice when there was no ice. They started to make their own skates, selling them to friends, and eventually set up their own company, Rollerblade, to market them. They were so successful that in-line skates are often known simply as 'Rollerblades'.

As a competitive sport, in-line skating is actually several sports. There are in-line versions of the traditional roller skating events: speed skating, artistic (figure) skating, and roller hockey. However, the best-known and most popular of the competitive sports is aggressive in-line skating, also known as 'aggro'. 7 ____ There are two events, street and vert (short for 'vertical'). In street competition, skaters perform tricks while jumping over boxes, ramps, and rails, while in vert they do a 60-second routine of tricks and stunts in a half-pipe, like that used in skateboarding and snowboarding.

It seems certain that extreme sports will continue to grow in popularity and bring even more heart-stopping action to more people. So, what are you waiting for? Go to extremes!

WORK IT OUT!

Find these words and phrases in the text and underline them. Can you work out what they mean from the context?

taken off • coined • versions • originated • stands for devoted to • went from strength to strength

Have your say!

- Have you ever tried any extreme sports?
- Which of the sports mentioned in the text would you like to try?

G Grammar 1

Modals (2): degrees of certainty

Look at the following sentence and choose the correct meaning.

'Ian must be playing football,' said Maria.

a Maria thinks that Ian has no choice about playing football.

b Maria is almost certain that Ian is playing football.

These modal verbs can be used to express an opinion about what we think is:

almost certainly true or not true.
*'That **can't** be Ruth at the door. She's playing tennis.'*
*Basketball **must** be the number one sport in this country.*
*'You **must have** been very pleased when you won the match.'*
*'Richard **can't/couldn't have** been very happy when you beat him.'*

probably true or not true.
*'Tom **ought to/should be** arriving back from the game any minute now.'*

possibly true or not true.
*'This **could/might/may** be the greatest final ever!'*
*'Dad **could/might/may** have been delayed at the tennis club.'*

See *Grammar database 19* on page 184 for more information.

1 **Find an example of a modal being used to express an almost certain opinion in the text on page 91. Underline the sentence.**

2 **Use the prompts and your imagination to answer the questions about the photograph.**

1 Where was this photograph taken? **might**
2 How do you think the people are feeling? **must**
3 What were the people doing before the photo was taken? **may**
4 Who do you think these people are? **could**

3 **Complete the second sentence so that it has a similar meaning to the first sentence, using the word given. You must use between two and five words, including the word given.**

1 Perhaps Len has forgotten about basketball practice.
have
Len __________ about basketball practice.

2 I imagine it was depressing to lose by six goals.
been
You __________ after losing by six goals.

3 I don't believe that Oliver beat Simon at squash!
beaten
Oliver __________ Simon at squash!

4 Perhaps Carol didn't know that the match had been rearranged.
may
Carol __________ that the match had been arranged.

5 I suppose Tim was unhappy when his BMX bike was stolen.
happy
Tim __________ when his BMX bike was stolen.

4 **Use the words in brackets in the correct form to complete this dialogue.**

Kelly: Well done, Fran. You've improved! You __________ (**must / practise**).

Fran: Well, I think you __________ (**might / let**) me win.

Kelly: Maybe next time! But honestly, you were really good. You __________ (**can't / miss**) more than a few shots.

Fran: It was a lot of fun. You __________ (**must / be**) exhausted, though. That's your second match today, isn't it?

Kelly: Yes. I __________ (**must / be**) mad! I've got another match tomorrow, as well. I'm playing Wendy. She __________ (**can't / be**) very good because I heard that Amy beat her last week.

Fran: She __________ (**can't / do**)! Amy is a complete beginner!

Kelly: Yes, I know. Look! There's Wendy's car. She __________ (**must / play**) at the moment. Let's see if we can find her.

Fran: Okay.

V Vocabulary

People in sport

1 Match the following words to the correct definitions.

1	referee	a	the person or team who most people think will win
2	coach	b	a person who has won a major competition
3	opponent	c	someone who controls a tennis match
4	favourite	d	the person who comes second
5	runner-up	e	the person you are playing against
6	champion	f	the person who is winning a race
7	competitor	g	someone who controls a football match
8	umpire	h	someone who trains athletes
9	leader	i	someone who takes part in a sporting competition

2 Phrasal verbs

Complete these sentences using the phrasal verbs to do with sport in the correct form.

give up • take on • put off • join in
drop out • catch up

1 The other runners gradually ____________ with the leader.
2 This is the first time this team ____________ such a difficult challenge.
3 The final ____________ until next weekend because of the weather.
4 John and Mark started playing football and all the other children soon ____________ .
5 If you want to win a marathon, it's important never to ____________ but to believe that you can keep going.
6 Everyone was shocked when the leader ____________ of the race with only two laps to go.

3 Word formation

Complete each sentence using a form of the word in bold.

1 This ____________ will really damage our chances of winning the championship. **lose**
2 I'm really quite ____________ and I can't stand losing. **compete**
3 We need a great ____________ from everyone if we're going to win this match. **perform**
4 Regular training helps to build and ____________ muscles. **strong**
5 Both our key players are out of action at the moment with serious ____________ . **injure**
6 The important thing in any sport is to get your ____________ right. **prepare**

4 What other words can be formed using the words in exercise 3? Make a note of as many as you can. Don't forget to include any negative forms.

5 Collocations

Complete these phrases using *go*, *play* or *do*.

1	____ skateboarding	5	____ windsurfing
2	____ karate	6	____ skiing
3	____ horse-riding	7	____ water polo
4	____ squash	8	____ the long jump

6 Match each sport to the place where it is played.

1	football	a	rink
2	basketball	b	court
3	hockey	c	course
4	volleyball	d	pitch
5	cricket	e	ring
6	golf		
7	skating		
8	boxing		
9	tennis		
10	wrestling		

Listening

Wordpower!

gender • sexism • (un)fair • physical strength

Starting point

Is it unusual to see women taking part in certain sports?
Do women get the same sporting opportunities as men in your country?

1 2.14 **Listen to these three extracts and match each speaker to one of the pictures below.**

2 2.15 **Listen to extracts from the other two speakers. Which sports do they mention?**

3 **Read statements A–F in exercise 4. For each statement, suggest what the speaker might be talking about.**

Example: **A** She did badly in a competition because she lost concentration.

Perhaps she was playing a sport professionally, such as tennis, and she was distracted by one of the spectators.

> **EXAM EXPERT**
>
> **How should you do the exam practice task?**
>
> a Read any statements you are given about the speakers before you listen so that you know what to expect.
>
> b Only read any statements you are given about the speakers after listening so that you don't get confused.

4 2.16 **exam practice**

You will hear five different women talking about sports. For questions 1–5, choose from the list (A–F) what each speaker says. Use the letters only once. There is one extra letter which you do not need to use.

Speaker 1 ____ Speaker 4 ____
Speaker 2 ____ Speaker 5 ____
Speaker 3 ____

A She did badly in a competition because she lost concentration.
B She discovered something was harder than she'd imagined.
C She regrets not being in better shape.
D She wants to improve her mind as well as her body.
E She recently tried a new sport for the first time.
F She won something due to someone else's misfortune.

5 **Listen again and note down the words and phrases that helped you find the answers to exercise 4.**

Have your say!

- Which of the sports mentioned by the women can you do in your area?

Speaking

Starting point

How do you think the people in the photographs on this page feel?
Do you prefer to take part in sport or watch sport as a spectator?

1 Choose true (T) or false (F).

In an English exam interview or Speaking paper, ...

1 you will lose marks if your answers are untrue. T/F
2 you should give one-word answers to save time. T/F
3 your answers should be clear and relevant. T/F
4 if you don't understand the question, talk about your family or interests. T/F
5 never admit that you're not sure about something – always express a firm opinion. T/F

2 2.17 Listen to extracts from a candidate talking in a Speaking test. As you listen, put the following questions the candidate was asked in the correct order.

a Do you follow any sports as a spectator?
b Do you play much sport?
c Have you ever tried any unusual sports?
d What are the sporting facilities like in your area?

3 2.18 Now listen to the whole of the discussion and check your answers. Which candidate do you think performs better, Michael or Sonia? Why?

4 You are going to interview each other using the questions in exercise 5. Before you do, make brief notes of your answers and the reasons for them.

5 exam practice

Do you come from a large family?
What do you like doing in your free time?
Do you play any sport?
Do you prefer team or individual sports?
Do you follow any sports as a spectator?
What do you think of extreme sports?
What are the sporting facilities like in your area?

EXAM EXPERT

How should you do the exam practice task?

a Walk into the interview room chewing gum, sit down and say 'Hi. Is it difficult?'
b Walk into the interview room, smile, greet the examiners and sit down when invited, ready to begin the interview.

See *Speaking database* on page 193.

Reading 2 2.19

Wordpower!

injury • pressure • privacy • stress • uncertainty

Starting point

What problems do successful sportsmen and -women face?

1 **You are going to read a text about problems faced by sportsmen and -women. Read the text quickly and note down the main problem each person describes.**

1 Sandra McNaughton
2 Benjamin Bailey
3 Karen Rush
4 Marcus Jordan
5 Helen Tyler
6 Gordon Clarkson
7 Luke Zafelli
8 Angela 'Tornado' Wilson

2 **Look at the questions in exercise 3. Which of them refer to the following things?**

a the future
b success
c uncertainty
d happiness
e other people

3 exam practice

You are going to read a newspaper article about different sportsmen and -women. For questions 1–15, choose from the people (A–H). The people may be chosen more than once.

Which person
1 was lied to by someone close? ____
2 was affected by the weather? ____
3 predicts that their performance will improve? ____
4 was accused of wrongdoing? ____
5 didn't know if two things would work together? ____
6 will continue with their sport but in a different way? ____
7 felt uncertain because of something they read? ____
8 made a choice to stop something? ____
9 had an accident? ____
10 was very excited by an announcement? ____
11 was advised not to worry? ____
12 missed an important sporting event? ____
13 was unsure that they would achieve victory? ____
14 met someone who changed them? ____
15 felt pressure from journalists to do well? ____

Eight sportsmen and -women describe the challenge they've faced this year.

A Sandra McNaughton – tennis player

'I was on such a high at the start of the year. I'd won the Ladies Open back in December, and Dave Barbeck and I won the Mixed Doubles in February. Everything seemed to be going right. And then I tripped during training and sprained my ankle. Suddenly my prospects for the rest of the year seemed worse than ever. I didn't get to compete at Wimbledon, of course, but I have now totally recovered, thank goodness.'

B Benjamin Bailey – footballer

'Things weren't so good in September, when the rumours started in the press that I was to be dropped from the team. I don't know where they came from, and my coach and the manager both reassured me they weren't true, but it's a horrible feeling thinking you might not be wearing the club's strip for much longer. I had sleepless nights about it. I've learned an important lesson, though: never believe what you read in the papers.'

EXAM EXPERT

How should you do the exam practice task?

a Underline the sentences that give you the answers and write the question number next to them so that you can check your answers easily.

b Don't waste time underlining the sentences that give you the answers because it's important you do each task very quickly.

Professional challenges

C Karen Rush – boxer

'The biggest challenge I've had to face this year is staying focused. I fell head over heels in love in March, and all of a sudden there was something in my life apart from boxing. Training's extremely demanding, and you have to be utterly single-minded, so I had to work out if I'd have to sacrifice either my relationship or my career, or if I could have both. So far I've managed to keep both, but I know it's not going to be easy.'

D Marcus Jordan – rugby player

'It was a very weird year for me, knowing it was my last season playing professionally. I don't regret taking the decision to retire – you can't go on forever – but with every game I just felt a little sadder. The end was drawing near. I'm not going to completely disappear, though, as I'll be playing as an amateur for the Lincolnshire Warriors, a club for older players.'

E Helen Tyler – long-distance runner

'The marathon in Lisbon. The media had built it up into such a big thing, and of course I was desperate to win, but I just wasn't prepared for running in that kind of heat and I found it really difficult to keep up the pace. There were moments when I thought I wouldn't make it. Thankfully, I just kept going, and it paid off. I cried when I was awarded the trophy.'

F Gordon Clarkson – basketball player

'Discovering that the person I most trusted – my business manager – had been stealing from me. I always just signed the contracts without reading them, and left the business side of things to him. Now I feel betrayed, and have lost one of my best friends. I'll be a lot more careful in future, that's for sure.'

G Luke Zafelli – sprinter

'My whole world fell to pieces when they told me I'd failed a drugs test, wouldn't be able to compete in the European Championships and that my career was over. I felt anger, shock and resentment, but knew I had to stay strong to clear my name. When they finally admitted there'd been a mix-up with the blood samples and I was reinstated, just before the Championships, I was thrilled. I never want to go through anything like that again.'

H Angela 'Tornado' Wilson – snooker player

'Last year, I was World Snooker Champion. This year, I haven't won a single major championship. When you suffer one defeat after another, it really affects your mood, making it even more difficult to win the next time. I'm just beginning to learn how not to let failure affect me, so I can continue to play. So – watch this space. I'll be back, and I'll be better than ever!'

4 Find words in the text to complete these definitions.

1 Your ________ are your chances of future success.
2 A team's ________ is the coloured clothes they play in.
3 A professional is paid for performing, whereas an ________ isn't.
4 A sports ________ is an organisation that consists of a team and other staff.
5 Another word for 'speed' is ________.
6 If you are ________ something, you are given it for your achievements.
7 ________ are written legal agreements.
8 If you suffer a ________, you lose a sporting contest.

WORK IT OUT!

Find these words in the text and underline them. Can you work out what they mean from the context?

rumours • reassured • demanding • single-minded
sacrifice • weird • paid off • resentment • mood

Have your say!

- Do you think professional sportsmen and -women are under a lot of pressure?
- Would you like to be involved in sport professionally?

Grammar 2

Prepositions of time and place

Which prepositions complete this sentence?
The match is ***on / at*** *Monday* ***to / at*** *the Millennium Stadium* ***at / in*** *Cardiff.*

at
a specific time:
at one o'clock/midnight/6.30

a public holiday:
at Christmas/Easter/New Year

a specific location or building:
meet at the airport/McDonald's/the cinema

group activities:
be at a match/party/concert

other phrases:
at the weekend, at work, at night, at dawn

on
days:
on Monday/Friday morning/my birthday

positions on a surface:
on the table/a bridge/the road

islands:
on Tenerife/Crete/the Isle of Man

other phrases:
on TV, on the phone, on time

in
periods longer than a day:
in 2012/the first week of March/summer

parts of the day:
in the morning/afternoon/evening

inside rooms, buildings or large areas:
in the cinema/London/the centre of town

other phrases:
in a week's time, in time

See *Grammar database 20* on page 184 for more information.

! Be careful!

☒ arrive at the airport/the station/your destination

☒ arrive in Manchester/Russia/Africa

☒ arrive to the airport/Manchester/your destination

1 Complete this dialogue using the correct prepositions.

Kyle: We're meeting Jonty (1) __________ the corner of his street (2) __________ one, aren't we?
Hailey: No, (3) __________ the stadium, outside the gate. He said he had to go shopping (4) __________ the morning.
Kyle: Oh, yeah. He's never (5) __________ time for anything, though. We'd better get the tickets.
Hailey: Did you see the other game (6) __________ TV? It was one-one (7) __________ half-time and we scored two (8) __________ the second half!
Kyle: I missed it. I was (9) __________ work. I deliver pizzas (10) __________ the evenings, remember?

Indirect questions

What is wrong with this sentence?
Could you tell me what time is basketball training this week?

Indirect questions are more formal than direct questions. They are formed using an introductory phrase, such as:
Could you tell me …
Do you know …
I wonder if you could …
Would you mind telling me …
Could I ask …
Do you think you could …

This is followed by a question word clause. Notice the word order.

Could you tell me what ***time the match starts****?*

I wonder if you could let me know ***how much the tickets are****.*

When an indirect question begins with a question form, it needs a question mark at the end. Otherwise, we do not use a question mark. Compare:
Could I ask how you play this sport?
I wonder if you could tell me how you play this sport.

See *Grammar database 21* on page 185 for more information.

2 Imagine you are going to interview one of the people in the text on pages 96–97. Choose the person to interview and write indirect questions you could ask, using these phrases.

1 Could you tell me …
2 Would you mind telling me …
3 Could I ask …
4 I wonder if you could tell me …

3 Now role-play the interview in pairs. One of you should take the part of the sportsman or -woman, and the other the part of a reporter interviewing them for a national newspaper.

Use of English

1 Read the text in exercise 2 quickly to find the answer to this question.

Are professionals allowed to compete in the Olympic Games™?

2 exam practice

Read the text on the right and decide which answer (A, B, C or D) best fits each gap.

Money and the Olympics®

Today, the distinction between the professional and the (1) ___ is purely a matter of sporting success. Most (2) ___ start their careers by winning competitions for non-professionals before deciding to (3) ___ themselves to their chosen sport. However, for a long time many people believed that getting paid for a sporting (4) ___ destroyed the ancient Olympic® ideal of people simply trying to do their best for the love of the sport.

In fact, even (5) ___ in ancient Olympic® (6) ___ were able to make large amounts of money from winning. At the Games themselves, only a laurel wreath was (7) ___ to the winner, but back in his home town he could become very rich.

During most of the 20th century, professionals were (8) ___ from entering the Olympics®. This gave the wealthy an advantage (9) ___ they could afford to train and compete without needing to earn money. In 1986, the IOC (which (10) ___ for International Olympic® Committee) decided to allow professionals to take (11) ___ in the Olympics®. Only boxing still restricts the (12) ___ of professionals allowed to compete, as boxing excludes professionals altogether.

1	**A** champion	**B** amateur	**C** umpire	**D** volunteer
2	**A** opponents	**B** rivals	**C** runners-up	**D** athletes
3	**A** concentrate	**B** devote	**C** focus	**D** aim
4	**A** match	**B** action	**C** activity	**D** recreation
5	**A** players	**B** members	**C** participants	**D** attendants
6	**A** sessions	**B** acts	**C** plays	**D** events
7	**A** earned	**B** awarded	**C** gained	**D** rewarded
8	**A** prevented	**B** denied	**C** refused	**D** disallowed
9	**A** but	**B** since	**C** despite	**D** although
10	**A** goes	**B** takes	**C** means	**D** stands
11	**A** part	**B** account	**C** place	**D** sides
12	**A** amount	**B** degree	**C** number	**D** quantity

> **EXAM EXPERT**
>
> **How should you do the exam practice task?**
>
> Leave yourself **very little / enough** time to transfer your answers to the answer sheet and do it as **carefully / quickly** as possible because any mistakes **will / won't** cost you marks.

3 Look at the title of the text in exercise 4. What do you know about this subject already?

4 exam practice

Read the text below. Use the word given in capitals at the end of some of the lines to form a word that fits in the gap in the same line. Write your answers IN CAPITAL LETTERS.

> **EXAM EXPERT**
>
> **How should you do the exam practice task?**
>
> **a** If you really don't know the form of the word that is needed, leave the gap blank.
>
> **b** If you're not sure of the word that is needed, take a guess using your knowledge of ways of forming words.

Drugs and the Olympics®

In 1967, the use of drugs by (1) ___ in the Olympics® was banned. Before modern drugs	**COMPETE**
became a problem, athletes had tried all sorts of ways, including drinking a (2) ___	**MIX**
of alcohol and raw egg before a race, in order to get an unfair advantage and an (3) ___	**IMPROVE**
in their time. In the marathon in 1904, Thomas Hicks, who became the gold (4) ___ ,	**MEDAL**
actually drank brandy during the race! (5) ___ , in 1960, a Danish athlete died after taking	**FORTUNE**
drugs and the (6) ___ was taken to outlaw certain substances. Today, there are	**DECIDE**
(7) ___ chemicals which athletes are not allowed to take – not only during competitive	**COUNT**
events but also during (8) ___ . Olympic® officials randomly test athletes' blood for	**TRAIN**
(9) ___ of these drugs. Any athlete found to have these substances in their system	**EVIDENT**
will almost certainly be banned from competing, partly because they give the athlete	
an unfair advantage, and partly because they are so (10) ___ .	**HARM**

Writing: formal email

Starting point

Choose one of the following and tell your partner about it.

- What reasons are there for writing formal letters and emails?
- Do you like writing emails or do you prefer other means of communication? Why? / Why not?

1 **Read this email. What features of formal language can you find in the email?**

write reply send

From: Michelle Greene
Sent: 15th March

Subject: Interview

Dear Mr Peterson,

Thank you for your email agreeing to be interviewed for our school magazine.

In answer to your questions, the interview should last approximately half an hour. What we are interested in is how you felt winning a gold medal in the Olympics®. We would also welcome any advice you have for young people on becoming a professional athlete.

We would like to hold the interview at the school. Do you think you could be here on either 13th or 14th May?

____

____

I wonder if you could possibly bring your gold medal with you. We are planning to take photographs during the interview and our readers would be very interested to see the results of all your hard work.

Please do contact me if you have any further questions regarding the interview.
Yours sincerely,
Michelle Greene

2 **Answer these questions.**

1 Who do you think Mr Peterson might be?
2 Who do you think Michelle Greene might be?
3 What questions do you think Mr Peterson asked in his last email?
4 What suggestion and what request does Michelle make?

3 **Complete Michelle's email by writing a paragraph about the time of the interview. Include the following points.**

- afternoon (4pm) better because of lessons
- morning possible, if before 9am

Plan ahead

1 exam practice: formal email

The editor of your school magazine has asked you to arrange an interview with a local sportswoman. Below is the email the sportswoman has sent you.

write reply send

From: Penny McDougal
Sent: 12th February

Subject: Interview

I am very happy to be interviewed, but there are one or two pieces of information I will need. Could you let me know where and when you would like the interview to take place? I would be grateful if you could give me a choice of dates since I am quite busy. I would also like to know what I am going to be asked about and whether there is anything I should bring with me to the interview.

I look forward to hearing from you soon.

Yours sincerely,

Penny McDougal

Read Mrs McDougal's reply and the note below from the editor of the magazine. Then write an email to Mrs McDougal, arranging the interview and answering her questions.

We want to know about Mrs McDougal's career, especially being a woman in football. Does she have any advice for us? We've got a special issue on sport in March, so around the middle of February would be a good time to interview her. You suggest some dates and times. Oh, and does she have any photos of herself playing? They'd look great in the magazine. Good luck, and speak to you later.

Carol

EXAM EXPERT

How should you write a formal letter/email?

a From the notes you are given, you need to choose the information you think is the most important and write about that.

b You need to include all the information you are given in notes, perhaps adding other relevant information from your imagination.

See *Writing database* on pages 196–197 for further information.

2 Look at the writing task in exercise 1 and answer these questions.

1 Who are you writing to and why?
2 What four things does she want to know?
3 What are the answers to her questions?
4 How are you going to start your email?
Dear ________
5 At the end of your email, what should you write above your name?
Yours ________

3 Make a paragraph plan. Decide what information you will include in each paragraph.

4 Write your email in 120–150 words. You must use grammatically correct sentences with accurate spelling and punctuation in a style appropriate for the situation.

5 When you have written your email, make sure that you have:

- used formal language ☐
- answered all of Mrs McDougal's questions ☐
- added any other relevant information ☐
- checked your grammar, spelling and punctuation ☐
- written the correct number of words. ☐

8

Communication

Wordpower!

telecommunications • the media
global • satellite • text messaging

Starting point

What means of communication can you think of?
How do they affect our lives?
How do you think they will develop in the future?

1 **Look at the headings in the text opposite. Do you know what any of these jobs involve?**

2 **Look at the text quickly to match these people to the jobs they do.**

1	Mike Rae	**a**	director
2	Lisa Jenkins	**b**	special effects manager
3	Todd Barnes	**c**	camera operator

3 **exam practice**

You are going to read an article about jobs in the media. For questions 1–15, choose from the jobs (A–F). The jobs may be chosen more than once.

Which job(s) would you recommend for someone who:

is good at coming up with new stories? 1 ___
is interested in how action films are made? 2 ___
doesn't mind working in different places? 3 ___ 4 ___
can quickly decide what to do? 5 ___ 6 ___
is good at understanding instructions? 7 ___ 8 ___
is able to work with computers? 9 ___
can communicate well with people? 10 ___ 11 ___ 12 ___
is interested in politics? 13 ___ 14 ___
has a qualification in a scientific subject? 15 ___

Reading 1 3.01

How would you like to be involved in making the latest Hollywood blockbuster? Or how about reading the news on TV? Working in the media can be a great career move, as Isabel Pettifer finds out!

There are many jobs in the media, some of which you may never have thought of as a career option. I went along to Planet Productions to speak to the people there about what it takes to get to the top.

A Special Effects Manager
Want to crash a car, or destroy a spaceship? People who work in special effects design, make and operate the special effects equipment required for a production. Many of the people working in special effects are experts in specialised areas (electronics, explosives, etc). Mike Rae, special effects manager at Planet Productions, told me that you had to be able to use computers, be creative and have a good imagination, as well as understand what the director is telling you. He said he had learned what looked good on screen by watching films like *Star Wars* when he was a child.

B Camera Operator
Think you can get the perfect shot? It is the camera operator's job to produce the visual images that make films and television programmes possible. Camera operators set up, position and operate camera equipment in studios or on location to shoot required scenes. Tasks will vary considerably depending on whether they are working in film or television. You might have responsibility

EXAM EXPERT

How should you do the exam practice task?

When there is more than one answer to a question

a it doesn't matter what order you put them in.

b you should be careful to put them in the correct order.

Media matters

for interpreting the director's intentions. Lisa Jenkins, one of the few women camera operators in the industry, said she had done a photography degree course before landing a job with Planet Productions. I asked her whether qualifications were important. 'What really counts is experience,' she told me. 'Most people follow the traditional "start at the bottom and work your way up" approach.'

C Journalist
Journalists work across a range of factual, news and current affairs programmes for radio, television and the print media, reporting on local, national and international stories. They may be expected to contribute ideas, write scripts and news bulletins, direct news items on location and interview on camera. Planet Productions has a staff of five journalists and they agreed that vital qualities were an eye for a story, a focus on the reader, viewer or listener and the ability to decide in a split second how to cover a story. If you also have excellent communication skills and can write well, then maybe journalism is for you!

D Presenter
Presenters introduce, present and host productions for radio or television. They may, depending on the production, introduce programmes, host shows, read news, interview people, report on issues and events, research and write scripts, attend production meetings and find guests to appear in a production. Good organisational skills, a good memory and a good sense of timing are essential here. You've also got to look right and sound right, of course. A good presenter makes the viewers feel that he or she is talking directly to them, so you have to come across as a likeable person.

E Scriptwriter
Maybe you'd like to see your ideas up on the big screen. It's scriptwriters who work to produce scripts for a variety of radio, TV or film productions. Their tasks may include choosing themes for written work and conducting research into the subject. Then, of course, they have to plan and organise the material and write, revise and edit the script. Good knowledge of story structure is important, along with the ability to produce fresh and original ideas. Good communication skills and an excellent understanding of English, particularly grammar and spelling, is also vital. The pressure can be intense, so you have to be able to work to deadlines.

F Director
See yourself as a leader? The director takes overall responsibility for the creative, visual and audio effect of a production. They are responsible for managing both human and technical resources on a production and reporting to the producers. Directors take creative decisions and may be responsible for writing or rewriting parts of the script. One of the directors at Planet Productions, Todd Barnes, told me you had to keep calm and think straight under pressure. He said he had to make important decisions every minute of every day. Have you got what it takes?

Whatever your skills, working in the media can be a rewarding experience. For more information, try searching online for 'careers in the media' and see what comes up!

WORK IT OUT!

Find these words and phrases in the text and underline them. Can you work out what they mean from the context?

explosives • qualifications • likeable
contribute • vital • a split second
deadlines • overall • comes up

4 **Find forms of these words in the text. Match them to the correct definition.**

1	blockbuster	a	take pictures of
2	image	b	picture
3	shoot	c	important events in the news
4	current affairs	d	short news report on television or radio
5	script	e	the written words of a news report, film, etc
6	bulletin	f	very successful film

Have your say!

- Discuss which of the jobs you would like to do.

G Grammar 1

Reported speech

He said he wanted to work in the media.

What did he actually say?

a *I wanted to work in the media.*
b *I want to work in the media.*

When we report (tell somebody else) what a person said to us, we often have to change the tense of the verb, together with other words which refer to time and place.

present simple	→ past simple
present continuous	→ past continuous
present perfect past simple past perfect	→ past perfect
present perfect continuous past continuous past perfect continuous	→ past perfect continuous

Other words we have to change include pronouns and:

here	→ there		
now	→ then, at that moment		
today	→ that day		
yesterday	→ the day before, the previous day		
tomorrow	→ the day after, the following/next day		
next week/month/year	→ the following week/month/year		
ago	→ before	may	→ might
this	→ the, that	will	→ would
can	→ could	must	→ had to

See *Grammar database 22* on pages 185–186 for more information.

1 Find this sentence in the text on page 102 and underline it.

He said he had learned what looked good on screen by watching films like Star Wars *when he was a child.*

Find three other examples of reported speech in the text and underline them.

2 These are things your friends have said to you. Use the words in bold to rewrite them as reported speech.

1 **Kevin:** 'I am starting my job at the TV studio next week.' **said**
2 **Alysia:** 'This is my favourite episode.' **told**
3 **Terry:** 'I think the media have a great influence on public opinion.' **thought**
4 **Richard:** 'I love special effects and I think they'll get better in the future.' **said**
5 **Cheryl:** 'I have been working for this radio station for two years.' **told**

Reported questions G

Dave asked her whether qualifications were important.

What did he actually say?

a *Are qualifications important?*
b *Were qualifications important?*

In this kind of *yes/no* question, which word could we use instead of *whether*?

When we are reporting a question that uses a *wh-* question word (*what*, *why*, *where*, *when*, *how*, etc), we repeat the question word. Notice the word order in the second sentence.

How did you get into the media? → *I asked her how she had got into the media.*

See *Grammar database 23* on page 186 for more information.

3 Correct these sentences.

1 I asked to Lisa what was it like working in the media.
2 The director asked me that did I work in films before.
3 The producer asked me what are you doing tomorrow?
4 I asked the journalist if was he ever frightened.
5 The presenter asked the contestant what will she do with the money if she wins?

4 Rewrite these questions as reported questions.

1 'Do you work in the media?'
I asked her ____________________
2 'Which channel do you work for?'
I asked her ____________________
3 'Who wrote the script for this show?'
I asked her ____________________
4 'Has the show ever won any awards?'
I asked her ____________________
5 'How long does it take to record each episode?'
I asked her ____________________

Have your say!

Discuss these statements. Tell the class what another student said using reported speech.

- TV keeps getting better and better.
- I can't stand watching old films in black and white.
- I try to watch the news at least once a day.

V Vocabulary

Communication

1 Put these words into the right categories. Some words might go in more than one category.

channel • presenter • bulletin • newsreader
viewer • surfing the internet • chat room
talk show • documentary • reality TV • email
editor • reporter • text message • studio

TV	Means of communication	People

2 Phrasal verbs

Match each phrasal verb to do with communication to the correct meaning.

1 Could you **turn** the TV **on**? I want to watch the news.
2 I keep trying to **log on** to check my email but it isn't working.
3 Members of the audience are requested to **turn off** all mobile phones.
4 As the politician spoke, the journalists **took down** what he said.
5 Could you **put** me **through** to Mr Thorpe, please?
6 I don't think you should **bring** the argument **up** again when we see Ray and Scott.
7 I couldn't hear anybody on the line so I decided to **hang up**.
8 Oh, this show is rubbish! Why don't you **turn over**?

a connect someone on the phone
b stop a TV, etc, from working by pressing a button
c write what someone says
d put the phone down
e change channel on a TV
f start a TV, etc, working by pressing a button
g mention in a conversation
h connect to the internet

3 Word formation

Complete this table. Include all possible forms you can think of, including negative forms.

Noun	Verb	Adjective
		active
	argue	
	communicate	
	converse	⊠
	correspond	
	direct	
	discuss	⊠
	enthuse	
	⊠	journalistic
responsibility	⊠	
	say	⊠

4 Synonyms for *get*

Use these verbs in their correct form to replace the words in bold.

arrive • become • buy • find • receive • take

1 I think we should **get** a satellite dish so that we can **get** more channels.
2 I'd like to **get** a job in the media and learn more about current affairs.
3 When the journalist **got** home, she turned on the TV to watch the news.
4 Georgia didn't want to be late for the interview so she **got** a taxi.
5 Mike **got** annoyed when he was given a low mark for his essay on the media.

Listening

Wordpower!

reality TV • series • nominate • vote

Starting point

Would you like to go on a show like the one in the photograph?
Do you ever watch reality shows?

1 **Read the questions in exercise 3. Who is on the radio programme? What are they talking about?**

2 **3.02 Listen to this extract. What is Jenny's connection to the media?**

EXAM EXPERT

How should you do the exam practice task?

a Always read the questions before you listen so that you know what to expect.

b Never read the questions before you listen so that it sounds fresh to you.

3 3.03 exam practice

You will hear a radio discussion about the media. For questions 1–7, choose the best answer (A, B or C).

1 What has Jenny not done since the programme ended?
A presented a TV programme
B talked on radio and TV
C been recognised in the street

2 What prompted Jenny to appear on the TV programme?
A She had heard about the financial benefits for contestants.
B She felt she represented young British people.
C She thought she would learn more about herself.

3 What worries Tony about reality TV?
A People develop very strong relationships on these programmes.
B The programmes should be more educational.
C People have to behave in ways that he disapproves of.

4 What does Jenny say about nominating the other housemates?
A It was difficult because it took place at the end of the day.
B The relationships they had developed made it difficult.
C It made it difficult for people at home to take it seriously.

5 How does Tony react to the suggestion that everyone knows the show is a game?
A He gives an example of negative behaviour in children.
B He questions whether all adults realise this.
C He doubts that children take the game seriously.

6 How does Jenny think that young children benefit from the programme?
A They develop useful social skills.
B They understand that they shouldn't talk to strangers.
C They learn how to defend themselves.

7 What does Airwave want?
A a complete ban on this kind of programme
B a ban on these programmes in the early evening
C a ban on programmes involving young children

Have your say!

Imagine you are going to produce a new reality TV show. Decide what your show is going to be like. Think about

- where the contestants are going to live
- a name for your show
- what the contestants have to do.

Speaking

Wordpower!

subtitles • translate • pronunciation

Starting point

What is happening in this photograph? Do you ever learn anything from TV programmes in English?

1 **Complete these phrases using *agree* or *disagree*. Some phrases can take both.**

1 I completely/totally __________ .
2 I __________ with you up to a point.
3 I have to __________ .
4 I'm afraid I __________ .
5 I couldn't __________ with you more.
6 I'm sorry to __________ , but …
7 To a certain extent, I __________ with you, but …

2 **3.04** **Listen to this extract from an interview. What do you think the two candidates, Anne and Rob, are discussing? Which candidate do you think does better? Why?**

3 **Discuss these statements. Do you agree or disagree with them? Use the phrases from exercise 1.**

Watching TV in English is a waste of time.

English has become the language of the internet.

You can't learn anything from the internet.

Books and magazines are an old-fashioned way of learning English.

Listening to the radio in English is a good way to practise.

4 exam practice

I'd like you to imagine that your English school is considering what to buy to help students with their English. Here are some of the things that have been suggested. Talk to each other about the advantages and disadvantages of each type of media and then decide which three you would recommend to the owner of the school. You have about three minutes.

- What are the advantages and disadvantages of each type of media?
- Which three would you recommend to the owner of the school?

> **EXAM EXPERT**
>
> **How should you do the exam practice task?**
>
> **a** It's a good idea to develop the discussion by asking your partner questions about what they say.
>
> **b** Give your opinion about all the choices while your partner listens in silence, and then you should listen in silence to your partner.

5 exam practice

What are the best ways to get the news?

Is it important to keep up to date with the news?

Do you think young people are influenced by what they see in the media?

Do you think we should control what time certain programmes are shown?

Would you ever consider a career in the media?

> **EXAM EXPERT**
>
> **How should you do the exam practice task?**
>
> You should always
>
> **a** give very short answers because there isn't much time.
>
> **b** develop your answers, giving examples and reasons.
>
> See *Speaking database* on page 193.

Reading 2 3.05

Wordpower!

annoying • convenient • easy to use
file sharing • cheap • instant • uploading

Starting point

Put the following in order (1–4) according to how much you use them. What do you like/dislike about them?

SMS (text messages) ____
email ____
instant messaging ____
social networking sites ____

Which companies/services do you use (eg Facebook, Google, etc)?
If you use email, do you ever have a problem with spam?

1 **Read the title and the first paragraph of the main article. Then read the section called *How to switch: The alternatives to email*. What do you think the article is going to be about?**

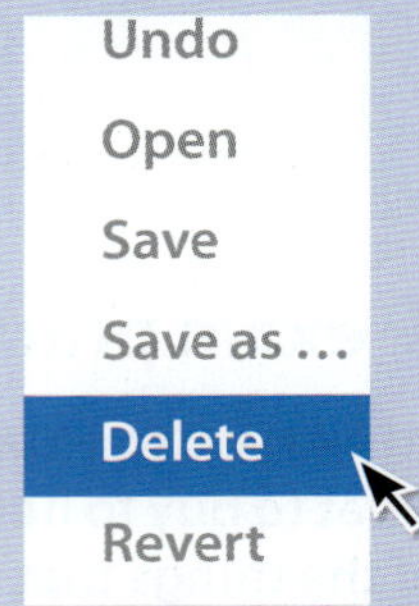

Are we facing the death of email?

First, people started leaving email for Twitter. Now a high-tech office has abandoned it altogether. Adam Sherwin gets the message.

Imagine it: no more deleting an inbox full of 'unbeatable offers'. Email could soon be a thing of the past if Thierry Breton, CEO of the information technology services company Atos, is accurate in his predictions.
Breton has told his staff to stop sending each other emails, complaining that they waste time and are outmoded. **1** ____ He also predicted that companies would have a problem in the future because of all this useless information.
Internal email will be phased out over 18 months at Atos. The 75,000 staff will instead use instant messaging and chat-style services inspired by social networking sites such as Facebook or Twitter. Atos staff used to spend between 5 and 20 hours a day dealing with email, but Breton's replacements have cut this by up to 20%, the firm claims. **2** ____ Email use is down 31% among the 12–17 age group, with a further 21% slump among those aged 18–24. Mobile Instant Messaging (IM) services such as Blackberry Messenger and Yahoo! Messenger were designed to allow low-cost, real-time communication. **3** ____ Mobile IM users are predicted to exceed 1.3 billion worldwide by 2016. Clearly, Mark Zuckerberg had this in mind when he developed Facebook messages. The social network's 'modern messaging system' merges text messages, IM and email into a single interface for 750 million users. **4** ____ 'They want things like SMS and IM to message each other.'
However, when they start working, those teens are likely to find that emails, and all that spam, haven't gone away. The proportion of companies sending more than 50,000 emails each month is increasing and is currently around 60%. Although this looks good

2 **Look at these missing sentences from exercise 3 and answer the questions about them.**

1 **He** claimed that only 10 per cent of the 200 electronic messages his employees received per day turned out to be useful.

What kind of person could 'he' be? There is information in the sentence to help you.

2 **For example**, without a ready audience through email, the website Groupon would not have built a network of 143 million subscribers.

What could this be an example of? Does it suggest email is a positive or a negative thing?

for the future of email, the majority of what is sent is unwanted. 5 ____ Tim Walters, senior analyst at the technology research company Forrester Research, said that, even though email wastes a great deal of time, it's still used daily by 85% of workers. He added: 'Email isn't a beast to be killed. Sometimes it's the most appropriate tool for communication.'

What could replace email in the workplace? 6 ____ 3reton has introduced the \tos Wiki, which allows all employees to communicate with each other, and Office Communicator, the company's online chat system which allows video conferencing, file and application sharing.

Although email might be dying, it will take time to disappear, thanks to its proven success. 7 ____ and more than 107 trillion emails will be sent this year. Dn the other hand, despite the popularity of instant messages, the IM industry is hampered by services which do not communicate with each other.

How to switch: The alternatives to email

Twitter
Widely used for newsgathering, broadcasting and simply passing time, but has not become a major communications tool, although it does have a private messaging service.

Facebook
What unites most users is that it is a personal communications tool, rather than one to be used at work.

Google Docs
Create a document, save and publish it and allow people to share and edit it: simple and effective. Could be used to post messages to large numbers of people at once.

BBM/WhatsApp
Instant messenger services are already widely used. The newer version is mobile instant messaging apps.

3 Yammer, a kind of 'Facebook for business' which allows groups of employees to share ideas through private communication, is now used by more than 80,000 firms.

How is this connected to the subject of emails? What could have come before this sentence?

4 **These** are the kinds of services that are replacing email for the next generation.

What kinds of services might replace email? What do you think the previous sentence talked about?

EXAM EXPERT

When you've decided that a sentence fills a gap,

a cross out the whole sentence so you can't read it anymore.

b put a line through the letter of the sentence so you don't use it again by mistake.

3 exam practice

You are going to read an article about email. Seven sentences have been removed from the article. Choose from sentences A–H the one which fits each gap. (1–7). There is one extra sentence which you do not need to use.

A 'High school kids don't use email,' the 27-year-old technology pioneer said.

B For example, without a ready audience through email, the website Groupon would not have built a network of 143 million subscribers.

C None of the above methods were particularly popular with their users.

D Spam still accounts for an estimated 89% of all emails.

E Yammer, a kind of 'Facebook for business' which allows groups of employees to share ideas through private communication, is now used by more than 80,000 firms.

F His strategy has already been adopted by teenagers, who are increasingly rejecting email.

G He claimed that only 10 per cent of the 200 electronic messages his employees received per day turned out to be useful.

H These are the kinds of services that are replacing email for the next generation.

WORK IT OUT!

Find these words and phrases in the text and the removed sentences and underline them. Can you work out what they mean from the context?

unbeatable offers • a thing of the past • slump
exceed • proportion • pioneer • subscribers

4 Find words or phrases in the text which have a similar meaning to these words and phrases.

1 getting rid of or removing (paragraph 1)
2 old-fashioned (paragraph 2)
3 removed slowly (paragraph 3)
4 combines; puts together (paragraph 3)
5 suitable (paragraph 4)
6 talking to workmates using electronic equipment (paragraph 5)

Have your say!

- One reason some people prefer email is that it's easier to keep a record of communication, whereas people don't usually keep old text messages. Do you think this could help keep email alive?

G Grammar 2

Reporting verbs

Which is correct?

a *My dad told me to disconnect from the internet.*

b *My dad told to me to disconnect from the internet.*

suggest, deny
+ noun:
Simon suggested this instant messenger software.
+ *-ing*:
Marcus denied breaking the typewriter.
+ *that* clause:
Simon suggested that I should get this instant messenger software.

claim
+ *that* clause:
Carol claimed (that) she was a journalist, but in fact she wasn't!
+ full infinitive:
Carol claimed to be a journalist.

refuse, agree
+ full infinitive:
Aliki agreed to help me choose a new mobile phone.

tell, order, command, ask
+ *someone* + full infinitive:
I asked Aliki to help me choose a new mobile phone.

See *Grammar database 24* on page 187 for more information.

1 The words or phrases in bold are incorrect. Correct them.

Damian was in trouble. His parents had received their phone bill, and it was enormous. There were over a hundred calls to an astrologer. Damian denied **to make** the calls and claimed not **knowing** anything about them. He suggested that the phone company **making** a mistake and refused **admitting** doing something he hadn't done. His parents didn't believe him, however, and told him **go** to his room. His parents discussed what to do. They agreed **checking** with the phone company, so Damian's mum phoned up and asked **speak** to the manager. It turned out that there had been a mistake, so Damian's parents apologised to Damian for not **to believe** him and asked him **forgiving** them. He told **to them** he was glad it was all sorted out, and he was very relieved that they didn't have to pay the bill.

2 Use each of these reporting verbs once to rewrite the sentences in reported speech.

agree • claim • deny • refuse • suggest

1 'Why don't we check the time of the film on the internet?' Liam said.
2 'I have over a thousand names in my email address book,' said Nicole.
3 'No! I won't let you borrow my newspaper!' Darren said to Jamie.
4 'Okay. I'll let you use my computer to check your email,' Rob said to me.
5 'No, I didn't use your mobile phone,' Anoushka said to Scott.

although, even though, in spite of, despite, however G

Circle the correct word to complete this sentence.

I don't check my email often, ***despite*** */* ***however*** */* ***although*** *I know I should.*

Although/Even though *I have an instant messenger, I don't use it often.*

In spite of/Despite *the fact (that) I have an instant messenger, I don't use it often.*

In spite of/Despite *having an instant messenger, I don't use it often.*

In spite of/Despite *the benefits of instant messengers, I prefer to use email.*

I have an instant messenger. ***However****, I don't use it often. / I don't use it often,* ***however****. / I don't use it* ***often****, however, because I prefer to use email.*

See *Grammar database 25* on page 187 for more information.

3 Complete each sentence starting with the words given so that it means the same as this sentence from the text on page 108.

Online communities are a more recent development, but they've caught on fast.

1 Online communities are a more recent development. However, …
2 Although …
3 Despite the fact that …

4 Use the words in bold to connect the sentences.

1 I wrote to Mandy months ago. I still haven't received a reply. **despite**
2 Dan warned us not to swim there. We didn't take his advice. **although**
3 Most webcams are cheap. Some of them are very good quality. **however**
4 Rachel reminded me about the meeting. I forgot to go. **even**
5 Simon works very long hours. He loves his job on the newspaper. **spite**

Use of English

1 **Read the text in exercise 2 quickly, and decide whether these statements are true (T) or false (F).**

1 Sign language was invented recently. T/F
2 The same sign language is used all round the world. T/F
3 Sign languages are real languages. T/F
4 It's impossible to express emotions with sign language. T/F
5 It's easier to learn sign language than other languages. T/F

2 exam practice

Read the text below and think of the word which best fits each gap. Use only one word in each gap. Write your answers IN CAPITAL LETTERS.

EXAM EXPERT

How should you do the exam practice task?

a Don't waste time reading the text first; go straight to the first gap.

b Quickly read the whole text through to get a general idea of what it's about before filling the gaps.

Sign Language

Despite the fact (1) ________ sign language has been used for thousands of years in one form or another, not much is known about its history. Today, thousands (2) ________ deaf people around the world use sign language (3) ________ communicate. However, (4) ________ are many different sign languages, and a signer (5) ________ uses British sign language may well not be able to understand a signer from another country. Even (6) ________ some people believe that sign languages are not real languages, linguists who have studied (7) ________ say that they are. The only difference is that instead (8) ________ using speech or writing to express meaning, signers use (9) ________ hands. (10) ________ fact, anything that can be expressed through spoken language can also be expressed through sign language. Learning sign language is like learning any (11) ________ language – it (12) ________ time and practice.

3 **Read the text in exercise 4 and decide what part of speech (noun, verb, etc) is required to fill each gap.**

4 exam practice

Read the text below. Use the word given in capitals at the end of some of the lines to form a word that fits in the gap in the same line. Write your answers IN CAPITAL LETTERS.

EXAM EXPERT

How should you do the exam practice task?

Remember that adverbs

a are only used to give information about verbs.

b are used to give information about both verbs and adjectives.

Should we believe what we read?

When we read a newspaper story about something that's happened,
we usually presume that it's (1) ___ accurate. We tend to believe that the — FACT
(2) ___ has done his or her research, and that we can rely on the words — REPORT
written. However, some sections of the media see things rather
differently. There is a (3) ___ used in the tabloid newspaper industry — SAY
in Britain: 'The (4) ___ doesn't sell newspapers'. For tabloids, the aim is — TRUE
to create stories that shock the reader, even if they're not true.
(5) ___ who work for these papers often feel that their — JOURNAL
(6) ___ is not so much to present the facts as to produce the most — RESPONSIBLE
interesting story possible.
Can any form of spoken or written (7) ___ accurately present reality? — COMMUNICATE
Perhaps not. Producing a text always involves a (8) ___ . Which words — CHOOSE
we use and how we express them reflect our (9) ___ opinion. — PERSON
Indeed, we shouldn't even completely believe what we see on TV as
the selection of images shown or not shown will affect our (10) ___ . — RESPOND

Writing: report

Wordpower!

content • creative writing • in colour • issue
poetry • reviews • school news • section

Starting point

Does your school have a school newspaper, magazine or website?
What kind of articles and features should a school newspaper, magazine or website contain?

1 **Write these words and phrases in the gaps to complete the model report.**

Quality • Conclusion • Subject • To • Content
Introduction • From • Number of Issues • Date

(1) ________________ : Mrs Webster
(2) ________________ : Ben Parker
(3) ________________ : School Magazine
(4) ________________ : 24th September

(5) ________________
As requested, I have interviewed a number of students and parents regarding the quality of 'Together', the school magazine. My findings are outlined below.

(6) ________________
On the whole, comments about the quality of 'Together' were very positive. Readers find it an interesting and informative magazine. However, ...

(7) ________________
The majority of people interviewed would prefer 'Together' to come out more often. They would rather have three smaller issues per year than one large issue at the end of the school year.

(8) ________________
Although most parents enjoy the 'School News' section, many students commented that they would prefer shorter articles and more photographs. Secondly, some students suggested ....

(9) ________________
To sum up, we should consider bringing out 'Together' more often, and making it colour. We should also look into having more photographs and a creative writing section.

2 **Read the report again and answer these questions.**

1 Who wrote the report?
2 Who do you think Mrs Webster is?
3 Is the report formal or informal?
4 Why does the writer use headings?
5 What recommendations does the writer make?
6 In which paragraph are the recommendations made?

3 **Underline these words and phrases in the report. What do you think they mean?**

As requested • regarding • findings • outlined
On the whole • positive • consider • come out
Secondly • To sum up • The majority of • look into

4 **Look at the final paragraph and find two recommendations which are not mentioned earlier on in the report. Use these points to complete the two unfinished sentences in the second and fourth main paragraphs of the report. Use your own words and an appropriate formal style.**

Plan ahead

1 exam practice: report

You help produce your college newspaper. Your editor has asked you to interview students at your college to find out their opinions about the quality of the newspaper, and to present your findings in a report.

EXAM EXPERT

How should you write a report?

a Always have four main paragraphs.

b Choose an appropriate number of paragraphs for the information you want to present.

See *Writing database* on page 201 for further information.

2 **Look at the question in exercise 1 and use your imagination to answer these questions.**

1 What's the name of your editor?
2 What's the name of the newspaper?
3 What different features and content are currently in the newspaper?
4 What do the students like about this content?
5 What do they dislike about this content?
6 What would they like to see included which is not included at the moment?
7 How often does the newspaper come out?
8 Do they think that is often enough?
9 Did the students make any other points you want to include in the report?
10 What suggestions and recommendations for improvement will you make?

3 **Complete this information and decide what your paragraph headings are going to be.**

To: ______________________
From: ______________________
Subject: ______________________

Paragraph headings:

____
____
____
____

4 **Make a paragraph plan. Make a note of the main points you are going to include in each paragraph. Add more paragraphs to the table if necessary.**

Paragraph	Main points
1	
2	
3	
4	

5 **Write your report in 120–180 words in an appropriate style.**

6 **When you have written your report, make sure that you have:**

- used paragraph headings ☐
- presented your findings clearly ☐
- made suggestions and recommendations ☐
- used report words and phrases ☐
- used formal language. ☐

Check your progress! Units 7–8

1 Choose the correct word to fill the gap in each sentence.

1 Tom's been a(n) ____ golfer for two years and he's hoping to turn professional soon.
A volunteer B amateur C freestyle D trainee
2 Sending text ____ from your mobile is a great way to keep in touch with friends.
A letters B compositions C notes D messages
3 I found this great website when I was ____ the internet last night.
A travelling B driving C surfing D riding
4 Journalists are under a lot of pressure to meet ____ every day.
A limits B deadlines C barriers D times
5 Do you think parents should ____ their children from spending too much time online?
A deny B refuse C disqualify D prevent
6 The ____ in the 1500 metres waited for the starter to fire his gun.
A competitors B players C umpires D runners-up
7 *The Lord of the Rings* was filmed on ____ in New Zealand.
A place B spot C location D region
8 There was a report in the news that Beckham has joined a new football ____ .
A association B group C band D club
9 Publishing companies are always on the ____ for new writers.
A lookout B watch C view D outlook
10 One of the star players was ____ during the match.
A damaged B injured C spoiled D broken

10 marks

2 Write a word from the box in the correct form to complete each sentence.

come • go • be • lend • run • break • let

1 The man claimed ____ an Olympic® champion but I didn't believe him.
2 Tony suggested ____ to see a football match at the weekend.
3 The young boy denied ____ the window with his ball.
4 I thought you agreed ____ Victoria your skis, didn't you?
5 The coach told the players ____ around the pitch to warm up.
6 My mum refuses ____ me play basketball on a school night.
7 Could you ask Ashley ____ to training on Friday evening?

7 marks

3 Complete each sentence using a form of the word in brackets.

1 We practised hard in ____________ (**prepare**) for the big match.
2 The only thing Mark is ____________ (**enthuse**) about is chatting online.
3 If you can't behave more ____________ (**responsible**), you'll never be captain of the team.
4 Catherine's very popular and everybody says she's very ____________ (**like**).
5 I don't know what ____________ (**qualify**) you need to be a referee.
6 I think they made the wrong ____________ (**decide**) when they took my favourite show off the air.
7 Always respect your ____________ (**oppose**), whether you're winning or losing.
8 I love ____________ (**real**) TV because you get to see ordinary people in interesting situations.

8 marks

4 Write a word from the box in the correct form in each gap to complete the sentences.

drop • give • join • put
log • hang • bring

1 I don't believe it! I was just talking to Mary on the phone and she ____ up!
2 Finally, the pain was too much and I had to ____ out of the race.
3 You need to remember your password every time you ____ on.
4 Why don't you let your little brother ____ in your game of football?
5 You'll never become a professional if you ____ up so easily.
6 Good morning. Could you ____ me through to the Complaints Department, please?
7 When Bill arrives, don't ____ up the fact that his team lost yesterday.

7 marks

5 Choose the correct word to complete each sentence.

1 Is that Zoe's mobile? She **can't** / **must** / **should** have forgotten it when she left.
2 Sally said the score was ten-nil? That **shouldn't** / **mustn't** / **can't** be right!
3 If your mum left work half an hour ago, then she **should** / **must** / **can** be here soon.
4 Jack looks happy. He **can't** / **should** / **must** have won at golf.
5 I rang Diana but there was no answer. Do you think she **should** / **might** / **can** have gone out?
6 Jill **mustn't** / **can't** / **shouldn't** have known about your party or she wouldn't have arranged hers on the same day.
7 That's not the right web page. You **should** / **must** / **can** have put in the wrong address.
8 It **can't** / **shouldn't** / **mightn't** have been easy for you to lose after training so hard.

8 marks

6 Complete the second sentence so that it has a similar meaning to the first sentence, using the word given. Do not change the word given. You must use between two and five words, including the word given.

1 If your performance improves slightly, you'll be ready for the competition.
slight
If there is ______________________ your performance, you'll be ready for the competition.

2 I'm certain you didn't see Jacob at the match because he's in Canada.
seen
You ______________________ Jacob at the match because he's in Canada.

3 'I am the fastest runner in the class,' said Martin.
be
Martin ______________________ the fastest runner in the class.

4 Perhaps we should have the meeting tomorrow instead of this afternoon.
off
Perhaps we should ______________________ tomorrow.

5 'Are you happy with the result?' I asked the women's champion.
if
I asked the women's champion ______________ happy with the result.

6 Why do we always argue about the rules every time we play?
an
Why do we always ______________________ about the rules every time we play?

7 'No. I won't participate in the training session at the weekend,' said Carol.
part
Carol refused ______________________ in the training session at the weekend.

8 The runner in second place is almost at the same point as the leader!
caught
The runner in second place ______________________ the leader!

9 Although he's blind, Gareth can run 100 metres in under 11 seconds.
spite
Gareth can run 100 metres in under 11 seconds, ______________________ that he's blind.

10 'Why don't we call Erica and ask her if she knows the score?' said Jessica.
to
Jessica suggested ______________________ her if she knew the score.

20 marks

Total: 60 marks

9

Work

Wordpower!

babysitting • badly paid • earn • gain experience
mowing lawns / cutting grass • stacking shelves

Starting point

Look at the pictures. Which of these jobs would you like/not like to do part-time?
What other part-time jobs do teenagers sometimes do?

1 **The article you are going to read mentions several different jobs. Look through the article quickly to find all the different jobs mentioned and circle them.**

2 **Look at the sentences in exercise 3. Underline all the words and phrases which you think might refer to things in other sentences in the text.**

3 exam practice

You are going to read an article giving advice to teenagers about part-time jobs. Seven sentences have been removed from the article. Choose from the sentences A–H the one which fits each gap (1–7). There is one extra sentence which you do not need to use.

A This, however, depends on your having the appropriate qualifications.
B You might not even be able to find a job in an area that you enjoy.
C Indoor house painting is another option.
D In return, you can learn an amazing amount about the business.
E Try as many positions as possible and ask lots of questions about cash flow, staffing, etc.
F You won't earn any money, but you can gain valuable experience.
G This is a question which is best answered by doing a market survey.
H There are several things you can do to make your services more valuable.

Reading 1 3.06

As a teenager, you are likely to have both a fair amount of spare time and a desire to earn some money. By working to earn money yourself, you can learn a lot about the value of things as well as the world of business. Typical and obvious jobs for teenagers include working at a fast-food restaurant, working as a shop assistant or stacking shelves at a supermarket.

What you get out of a job like this depends on your attitude. If your attitude is 'I hate this job' then obviously you won't benefit much from it; if, on the other hand, you look at it as an opportunity to learn how a business works from the inside out, then the benefits can be great. Many of the new generation of millionaires, for example, are owners of franchise and private restaurants. Owning a restaurant is not easy, however, and it requires knowledge and skill to be successful, so start gathering these as a teenager. **1** ______ Applying this attitude to any job you have will really pay off; you'll learn a huge amount. For many teenagers, there are a variety of problems associated with getting a job. You may not be old enough or you may lack reliable transportation. You may not have enough total time available or a regular enough schedule for someone to be willing to hire you. **2** ______ If any of these problems hold true for you, then working for yourself on a part-time basis may be the best way to go.

Babysitting is a tried and tested way for responsible teenagers who like being with kids to make money. **3** ______ For example, think about taking a first-aid course so that you know how to handle emergencies.

EXAM EXPERT

How should you do the exam practice task?

If you think that two or more sentences can fit in the same gap,

a just choose one of them randomly as they will both be marked right.
b choose the one which cannot fit in another gap as well.

Part-time Jobs for Teenagers

Secondly, you might want to consider teaming up with some like-minded friends. That way your group will be able to say yes more often, increasing the amount of work you're offered.

If babysitting doesn't appeal to you, then you might want to consider garden care. During the summer you mow lawns, trim hedges and so on, in the autumn you rake leaves and in the winter you shovel snow! **4** ______ Before undertaking this, you need to make sure you know what you are doing by working with someone with experience and practising at home (but get your parents' permission first!). Other activities include providing in-home pet care when owners are on holiday; errand running for busy people; washing cars for neighbours or teaching people how to use computers or the internet.

One question you will have as soon as you choose an activity is 'How much should I charge?' **5** ______ You'll need to call around and ask potential customers what they are used to paying and/or willing to pay, or ask your friends what they charge for similar activities. In the case of an activity like car washing, you could also call garages in your area and ask what they charge.

Another way of gaining experience is to offer your services to a small business. Although it may not be obvious to you, every community has thousands of small firms which do all sorts of things: printing, plumbing, computer programming, advertising, and so on. Many of these could really benefit from a part-time helper who is reliable and mature. **6** ______ You will be surprised at how quickly you become a valued part of the team.

Volunteer positions are another option. You can volunteer your services at hospitals, old people's homes, and most charitable organisations or political groups. **7** ______ This will benefit you in the future, as colleges and universities will be impressed by any voluntary work you have done.

WORK IT OUT!

Find these words and phrases in the text and underline them. Can you work out what they mean from the context?

typical • hold true • tried and tested
mature • old people's homes

4 Find words in the article which are similar in meaning to these words and phrases.

1 gaining, getting (paragraph 2)
2 not have (paragraph 3)
3 deal with (paragraph 4)
4 with the same interests (paragraph 4)
5 starting to do (paragraph 5)
6 possible (in the future) (paragraph 6)

Have your say!

- What other advice would you give to a teenager thinking of getting a part-time job?
- Is the advice in the article useful for you and your friends?

Grammar 1

Relative clauses

In which of these situations is there more than one woman?

In which sentence can we replace *who* with *that*?

a *The woman who was offered the job had very good qualifications.*

b *The woman, who was offered the job, had very good qualifications.*

Defining relative clauses: essential information

Do not use commas:
The job which I turned down was very badly paid.
that can usually replace the relative pronoun:
The job that I turned down was very badly paid.
We can leave out the relative pronoun completely when it is the object of the clause:
The job I turned down was very badly paid.

Non-defining relative clauses: extra information

Use commas:
I've worked here for 20 years, which is a very long time.
that cannot replace the relative pronoun
We cannot leave out the relative pronoun.

! Be careful!

Which relative pronoun to use (*who*, *which*, *where*, etc) depends on what is being referred to.

See *Grammar database 26* on page 188 for more information.

1 **These phrases appeared in the article on pages 116–117. Without looking back, write in all the possible relative pronouns. Put a dash (–) if the relative pronoun can be left out. Then check your answers by looking back at the article.**

1 … a tried and tested way for responsible teenagers ________ like being with kids …
2 There are several things ________ you can do …
3 … increasing the amount of work ________ you're offered.
4 This is a question ________ is best answered by …
5 … these could really benefit from a part-time helper ________ is reliable …
6 … will be impressed by any voluntary work ________ you have done.

2 **Choose the correct word or phrase to complete each sentence.**

1 My boss is the Sales Manager, **who / which** actually spends most of his time abroad.
2 The position of Sales Director, **who / which** is very well paid, has been vacant for several months.
3 I'll have another interview next week, **which / when** they'll tell me if I've got the job or not.
4 There are several reasons **why / which** we decided not to offer you the position.
5 This is the desk **where / which** I work.
6 My new boss, **who's / whose** name is Alan, seems very nice.

! Be careful!

☒ the office in which I work
☒ the office which I work in
☒ the office where I work
☒ the office where I work in

3 **Write one word in each gap to complete the text. Do not write *that* and do not leave any gaps blank.**

My first paid job, (1) ________ I got when I was 14, was on a Christmas tree farm (2) ________ was run by Mr and Mrs Greenhow, (3) ________ were friends of my parents. People (4) ________ wanted to buy a Christmas tree would come to the field (5) ________ I was working and would tell me (6) ________ tree they wanted, (7) ________ I would then dig up for them and carry down to the farmhouse, (8) ________ Mrs Greenhow would sort out payment. The job, (9) ________ sounded easy when they offered it to me, was actually extremely hard work as the trees (10) ________ I had to dig up were always the really big ones – no-one (11) ________ wants a real Christmas tree wants a small Christmas tree! That was the time (12) ________ I realised I was better suited to working in an office. Doing that holiday job was the main reason (13) ________ I decided to work hard at school – so I wouldn't have to work on a farm for the rest of my life!

V Vocabulary

Employment

1 Make notes and discuss. What's the difference between …

1 being **unemployed** and **self-employed**?
2 a **permanent** job and a **temporary** job?
3 a **salary** and a **wage**?
4 a **part-time** job and a **full-time** job?
5 being **on commission** and getting **royalties**?
6 **getting the sack** or **being fired** and **being made redundant**?
7 **commuting** and **going on a business trip**?
8 **doing overtime** and **being on strike**?

2 Phrasal verbs

Choose the correct word to complete the phrasal verbs.

1 Is there an application form to fill **in** / **up** or should I just send you a CV?
2 The company took **up** / **on** over a hundred new members of staff last year.
3 I think I've taken **off** / **on** more work than I can actually manage.
4 Interviewing job applicants takes **over** / **up** a lot of my time.
5 Why don't you put **in** / **up** for promotion? You deserve it.
6 Their family firm was taken **up** / **over** by a huge multinational corporation.

3 Word formation

Complete each sentence using a form of the word in bold.

1 This company prides itself in the way it treats its ________________ . **employ**
2 I'm Mr Taggart's personal ________________ . **assist**
3 I've spoken to the ________________ director and she'd like to discuss the idea with you further. **manage**
4 I was a factory ________________ for over 30 years. **work**
5 If you've got a problem, talk to your ________________ . **supervise**
6 Dawn's a ________________ accountant at the moment. She won't qualify for another two years. **train**
7 We interviewed over a hundred ________________ for the position. **apply**

4 *have / take / make / do*

Put each phrase into the correct category: *have, take, make* or *do*. Some phrases can go in more than one category.

an appointment • an arrangement • a break • care • certain • a complaint • a day off • a decision • a difference
an effect • an effort • an experience • an experiment • a fortune • a holiday • your homework • an idea • a job
a mistake • money • part in something • a plan • research • sense • some work • someone a favour • a suggestion
sure • the best of something • the chance to do • the housework • turns • up your mind • your best • your duty

have	*take*	*make*	*do*

Listening

Wordpower!

working freelance • freedom • discipline
working hours • self-employed
take a break • have a day off
take on work • deadlines

Starting point

What are the advantages and disadvantages of working from home?

1 **Look at the gaps in exercise 2. What kind of information will you have to write in each gap?**

2 3.07 exam practice

You will hear part of a podcast giving careers advice. For questions 1–10, complete the sentences with a word or short phrase.

1 You can't choose your own __________ if you work for a company.
2 Being your own boss means you can __________ when it suits you.
3 Working from home means you can __________ domestic responsibilities.
4 The speaker likes the __________ that he has to organise his time.
5 Because he doesn't have to __________, he saves three hours every day.
6 The speaker has to take __________ if one of his children is ill.
7 He has to work long hours sometimes if he needs to meet a __________.
8 You can't spend the day playing games – you need to be __________ about your work.
9 The speaker's friends think he works __________, so he's free for visits.
10 He doesn't have as much __________ as he did when he worked in an office.

3 **Look at the words and phrases in italics in exercise 4. Think of another way of expressing each word or phrase.**

> **EXAM EXPERT**
>
> **How should you do the exam practice task?**
>
> Remember that the questions are **not always / always** in the same order as the information is presented in the recording.

4 3.08 exam practice

You will hear part of an interview with an office manager about how he developed his management style. For questions 1–7, choose the best answer (A, B or C).

1 What was *behind* the problems in Steve's first job?
A The staff refused to discuss matters with managers.
B The employees chose not to carry out tasks properly.
C Management did not give clear instructions to the workers.

2 What was the attitude of Steve's co-workers in his first job?
A They expected him to take matters up with the management.
B They weren't satisfied with the *standard* of his work.
C They wanted him to behave like them.

3 In his first job, how did Steve react to the pressure from his co-workers?
A by leaving
B by *taking their side*
C by making a complaint

4 Steve's supervisor's response was to tell Steve to
A behave like the other workers.
B stop causing problems.
C take care how he *approached* the manager.

5 Why did Steve think about getting a job in a factory?
A The money was better.
B He was disappointed with office work.
C He thought it would be a better way to get into management.

6 Steve mentions 'Jim in accounts' as an example of someone
A who helps the running of the office to go *smoothly*.
B whose work might suffer because of family circumstances.
C Steve had to *fire* because he didn't do his job properly.

7 Which of the following does Steve consider to be good use of his time?
A discussing personal matters in the office
B holding as many managerial meetings as possible
C socialising with staff after work

> **EXAM EXPERT**
>
> **How should you do the exam practice task?**
>
> If you aren't sure of the answer to a question,
>
> **a** keep listening. You don't want to miss the answer to the next question.
>
> **b** keep thinking about it as you'll probably get it right eventually.

Have your say!

- Based on the information you heard in exercise 2, do you think you would like to work from home? Why? / Why not?
- Do you agree with the things the office manager said in exercise 4? What do you think makes a good boss?

Speaking

Starting point

Think of as many places as you can where people work. Compare your list with a partner's.

1 3.09 Listen to a candidate talking about two photos in the Speaking paper of an English exam. How successful or unsuccessful is the candidate's answer? Give the candidate a score out of 5 for this part and explain your reasons.

2 Look at the photos in exercise 3 and complete the tables in note form.

Photo	This is a picture of ...	Similarities / differences	Which job do you prefer? Why?
A			
B			
Photo	**This is a picture of ...**	**Similarities / differences**	**Which job do you prefer? Why?**
C			
D			

3 exam practice

Candidate A, here are two photographs of different jobs. I'd like you to compare them and say which job you would prefer and why. You only have one minute for this.

- Which job would you prefer and why?

Candidate B, here are two photographs of different workplaces. I'd like you to compare them and say how you would feel about working in these places. You only have one minute for this.

- How would you feel about working in these places?

A

B

Candidate B, do either of these jobs appeal to you?

C

D

Candidate A, which place would you prefer to work in?

EXAM EXPERT

How should you do the exam practice task?

a When the other candidate is given two photos, don't look at them because they are not for you.

b When the other candidate is given two photos, look at them because you will have to talk briefly about them too.

See *Speaking database* on page 193.

Reading 2 3.10

Wordpower!

help out • contribute • share effort • earn • rate of pay

Starting point

How often do you do household chores? When was the last time you:

- tidied your room?
- made your bed?
- helped in the kitchen?
- took out the rubbish?
- washed the dishes?

Have your parents ever given you money for helping around the house? What things do you have done for you by your parents?

1 Read the article quickly and match to complete the sentences.

1 The writer of the article ___
2 The writer's son ___
3 Kate ___
4 Suzanne ___
5 Professor Frank Furedi ___
6 Sue Palmer ___
7 Karen Sullivan ___

a wrote a book called *Paranoid Parenting*.
b has three daughters.
c wanted money for a job he'd just done.
d had her cupboards cleaned out.
e has two sons who don't help in the house.
f is an expert on parenting.
g thinks teenagers have problems if they can't earn money.

EXAM EXPERT

How should you do the exam practice task?

a Remember that an option may be true, but it might not answer the question.

b As soon as you see an option that is true according to the text, choose that one as the answer.

Should parents pay kids for chores?

Should you pay your children to do household jobs, or should they do it out of love?

I could hear noises from the kitchen and I felt very proud. I was having my kitchen cupboards emptied and cleaned out by my 11-year-old son. When the job was over, he called me down to see it. 'How kind! What a big help you've been,' I exclaimed. He looked a little uncomfortable before replying in a businesslike manner, 'Do you think it's worth five pounds?'

I paid him, but grumpily, only after accusing him of employing the same tactics as people who clean your windscreen at traffic lights and then ask for money. At least it showed enterprise – earning and saving money to buy something he wants. But can enterprise and the getting of money coexist with family values?

Kate, a single working mum of three older teenagers, says she tried to offer money for chores, but didn't offer enough. 'I'm not going to pay five pounds for them to do the washing-up,' she said. 'The result is that the boys do nothing and the girl does a little, occasionally.'

2 exam practice

You are going to read an article about paying children to do jobs around the house. For questions 1–7, choose the answer (A–D) which you think fits best according to the text.

1 The writer's son
A often does jobs around the house.
B regularly earns a lot of money.
C was disappointed because he didn't get paid.
D did a job before discussing payment.

2 Kate's position is that
A she thought her children expected too much money.
B her boys shouldn't have to work.
C she is unable to work.
D her children didn't do their chores properly.

3 What does the writer mean by 'give and take' in line 30?
A telling children which jobs to do
B giving money for children to take
C helping others and others helping you
D lending and borrowing things

ꞔuzanne, a mother of three girls with ɔig age gaps between them, says: 'I have paid my kids for babysitting ɔecause I'd have to pay someone else o do this. I wouldn't pay for other ɔbs because I think they should do hem as a contribution to family life. ꞔut I don't think that it should just be about cash – give and take in a family s about caring and not money.' t's about caring and money. The ifficulty is in working out the ight balance. Professor Frank uredi, the author of Paranoid 'arenting, says, 'Anything that helps hildren understand that there is relationship between effort and utcome is to be welcomed, so aying children for jobs makes ense. Although it is important not ɔ place too much focus on financial ncentives.'
ue Palmer, the author of *Detoxing 'hildhood*, says that, for teenagers, ot being able to earn money can ead to a feeling of lack of control. he says, 'In our society, we often see e worth of people according to how uch they earn and we are inclined to ink that something isn't worth doing nless it's paid.'

How can this be a good message to pass on to the kids? 'It's important that children learn that money doesn't grow on trees, that you have to earn it,' says Palmer. 'However, there are jobs that everyone should do with the agreement that nobody gets paid for doing them, that everyone shares responsibility.'
What kind of jobs are those, then? On this, there does seem to be parental and expert agreement. Karen Sullivan, a parenting expert, says: 'Children should take responsibility for themselves and their belongings, so clearing up toys, games and clothes is a given.' She added that they shouldn't expect to have their room tidied or their bed made for them.
But when does all this start? The idea of contributing to the household, not for money, but for helping, should begin early, according to Palmer. 'It does have to start very young, when they love to help, but they are not actually helping but slightly irritating you. It's worth encouraging that.' Palmer thinks the rates for paid jobs should be set by the parents. 'That's how it works in the working world. Your boss offers you a rate; you accept it or you don't.'

Jobs for money
Washing the car
Tidying and cleaning the garage
Gardening
Ironing
Big sort-out of the kitchen cupboards or bedroom wardrobes
Babysitting younger siblings

Jobs to keep the family home in order
Taking out the rubbish, recycling
Sorting the laundry, loading the washing machine
Washing up, loading or unloading the dishwasher
Setting the table
Keeping your own room tidy
Keeping the bathroom tidy after use
Feeding pets
Helping to prepare dinner
Making your own packed lunches for school
Helping out with a 'Saturday morning blitz' – vacuuming, dusting, tidying as a whole family

4 What worries Professor Frank Furedi?
A that children will never learn to work
B that chores might be too difficult for children
C that money might become too important
D that we don't pay children enough

5 Which point do Sue Palmer and Karen Sullivan agree on?
A Children should do some jobs without being paid.
B Teenagers often feel a lack of control.
C Children must be paid for all jobs they do.
D Children are too young to take on responsibility.

6 What does Palmer say about very young children who try to help in the house?
A They should be given money.
B It can be annoying because they don't really help.
C We should tell them not to do these jobs.
D They are only doing it for the money.

7 What does 'it' in the last line refer to?
A encouragement given by parents
B the power that parents and bosses have
C the amount being offered for doing a job
D conditions in the working world

WORK IT OUT!

Find these words and phrases in the text and underline them. Can you work out what they mean from the context?

manner • grumpily • coexist
money doesn't grow on trees • a given

3 Find words or phrases in the text which have a similar meaning to these words and phrases.

1 good business sense; a positive attitude to work (paragraph 2)
2 calculating; finding (paragraph 4)
3 result (paragraph 4)
4 money offered to do a job (paragraph 4)
5 home; family unit (paragraph 8)
6 amount of money (paragraph 8)

Have your say!

- What do you think about the opinions in the text?
- Who do you agree or disagree with most? Why?

Grammar 2

The causative

Look at this sentence. Who did the actual painting?

The boss has just had the office repainted.

The causative = **have/get** + **object** + **past participle** (by / with)

We usually use the causative to show that someone pays or asks someone else to do something.

I'm going to get the car repaired by a mechanic. = I'm going to pay a mechanic to repair the car.

have is more formal than *get*

See *Grammar database 27* on pages 188–189 for more information.

! Be careful!

We can also sometimes use the causative for unpleasant situations which we did not arrange

eg *We had our office broken into last week.*

1 **Look back at the article on pages 122–123 and find one example of the causative.**

2 **For each section, find the person who probably does the work.**

1 Have you had your hair cut?
   A hairdresser
2 We got all the cats vaccinated last week.
3 I'm going to have my eyes tested tomorrow.
4 We're having the new cooker installed later today.
5 Did you have all the water pipes replaced?
6 They had all the wedding photos taken by a professional.
7 Managers usually have all their letters typed for them.

3 **Complete each second sentence using the causative.**

1 Our neighbours paid a famous architect to design their new house.
   Our neighbours ______________ a famous architect.
2 Are you going to get a plumber to fit your washing machine?
   Are you going to ______________ by a plumber?
3 Someone delivers our newspaper every morning.
   We ______________ every morning.
4 Someone cut the tree down for my grandparents with a chain saw.
   My grandparents ______________ with a chain saw.
5 The judge told the guards to release the prisoner immediately.
   The judge ______________ immediately.

4 **Make sentences with the causative using these ideas. Use some of the verbs in the box if you wish, or come up with your own verbs. Try to use a different verb for each sentence.**

cut • deliver • design • make • paint repair • steal • take • wash

1 Sandy – her photograph – last week.
   Sandy had her photograph taken last week.
2 We – our new furniture – tomorrow.
3 They – their house – at the moment.
4 Emma – not – wedding dress – until next month.
5 Craig – car – recently.
6 You – ever – bike?
7 Dan and Margaret – usually – grass.

5 **Write a question using the causative for each of these answers.**

1 Yes, once. My passport, while I was on holiday. It was awful!
   Have you ever had anything stolen?
2 No, the dentist said it didn't have to be taken out after all.
3 Because the floppy disk drive stopped working.
4 Last week. I was at the optician's for over an hour!
5 No, I think the builders are going to do that next week.
6 Yes, she's the only person who knows how to cut my hair properly!

Use of English

1 Quickly read the text in exercise 2 and answer this question.

What's another way of describing an internet business?

2 exam practice

Read the text below and decide which answer (A, B, C or D) best fits each gap.

The dot-com bubble

In the mid to late 1990s, thousands of new companies were (1) ___ up with one purpose: to benefit from the explosion of interest in the internet. Large corporations were happy to (2) ___ millions in the weirdest website ideas, confident that they would make a (3) ___ over time. Most of them didn't. Indeed, the vast majority of them have gone (4) ___ , leaving their investors severely out of pocket. So what went wrong?

The main mistake that companies (5) ___ was to forget to ask how their dot com company (as internet-based companies are sometimes called) would actually make a (6) ___ . It sounds fairly obvious now, but in the rush to 'get on the net', the whole concept was (7) ___ . There was also a second problem which dot coms did not (8) ___ . Yes, internet traffic was (9) ___ enormously, but people still felt uncomfortable – many still do, in fact – about buying products and services online. Even if the dot coms had come up with sensible business ideas, it's unlikely they would have brought in enough to cover their (10) ___ investment.

There were some (11) ___ , of course. Some companies have been hugely successful on the internet. Most, however, found it wasn't as easy to (12) ___ an internet business as they'd thought.

	A	B	C	D
1	A held	B got	C set	D let
2	A throw	B add	C pay	D invest
3	A prosperity	B wealth	C treasure	D fortune
4	A ruined	B bust	C broken	D smashed
5	A made	B did	C had	D took
6	A profit	B salary	C commission	D royalty
7	A overseen	B unobserved	C overlooked	D reviewed
8	A hesitate	B anticipate	C regard	D maintain
9	A raising	B improving	C increasing	D extending
10	A novel	B initial	C authentic	D innovative
11	A endings	B differences	C exclusions	D exceptions
12	A run	B rule	C govern	D supervise

EXAM EXPERT

How should you do the exam practice task?

a Just think about the meanings of the words because this part tests vocabulary.

b Think about the meanings of the words but also think about their patterns and structures.

3 exam practice

Complete the second sentence so that it has a similar meaning to the first sentence using the word given. Do not change the word given. You must use between two and five words, including the word given. Write the missing words IN CAPITAL LETTERS.

1 The politician is going to pay a writer to write her speeches for her.
have
The politician is going to ________ her.

2 That woman's father made a fortune when he sold his business.
is
That ________ made a fortune when he sold his business.

3 They have the grass cut by a gardener.
get
They ________ the grass.

4 The company employed a further 20 people.
taken
A further 20 people ________ the company.

5 It seems to me that that suggestion isn't very sensible. **sense**
That suggestion ________ to me.

6 Penny has decided to get some experience working in a small business.
mind
Penny ________ to get some experience working in a small business.

EXAM EXPERT

How should you do the exam practice task?

Remember that **only** / **more than** one thing is usually tested in each question. For example, if they're testing whether you know a phrasal verb, you **might** / **won't** also have to turn the sentence from active to passive.

Writing: review

Starting point

Choose one of the following and tell your partner about it:

- The best non-fiction book you have read
- The most interesting TV programme you have seen recently

Make sure you mention:

- The name of the book/programme
- Who wrote it / Who appeared in it
- What it was about
- What made it so good
- Why you would recommend it

1 Read the review below and answer these questions.

1 Is this a review of a book or a TV programme?
2 What is it called?
3 What does Tony Robinson do?
4 What is it about?
5 What example of a difficult job does the writer give?
6 What does the writer like about it?
7 Which adjectives does the writer use? Underline them.
8 Does the writer make a recommendation?

The Worst Jobs In History

One of the most interesting programmes that I've seen on TV recently is called 'The Worst Jobs In History'. It's actually quite an old programme, but it's being repeated on Channel 3. Presented by Tony Robinson, the show looks at some of the more difficult or disgusting jobs that people had to do in the past.

Each episode takes a different period of history and examines ______________________. For instance, the episode last week showed us how hard life must have been in the dark ages. We saw how a poor man spent hours farming the land and had to build a house by hand in order to provide for his family.

One of the best things about the programme is that they get experts to explain to viewers exactly how the jobs were done. In order to do this, they show us the tools and methods people used and, of course, the presenter has a go too, sometimes making it quite funny to watch.

This series teaches you a lot about how we made a living in the past. Look out for it – you'll never complain about your job again!

2 Find words or phases in the review that have a similar meaning to these words and phrases.

1 shown again (paragraph 1)
2 programme (paragraph 1)
3 looks at (paragraph 2)
4 For example (paragraph 2)
5 people watching (paragraph 3)
6 to achieve this (paragraph 3)
7 attempts the task (paragraph 3)
8 worked, earned money (paragraph 4)

3 How would you describe the style of this review?

1 Formal and academic
2 Informal but informative
3 Very friendly and chatty

4 One of the writer's sentences is incomplete in the review. Discuss what she/he might have wanted to say and write an appropriate ending to the sentence.

Have your say!

- Have you seen this programme? If you have, did you enjoy watching it? Why? / Why not? If you haven't, would you like to watch it? Why? / Why not?

Plan ahead

1 exam practice: review

Your school or college magazine has asked its readers to send reviews of TV programmes they have seen or books they have read that they learned something from. Write a review of a book or a programme that you have read/seen and say what you learned from it.

Write your review.

> **EXAM EXPERT**
>
> **How should you write a review?**
>
> **a** Make sure you have an equal balance of positive and negative points about the programme/book you're reviewing.
>
> **b** It doesn't matter if you have / don't have any negative points to make about the programme/ book you're reviewing.
>
> See *Writing database* on page 198 for further information.

2 Look at the exam task in exercise 1 and answer these questions.

1 What do you have to write?
2 What information do you have to include?
3 Who is going to read it?
4 What style should you use?

3 Write B for book, T for TV programme, or B/T for both next to the words below.

1 episode __ 4 presenter __
2 chapter __ 5 story __
3 writer __ 6 description __

4 Decide on the book or TV programme that you're going to write about. Which of the words from exercise 3 could you use to describe it?

5 Complete some of these phrases about your choice in exercise 4.

1 This book/programme ____________
2 We learn ____________
3 One of the best things ____________
4 It shows us ____________
5 I felt ____________
6 You will ____________

6 Make a paragraph plan. Decide what information you will include in each paragraph.

7 Write your review in 120–180 words in an appropriate style.

8 When you have written your review, make sure that you have:

- given the basic information in the introduction ☐
- included more details in the middle paragraphs ☐
- used suitable adjectives ☐
- used a variety of sentence structures ☐
- explained what you learned ☐
- written in a style suitable for the reader ☐
- concluded your review in an effective way. ☐

10

Health

Wordpower!

emergency • panic • broken bones
fractures • bleeding • unconscious

Starting point

Do you know any first aid? Would you know what to do in an emergency?
Do you think everyone should know some first aid? Why? / Why not?

Reading 1 3.11

FIRST AID FOR ADVENTURE TRAVELLERS

Aware that injury can ruin any adventure holiday, Richard Madden decides it is time to sign up for some training on first aid in faraway places.

Imagine this scenario. It is spring and you are walking with your two teenage children in the mountains. It has been a terrific day's walking and you stop to enjoy a final view before heading back to base. The sun has been beaming down all day, but now the air temperature is beginning to drop rapidly. Suddenly, you hear a scream. You look around to see Kate clutching her leg and writhing in agony on the ground. What started as a playful snowball fight with Ben is now an emergency. You rush over, shouting to your partner to find the mobile and ring for help. Now you struggle to suppress a rising sense of panic. Is Kate's leg (or ankle? or foot?) broken or just sprained? She can hardly move, let alone walk, but how can you ease the pain? Should you move her? If so, how? Is she suffering from shock? If so, what should you do? If you had learned first aid, you would know what to do. Then the killer blow: there is no mobile signal and anyway the battery is about to run out.

1 Read the first three paragraphs of the article and choose true (T) or false (F).

1 The accident is something that really happened to the writer. T/F
2 The injury to Kate's leg is serious. T/F
3 The writer has been in many life-threatening situations. T/F

2 Read the whole article quickly and fill in the gaps.

1 ____________ % of people know what to do in an accident.
2 The writer has suffered cuts, bruises and ____________ while doing adventure activities.
3 FFH stands for ____________.
4 Medical shock is when ____________ drops.
5 James Moore is the writer's ____________.

EXAM EXPERT

How should you do the exam practice task?

a Remember that an option may be true, but it might not answer the question.
b As soon as you see an option that is true according to the text, choose that one as the answer.

3 exam practice

You are going to read an article about learning first aid. For questions 1–7, choose the answer (A–D) which you think fits best according to the text.

1 In the first paragraph, the writer describes
A something that happened to him and his family.
B how the weather often causes accidents.
C the correct thing to do in an emergency.
D how a day out in the mountains can end in disaster.

2 In the scene in the mountains,
A they are unable to call for help.
B they do not have a phone with them.
C someone has died.
D someone runs for help.

3 What does the writer say about previous accidents doing adventure activities?
A He has never had an accident.
B They have been life-threatening.
C He used his first-aid skills.
D They have mostly been small.

4 On the FFH course, the emphasis is on teaching people
A what to do if you cannot get to a doctor.
B how to use basic first-aid skills.
C how to cover wounds.
D to keep safe so that accidents do not happen.

Adventure activities, by definition, bring with them an element of risk. Having tried almost everything from trekking to skydiving, I consider myself extremely lucky to have suffered little more than cuts and bruises and a spell of amnesia over the years. If there had been a life-threatening accident, I would have relied on others who had first-aid skills. Not good enough. Not good enough at all.

So I booked a Far From Help (FFH) course run by Wilderness Medical Training (WMT). Our WMT tutor for the weekend is James Moore. 'Because we are aiming to go beyond basic first-aid skills, we concentrate on assessment and diagnosis, including how and when to start treatment for common injury and illness problems when medical help is not readily available,' he explains. There is a lot to cover: wounds; shock; fractures; head injuries and unconsciousness; seriously ill casualties; chest and abdominal injuries; multiple injuries; common infections.

'What exactly is shock?' James asks. We all start to reply and then hesitate. As with many of the conditions we cover, we think we know but then find we're not sure. James smiles. 'Medical shock is when your blood pressure drops, causing an inadequate supply of oxygenated blood to the vital organs. This can happen for a number of reasons. In extreme cases, it can be life-threatening.'

After the FFH weekend, I could now make a reasonable job of playing a television doctor. Give me that white coat and I would know how to take your blood pressure, or use a stethoscope to check your lungs and listen to your heartbeat. I might even peer inside your ears to check you haven't got an insect crawling around in there. I could bandage your arm (making sure I haven't stopped your blood supply to your fingers in the process), and make a sling for it. 56
More importantly, perhaps, I would know how to deal with Kate's leg injury, late in the afternoon on that mountain trail. I would know how to diagnose the problem, treat her in the appropriate manner, make her as comfortable as possible and assess the best way of getting us all off the mountain safely. Above all, perhaps, my calmness and confidence that we could cope with the situation would increase our chances of a happy outcome.

It is a sobering statistic that in disaster scenarios about 15% of us become hysterical, 70% are stunned and bewildered, while only the remaining 15% will react effectively. Had I not gone on the course, I would almost certainly have been one of the 70%, lacking the confidence to make an informed decision about what to do. How much better it feels to be among the 15% who might one day be in a position to save someone's life.

5 Why do you think James smiles after he asks what shock is?
  A because it is not as serious as people think
  B because he doesn't want to frighten the others
  C because the people in the group realise they don't know
  D because he is pleased that he has just taught the others something new

6 What does 'it' in line 56 refer to?
  A someone's arm
  B a bandage on someone's arm
  C someone's blood supply
  D the process of applying first aid

7 How does the writer say he has changed because of the course?
  A He has started to worry about the number of accidents that happen.
  B He feels he would be more capable and more confident in an emergency.
  C He now gets angry at people who don't take things seriously.
  D He no longer thinks walking in the mountains is a fun activity.

WORK IT OUT!

Find these words and phrases in the text and underline them. Can you work out what they mean from the context?

beaming • suppress • run out • go beyond
hesitate • cope with • sobering

4 Find words or phrases in the text which have a similar meaning to these phrases.

1 holding tightly (paragraph 1)
2 extreme pain (paragraph 1)
3 the worst news of all (paragraph 2)
4 small injuries to the skin (paragraph 3)
5 losing your memory (paragraph 3)
6 not enough or not good enough (paragraph 5)
7 instrument for listening to the chest (paragraph 6)
8 out of control (paragraph 7)

Have your say!

- What would you do in the situation described at the beginning of the text? Would you be among the hysterical, the stunned and bewildered, or would you react effectively?

G Grammar 1

Conditionals (2): third, mixed and inverted

Is this sentence about the present or the past?
If I had known about nutrition, I would have eaten more fruit.

Third conditional

hypothetical (unreal) past

if + past perfect + modal + *have* + past participle
If you had been careful, you wouldn't have hurt yourself. (= You weren't careful so you hurt yourself.)

Mixed conditionals

hypothetical (unreal) past condition, present result

if + past perfect + modal + present
If I had eaten more meat as a child, I would be taller now.

hypothetical (unreal) present condition, past result

if + past (simple or continuous) + modal + *have* + past participle
If you were fitter, you might have won the race.

Inverted conditionals

We can use inversions (question word order) to make formal conditional sentences, instead of using *if*.
Were I in your position, I would change my doctor.
Had you been more careful, you wouldn't have hurt yourself.

See *Grammar database 28* on page 189 for more information.

1 Choose the correct word or phrase to complete these sentences.

1 If people had known about nutrition in the past, they _____ so many health problems.
  a might not have had c would not have
  b may have had d could have

2 You might have been all right if you _____ a doctor sooner.
  a didn't see c would see
  b had seen d saw

3 If you had known about the health risks, _____ smoking?
  a would you start c would you have started
  b did you not start d could you not start

4 I _____ a broken leg if I had been more careful.
  a wouldn't have c couldn't have had
  b didn't have d might have had

2 Rewrite these sentences beginning with the words given.

1 I didn't get any aspirin because I didn't have enough money on me.
If I __________
2 I caught a cold because I went out in the rain.
I __________
3 The doctor gave me a prescription because I needed some medicine.
If I __________
4 I was ill last Friday so I couldn't go to school.
I could __________
5 You feel sick now because you ate so much junk food yesterday.
If you __________
6 You didn't take your medicine and that's why you didn't get better.
If you __________
7 They did not apply for permission in time so the town council did not allow them to open the new gym.
Had __________

3 Complete these sentences in an appropriate way.

1 If people had known about bacteria hundreds of years ago, __________
2 If you had told me you were ill, __________
3 If I hadn't taken the pills my mum gave me, __________
4 If I'd known pasta was so high in calories, __________
5 If I hadn't eaten that fifth ice-cream, __________
6 If my parents hadn't taught me about healthy eating, __________
7 Had people known smoking was bad for them, __________

4 Make four sentences about you and your health using different conditional forms.

V Vocabulary

Health

1 Use the words in the box to complete these sentences.

alternative • check-up • clinic • disabled • first aid
germs • infection • prescription • surgery • tablet

1 I felt a little nervous as I went into the doctor's ____________ , but she was actually really friendly.
2 Wash your hands to get rid of ____________ before you start cooking.
3 The doctor gave me a(n) ____________ for some cough medicine.
4 The pills the doctor gave me aren't working so I'm thinking of trying ____________ medicine, like acupuncture.
5 The waiting-room at the health ____________ was full of people with flu!
6 Everyone should know some ____________ in case of an emergency.
7 I got an eye ____________ and had to go and see the doctor.
8 The doctor told me to take one ____________ three times a day after meals.
9 We need to do much more in this city to help ____________ people travel around.
10 I go to the doctor every six months for a(n) ____________ , just so that I know that I'm healthy.

! Be careful!

a surgery = a doctor's office
surgery = medical treatment involving an operation

2 Phrasal verbs

Each of these phrasal verbs to do with health is in the wrong sentence. Rewrite each sentence using the correct phrasal verb in the right form.

1 Lots of students have **passed out** flu over the last couple of weeks.
2 It was so hot that I thought I was going to **come down with** until the teacher opened a window.
3 John banged his head and was unconscious for a few minutes before he **broke out**.
4 Serious diseases often **get over** in countries in the developing world.
5 When Lisa was in hospital, I took her some sweets to try and **come** her **to**.
6 It took my grandma a long time to **cheer up** pneumonia.

3 Word formation

Find nouns that can be formed from these words.

allergic • operate • disabled • recover
fit • surgery (person) • ill • treat • inject

4 Word patterns

Choose the correct word or phrase to complete each sentence.

1 My mum made me **take / to take** the medicine but it was horrible!
2 The doctor advised me **taking / to take** more exercise.
3 I don't think there's any point in **telling / to tell** Scott to eat less junk food.
4 I don't always feel like **eating / to eat** healthy food.
5 You can't force people **stopping / to stop** smoking but you can encourage them.
6 It's not worth **worrying / to worry** about your health. Just enjoy yourself!
7 You are bound **catching / to catch** a cold if you go out in this weather without your coat.
8 Another burger? It's not like you **eating / to eat** so much junk food.

Listening

Starting point

Why might you phone a health clinic or doctor's surgery?

1 **For each question in exercise 2, discuss what the situation might be. Predict what you might hear each person say.**

2 3.12 exam practice

You will hear people talking in eight different situations. For questions 1–8, choose the best answer (A, B or C).

1 You hear someone talking on the phone. Who is she talking to?
- **A** a doctor
- **B** a receptionist
- **C** a nurse

2 You hear a man talking to his doctor. What is the doctor's advice?
- **A** keep using the cream
- **B** change washing powder
- **C** start taking tablets

3 You hear this conversation in a supermarket. What does the man want to do?
- **A** buy some fruit juice
- **B** study nutrition
- **C** start a special diet

4 You hear a patient in a doctor's surgery talking to the receptionist. Who does the woman want to make an appointment for?
- **A** herself
- **B** her husband's colleague
- **C** her son

5 You hear this woman talking to a friend on a bus. What is the woman's problem?
- **A** One of her colleagues is off work.
- **B** She keeps taking days off work.
- **C** She doesn't get on with her doctor.

6 You hear this extract from a radio programme. What is the caller's question about?
- **A** losing weight
- **B** stopping smoking
- **C** alternative medicine

7 You hear a girl talking about a TV programme. What does she say about the programme?
- **A** The advice it gave was wrong.
- **B** The advice it gave seemed unnecessary.
- **C** She couldn't understand the advice.

8 You hear this recorded message when you ring your doctor. Why is the surgery closed?
- **A** The doctor is ill.
- **B** It is a public holiday.
- **C** The doctor is on holiday.

EXAM EXPERT

How should you do the exam practice task?

a Read all the questions before you listen so that you know what to expect.

b Don't read the questions before you listen so that you can keep an open mind.

3 3.13 exam practice

You will hear five people talking about health issues. For questions 1–5, choose which of the options (A–F) each person says. There is one extra letter that you do not need to use.

- **A** Prevention is an investment for the future.
- **B** Doctors are not good at dealing with the public.
- **C** The situation was life-threatening.
- **D** Medical insurance is worth having.
- **E** The mind plays an important role in our physical health.
- **F** People are ignorant about disabilities.

Speaker 1 ____
Speaker 2 ____
Speaker 3 ____
Speaker 4 ____
Speaker 5 ____

EXAM EXPERT

How should you do the exam practice task?

a Use a pencil to point to the speaker you are listening to so that you don't get confused.

b Don't worry about remembering which speaker you are listening to because there are only five of them.

Have your say!

- What do you think are the main health risks people face today?

Speaking

Wordpower!

graphics • have an impact • slogan
warn of the dangers

Starting point

Imagine you had to design an anti-smoking poster aimed at teenagers. What would your poster be like?

1 3.14 **Listen to this extract from two candidates doing exercise 3. Make a note of any questions they ask each other.**

2 Read what you have to do in exercise 3 and choose true (T) or false (F).

1 You have to decide what should go in the book. T/F
2 You have to talk about how healthy your life is. T/F
3 You have to decide on one picture for the cover. T/F

EXAM EXPERT

How should you do the exam practice task?

a It's important to use unusual words to show your vocabulary, even if it sounds unnatural.
b It's important to sound natural, while showing that you have a good vocabulary at the same time.

See *Speaking database* on page 193.

3 exam practice

I'd like you to imagine that a book is going to be published about teenagers and the health risks they face. Talk to each other about how you think each of these things might affect teenagers' health and then decide which picture you would choose for the cover of the book.

- How might each of these things affect teenagers' health?
- Which picture would you choose for the cover of the book?

EXAM EXPERT

How should you do the exam practice task?

a Ask your partner questions now and again to keep the conversation going.
b Never ask questions because that's the examiner's job.

4 exam practice

Would you say you generally live a healthy life?

Do you think teenagers know enough about healthy living?

What advice would you give someone who wanted to improve their diet?

Do people worry too much about their health these days?

Are we healthier than people were fifty years ago?

Reading 2 3.15

Wordpower!

GP • surgeon • specialist • ward

Starting point

What different kinds of doctor can you think of?
What do you think the daily routine of a doctor is like?

1 **Look at the title of the article that you are going to read. What do you think the article might be about?**

2 **Read the first two paragraphs of the article and answer these questions.**

1 Who are Abigail and Gillian Doyle?
2 What scheme were they involved in?
3 What is the goal of the scheme?

3 exam practice

You are going to read an article about an unusual scheme. Seven sentences have been removed from the article. Choose from sentences A–H the one which fits each gap (1–7). There is one extra sentence which you do not need to use.

A She says that one thing that surprised her was the amount of medical knowledge most people have.
B Even so, Abigail is also very aware of the plus side.
C You can never predict exactly what cases are going to come up, although the appointment system means that Dr Doyle has some idea of what to expect.
D Abigail had her doubts at first, and she wasn't sure how she would react to the sight of blood.
E It's important for a doctor like Gillian to keep up with developments in medicine by reading medical journals.
F Her mother's duties include visiting patients on the wards and checking on their progress.
G The aim is to better equip teenagers to make decisions about their own futures.
H I explained to the patients why Abigail was there and they all thought it was a really good idea.

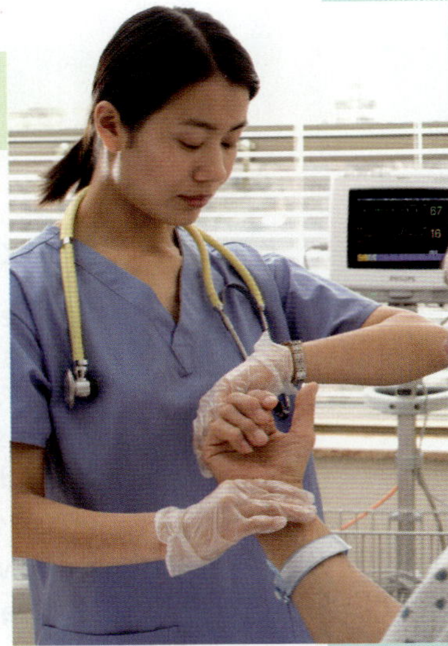

Abigail Doyle spent last Wednesday examining patients, taking temperatures and looking at X-rays. Not unusual, perhaps, for a doctor, but it is unusual when you are just thirteen years old.

Abigail and her mother, Dr Gillian Doyle, were taking part in 'Take Your Child To Work Day', a scheme designed to give children an idea of the jobs their parents do. **1** The scheme was first suggested by the local council after the success of similar schemes in America.

Dr Doyle thinks it's very useful. 'I don't mind what Abigail does as a profession, but at least she can base her decisions on experience. She got to see a lot of my day-to-day work, with patients coming in with everything from a sprained ankle or a sore throat to a fractured arm. **2** ' The positive response helped Abigail feel more comfortable in a strange situation.

'It was fascinating,' says Abigail. 'I'd been to the surgery before, of course, to meet Mum after school, but I'd never been there and met patients.' **3** In the end, it all went smoothly, although she's still not entirely comfortable with injections.

EXAM EXPERT

How should you do the exam practice task?

a Never choose a sentence to fill a gap unless it is talking about exactly the same thing as the sentence before.

b Remember that the correct sentence to fill a gap may be talking about something related to the sentence before, even if it isn't talking about exactly the same thing.

Doctor for a day

The surgery is open to patients from nine in the morning and a steady stream of them comes through the doors until they close at one. **4** ______ 'It's a job with a great deal of variety,' says Gillian, 'and I think Abigail liked that. There certainly isn't much time to get bored!'

The work at the surgery is only half of Dr Doyle's day. The other half is spent at a local hospital and Abigail accompanied her there, too. **5** ______ Abigail found this the most interesting aspect of the day. 'The surgery is quite a calm place, but I thought the hospital was full of activity. I could see how Mum must get a lot of satisfaction from seeing the improvement in the people she's treating.'

As part of the scheme, Abigail is creating a school project out of what she learned. **6** ______ She also found that it was hard to remain uninvolved. 'You have to care,' she says, 'but at the same time it's possible to care too much. It's not always easy to keep your emotions out of the work, and I see that with Mum sometimes.'

On the question of whether it has encouraged her to become a doctor herself, Abigail is undecided. 'It requires a lot of commitment. The training is quite long and the work is really demanding. At the end of the day, I was shattered!'

7 ______ 'There was one little boy who came into the surgery with an ear infection and he was in a lot of pain. While Mum got the details from his parents, I played with him and helped to calm him down. I felt like I was doing my bit and after Mum had treated him he left with a big grin on his face. It's a special feeling to be able to do something like that.'

4 Complete these sentences using words from the text and the removed sentences.

1 The __________ showed that John had broken his leg in two places.

2 You haven't broken anything, but you've got a __________ wrist. Try to rest it.

3 My eyes were __________ from studying so much. That can't be healthy!

4 The doctor said my leg was __________ so I had to go to hospital.

5 All the __________ in the new hospital have a view of the harbour, so patients can watch the boats coming in.

6 A nurse's job can be quite __________ and you often have to work very long hours.

WORK IT OUT!

Find these words and phrases in the text and underline them. Can you work out what they mean from the context?

taking temperatures • scheme • fascinating • grin
aspect • commitment • shattered • doing my bit

Have your say!

- Would you like to try a scheme similar to this one?
- What do you think you would learn?

G Grammar 2

Direct and indirect objects

How could you rewrite this sentence without *to*?

The doctor gave a prescription to me.

Some verbs can be followed by both a direct and an indirect object (usually a person).

The nurse showed me (indirect object) *the X-rays* (direct object).

When the indirect object comes last, we usually use a preposition (often *for* or *to*).

She handed some tablets to me.

When these verbs are used in the passive the subject of the sentence is usually the **indirect object** of the active sentence and not the **direct object.**

The nurse handed ***me*** *some tablets.*

I was handed some tablets by the nurse.

See *Grammar database 29* on page 189 for more information.

Infinitives of purpose

When we want to talk about someone's purpose, we can use the full infinitive:

I went to the surgery ***to see*** *the doctor.*

We can also use:

in order + full infinitive

The doctor got out her stethoscope ***in order*** *to listen to my chest.*

so as + full infinitive

Many people exercise ***so as to stay*** *in shape.*

With a negative purpose or with stative verbs, we don't normally use the infinitive alone.

☒ I take vitamin tablets in order/so as not to get ill.

☒ I take vitamin tablets not to get ill.

See *Grammar database 30* on page 190 for more information.

1 Rewrite these sentences putting the indirect objects earlier in the sentence where possible. If it is not possible, put a tick (☒).

1 My mum made an appointment at the doctor's for my dad.
2 The doctor wrote a prescription for me for some cough medicine.
3 Could you suggest a healthy diet to me?
4 My uncle sent a book about teenagers and health to my sister.
5 Why don't I lend my exercise bike to you?
6 Our teacher explained the food pyramid to us.
7 Would you mind passing the toothpaste to me?
8 I'd like you to describe the symptoms to me.

2 Put these words in the correct order to make sentences.

1 in/€200/my/cost/fees/over/doctor's/it/parents
It ________
2 permission/their/refuse/vegetarian/become/parents/children/some/to
Some ________
3 living/what/let/healthy/you/read/says/it/about/me
Let ________
4 me/my/sore/throat/for/mum/my/honey/made/lemon/a glass of/and
My ________
5 give/aspirin/you/doctor/to/some/the/ask
Ask ________

3 Complete these sentences in an appropriate way using the word given.

1 Doctors use a stethoscope ________ **order**
2 Doctors take X-rays ________ **as**
3 You should wash your hands regularly ________ **not**
4 Eat more vegetables ________ **order**
5 I work out twice a week ________ **to**
6 Put a plaster on your cut ________ **order**
7 You should brush your teeth every day ________ **as**
8 I rang the clinic ________ **in**
9 I'd like to become a doctor ________ **as**
10 Cover your mouth when you sneeze ________ **not**

Use of English

1 **Read the text in exercise 2, ignoring the gaps, and answer these questions.**

1 Which tastes are mentioned that we normally enjoy?
2 What do we get from the sugar in our diets?
3 Which tastes warn us of food that may be bad for us?

2 exam practice

Read the text below and think of the word which best fits each gap. Use only one word in each gap. Write your answers IN CAPITAL LETTERS.

Taste

We take it (1) ________ granted that when we put something in our mouths, we taste it. But why should our bodies be able to detect chemicals in this way? In order (2) ________ answer that question, we need to consider two things: the dietary requirements (3) ________ our bodies and the risks associated (4) ________ eating.

Our bodies need certain substances (5) ________ a regular basis, including vitamins, carbohydrates and salt. The flavour of food, (6) ________ as fruit, gives us important information (7) ________ the nutrients it contains. Sweet tastes mean sugar, which (8) ________ turn means high energy levels. Salty tastes indicate the presence of other chemicals we need besides sugar. Because we find these tastes pleasurable, we tend to eat food that (9) ________ high in these substances.

Bitter and sour tastes, on the other hand, usually act (10) ________ nature's warning devices. When something is poisonous, it usually has a bitter flavour, a taste (11) ________ we naturally dislike. Also, as food (12) ________ off it tends to develop a sour taste. This means that we are able to avoid food that could cause health problems.

> **EXAM EXPERT**
>
> **How should you do the exam practice task?**
>
> **a** Always complete the gaps in the order they appear in the text.
>
> **b** Complete the easier gaps first to give you more clues for the others.

3 **Quickly read the text in exercise 4. Which part of the body do auricular therapists focus on?**

4 exam practice

Read the text below. Use the word given in capitals at the end of some of the lines to form a word that fits in the gap in the same line. Write your answers IN CAPITAL LETTERS.

Auricular Therapy

If you've had an (1) ___ reaction to something, and don't know	ALLERGY
what it is, or if you suspect you've got some kind of (2) ___ or	ILL
(3) ___ , auricular therapists claim to be able to help. Auricular	INFECT
therapy is based on the idea that our ears can tell us a lot about	
our general level of health and (4) ___ . Auricular therapists	FIT
examine patients' ears with a special piece of (5) ___ for signs of	EQUIP
stress and pain in different parts of the body. The idea is that,	
once the cause of the stress or pain has been identified, (6) ___ is	TREAT
more likely to be (7) ___ . There are a number of recorded cases	SUCCESS
of patients making a full (8) ___ after being treated with auricular	RECOVER
therapy. However, critics claim it is not based on any proven	
(9) ___ principles and point out that to consult an auricular	SCIENCE
therapist rather than a qualified doctor may actually be (10) ___ .	DANGER

> **EXAM EXPERT**
>
> **How should you do the exam practice task?**
>
> If you're not sure whether, for example, the noun from *recover* is *recoverment*, *recovery*, or *recoverness*,
>
> **a** always choose the one with the most letters.
>
> **b** think about how the words look and sound.

Writing: story

Starting point

How often do you read stories or novels?
What can you learn from reading stories in English?

1 **Look at this writing task and the model answer. There are six extra words in the story that shouldn't be there. Cross them out.**

You have decided to enter a short story competition. The competition rules say that your story must begin with these words:
Jeff couldn't have got ill on a worse day.

Write your story for the competition.

Jeff couldn't have got ill on a worse day. He had been looking forward to the school party for weeks and now, all over his face, there were red spots! His brother noticed them and said, smiling, 'Oh, bad luck!'

Jeff called his mum, who came running. 'Oh, Jeff!' she said, so worriedly. 'Get dressed. We're going straight to the doctor's.' When they got there to the surgery, the waiting room was full. ______________________________
____
____

They went in to see the doctor when their turn came and sat down. 'What is it, Doctor? I thought that perhaps it was an allergy,' said Jeff's mum. Both Jeff and his mum couldn't believe in it when the doctor started laughing!

'I think someone's been playing a practical joke,' laughed the doctor. He took a towel and wiped away Jeff's face and the spots disappeared! Jeff realised that the spots had been drawn on with a red marker pen! His brother must have done it while Jeff was being asleep.

'I think it's going to be a great school party,' thought Jeff on the way home, as he planned on his revenge.

2 **Write one or two sentences to summarise the plot of the story.**

3 **Complete the second paragraph by writing a short description of the waiting room when Jeff and his mum arrive.**

4 **What would be a good title for this story?**

a An outbreak of disease
b A shocking trick
c The doctor's advice

Plan ahead

1 exam practice: story

Your English teacher has asked you to write a short story for your school magazine. The story must begin with the words:

There couldn't have been a better time for Emma to get toothache!

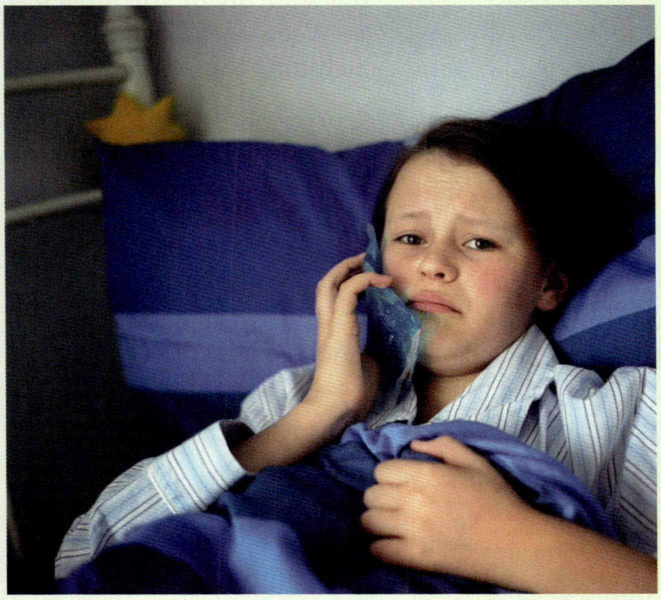

EXAM EXPERT

How should you write a story?

a Spend more time on the beginning of the story than the middle and the end.

b Try to have a balanced story with a good beginning, middle and end.

See *Writing database* on page 202 for further information.

2 Look at the writing task in exercise 1 and answer these questions using your imagination.

1 Why might having toothache be good?
2 What had Emma been planning to do before she got toothache?
3 What does she do instead?
4 What happens in the end?
5 How does Emma feel at the end of the story?

3 Write one or two sentences that summarise the plot of your story.

Emma wakes up with toothache on the morning of an important exam she hasn't studied for. She's happy because it means she can take the exam on another day.

4 Compare your plot with your partner's plot and ask each other questions about your stories.

What happens at the start of your story?

How does Emma feel?

What happens at the end of your story?

5 Tell the rest of the class what your partner's story is about. Give as much detail as you can. Listen to all the story ideas in the class and change your story if you hear any good ideas!

6 Make a paragraph plan. Make sure you have a good balance between the beginning, the middle and the end of your story.

7 Write your story in 120–180 words in an appropriate style.

8 When you have written your story, make sure that you have:

- used the sentence given at the start of your story ☐
- used paragraphs correctly ☐
- used direct speech where appropriate ☐
- written a story of the right length ☐
- used interesting adjectives and adverbs ☐
- checked your spelling and grammar. ☐

Check your progress! Units 9–10

1 Choose the correct word to fill in the gap.

While I was looking for another job after I had been made (1) ___ , I decided to do some (2) ___ work for a charity. I didn't (3) ___ any money, of course, but I gained some valuable skills and it helped me pass the time. Also, it was useful to be able to say in a job interview: 'Yes, I am (4) ___ at the moment, but I am spending my time in a constructive way.'

1	**A** full-time	**B** temporary	**C** redundant	**D** permanent
2	**A** amateur	**B** voluntary	**C** unprofessional	**D** recreational
3	**A** gain	**B** win	**C** add	**D** earn
4	**A** self-employed	**B** sacked	**C** fired	**D** unemployed

Sitting in the waiting room of the doctor's (5) ___ , Gary couldn't wait for his GP to see him. He felt so proud. At his previous (6) ___ , six months previously, the doctor had told Gary that he was seriously overweight. Since then, Gary had (7) ___ on a strict diet. He felt sure the doctor would be impressed by how (8) ___ and healthy he looked.

5	**A** surgery	**B** ward	**C** theatre	**D** office
6	**A** checkout	**B** check-in	**C** check-up	**D** checkpoint
7	**A** had	**B** taken	**C** gone	**D** come
8	**A** plump	**B** slim	**C** chubby	**D** obese

Andrew Carter got his first job – running (9) ___ for a small, local business – when he was fifteen. He was (10) ___ to a managerial (11) ___ in his early twenties, and then left to set up his own fast-food business, called *Carter's*. It's run as a (12) ___ , so other people pay him to open restaurants with his name on!

9	**A** errands	**B** tasks	**C** chores	**D** jobs
10	**A** enlarged	**B** improved	**C** increased	**D** promoted
11	**A** spot	**B** location	**C** position	**D** place
12	**A** firm	**B** franchise	**C** company	**D** partnership

Although this type of flu (13) ___ out over two years ago, scientists are still unsure how it is best (14) ___ . (15)___ who have been given antibiotics appear to (16) ___ after two or three weeks, but it is unclear whether the antibiotics are effective at preventing the disease from recurring.

13	**A** cracked	**B** smashed	**C** crashed	**D** broke
14	**A** operated	**B** fixed	**C** healed	**D** treated
15	**A** Customers	**B** Patients	**C** Guests	**D** Clients
16	**A** recover	**B** mend	**C** restore	**D** repair

16 marks

2 Complete the second sentence so that it has a similar meaning to the first sentence, using the word given. Do not change the word given. You must use between two and five words, including the word given.

1 Stay at home this week so you don't infect the other children at school.
as
Stay at home this week ________________ infect the other children at school.

2 The nurse said she would take my temperature in a few minutes.
have
I am going ________________ in a few minutes.

3 Lindsey was treated by that doctor.
is
That ________________ Lindsey.

4 Could you see if the woman with her leg in plaster needs any help?
whose
Could you see if the woman ________________ in plaster needs any help?

5 I don't want to do anything energetic.
feel
I don't ________________ anything energetic.

6 Fiona isn't usually rude to customers.
like
It is ________________ rude to customers.

7 The dietician suggested to Caroline that she shouldn't eat so much red meat.
advised
The dietician ______________ so much red meat.

8 Tim was sacked because he was continually late for work.
if
Tim would ______________ he hadn't been continually late for work.

9 Why didn't you ask to see a back specialist?
would
If I were you, I ______________ to see a back specialist.

10 You shouldn't apply for a job if you haven't got the right skills.
point
There ______________ for a job if you haven't got the right skills.

20 marks

3 Complete each sentence using a form of the word in brackets.

1 How many __________ (**apply**) were there for the job?
2 Isabelle works as a __________ (**surgery**) at the local children's hospital.
3 I think I'm going to need some __________ (**assist**) with this. Could you help me?
4 Is Rania __________ (**allergy**) to cheese?
5 I hate the thought of having __________ (**inject**), but they never actually hurt.
6 Although I'm physically __________ (**able**), I don't let that stop me from living a full life.
7 You'll start as a __________ (**train**), and after a couple of years, you'll be fully qualified.
8 Grandpa has to go into hospital for a minor __________ (**operate**) next week.

8 marks

4 Write a form of one of the verbs *have, take, make* or *do* in each gap.

1 Are you going to __________ part in the fun run to raise money for cancer research?
2 I've __________ up my mind. I'm going to be an actor!
3 Could you __________ me a favour?
4 We don't have one boss at our company. We __________ it in turns to make managerial decisions.
5 Scientists are __________ a lot of research at the moment into how we can slow down the ageing process.
6 I know it's difficult having a broken leg, but you just have to __________ the best of the situation.
7 Have you __________ an appointment to see the doctor?
8 __________ care, and get well soon! Lots of love, Mandy.

8 marks

5 Write a phrasal verb from the box in the correct form in each gap.

cheer up • come down with • fill in • get over
pass out • take on • take over • take up

1 The firm was __________ by a huge multinational corporation.
2 Mr Philips isn't here today. He's __________ flu, unfortunately.
3 __________! It's not that serious!
4 Writing prescriptions __________ a lot of a GP's time.
5 The business must be doing well – they __________ another twenty employees last year.
6 It was so hot on the bus, and I felt so faint, I was worried I was going to __________.
7 Could you just __________ your name and address, and sign at the bottom?
8 I hope she __________ her illness soon.

8 marks

Total: 60 marks

11

Learning

Wordpower!

lecture • secondary school • uniform • university

Starting point

Look at the photographs above. Use words connected to school and education to describe them.

1 **Read the article quickly and find words and phrases which fit into these categories:**

- Subjects
- Educational establishments

2 exam practice

You are going to read an article in which a novelist talks about his education. For questions 1–8, choose the answer (A–D) which you think fits best according to the text.

1 In the first paragraph, what does the author say he cannot remember at all?
  A his education before the age of ten
  B being at nursery school or primary school
  C going to playgroup for the first time
  D traumatic experiences in his childhood

2 What does the word 'This' (line 13) refer to?
  A being sent to a boys-only prep school
  B having to cope with being away from home
  C being the best in the class for most subjects
  D sitting at the front of the class for most subjects

3 What does Charles say about 'Getting a good Latin report' (line 14)?
  A It didn't make up for the bad treatment he received from his classmates.
  B The boys would start to be nasty to him as soon as he got his report.
  C It made him feel better about the fact that the boys didn't like him.
  D It was helpful that it was always given to him at the end of term.

Reading 1 4.01

Charles Li: *My education*

As part of our series looking at the education of successful people, novelist Charles Li looks back on his schooldays.

I have no recollection of my first days either at nursery school, which we called 'playgroup', or primary school That suggests that they were not too traumatic, at least In fact, I have few memories of being educated up to the age of about 10. The memories I do have from that period mainly relate to the playground or break time: asking Linda Clarkson if she wanted to be my girlfriend and falling off the climbing frame and breaking my arm.

When I was 11, my father, who was in the Navy, was posted abroad and I was sent to a boys-only prep school. Despite the initial difficulties of being away from home for the first time, I blossomed intellectually, and was at the top of my form for most subjects. This had its disadvantages Getting a good Latin report at the end of term is little consolation for the resulting bullying from the other boys

4 The writer suggests that, compared to his public school, his children's state school doesn't
  A employ teachers of such high quality.
  B offer such a range of academic subjects.
  C allow students to take so many exams.
  D organise so many additional activities.

5 What does the use of the word 'agonised' in line 42 suggest?
  A that the writer delayed thinking about the options
  B that the decision was a very difficult one to make
  C that the writer was experiencing great physical pain
  D that it was obvious what decision the writer would take

6 Charles Li says that teachers at boarding schools are different to other teachers because they
  A give their students much more freedom in the classroom.
  B have a very different view of what morality is.
  C care about more than just teaching their academic subject.
  D bring their own children up in a very different way.

I was unpopular both because I excelled academically and because I didn't excel at sport.

At thirteen, a public school decided I was bright enough to be awarded a scholarship. My new school was co-educational and, although there were occasions when having girls in the class was more of a distraction than an aid to learning, I much preferred being out of an all-boy environment.

Preparation for O levels (the equivalent of today's GCSEs) began immediately I arrived, and the standard of teaching was extremely high. At 16, I passed eleven O levels, all with an A grade. However, what I really value about my education there was the opportunity to take part in so many extra-curricular activities. It was the writing workshop, rather than English lessons, which made me consider becoming a writer. I also acted in school plays, debated in debating competitions, used a computer for the first time and became interested in photography. Now my children are at school – a state school – I wish they had the opportunities I had.

Just after my O levels, I had to make a decision. My parents were back in the UK and gave me a choice. I could either stay on at public school or move back home and go to the local sixth form college. I agonised over the summer, and came to the conclusion that a change would do me good. I decided to go home.

I've never regretted that decision. I thoroughly enjoyed the two-year A level course (English, maths and economics), particularly the freedom that comes from not going to a boarding school. Suddenly, the teachers were just teachers. They weren't interested in my moral upbringing, as teachers at private schools are.

I didn't study quite as hard as I should have done during that two-year period, but some last minute late-night revision enabled me to get good enough exam results to do a degree in English Literature at Dorkham University.

I loved it there. Most of my fellow first-year undergraduates were living away from home for the first time and often found it difficult not having their parents around to help them. Because I had been to boarding school, I was quite used to having to fend for myself. I enjoyed the course, I made some fantastic friends and, as with public school, I took advantage of all the clubs and societies on offer.

If I could do it all again, would I do anything differently? I certainly made the right decisions regarding going to sixth form college and choosing my A levels and degree course. If I were back at prep school, I would make more of an effort to be liked. Perhaps I did show off too much. There's one thing I do not regret, though: the decision to send my children to the local comprehensive school. Boarding schools may provide more opportunities, but one thing I've learned is that family is more important than anything. Even which school you go to.

7 How did the writer differ from the majority of first-year undergraduates at university?
   A He made full use of the clubs and societies provided.
   B He had experience of not relying on other people.
   C He loved the freedom of living away from home.
   D He didn't find studying for the course difficult.

8 What does Charles Li admit in the final paragraph?
   A that he may be partly responsible for how he was treated at prep school
   B that he should have stayed at public school for longer than he did
   C that schools actually make no difference to how you turn out in the end
   D that he should not have sent his children to the local state school

EXAM EXPERT

How should you do the exam practice task?

When the question ends with a question mark, find the answer in the text **before** / **after** looking at the four options. **Don't underline** / **Underline** it. Then choose the option that **is closest in meaning to** / **has the same words as** the answer in the text.

WORK IT OUT!

Find these words and phrases in the text and underline them. Can you work out what they mean from the context?

climbing frame • distraction • excelled • show off
moral upbringing • fend for myself • posted abroad

3 Find words or phrases in the article which have a similar meaning to these words and phrases.

1 class
2 a document describing your progress
3 an amount of money a school gives you to study there
4 with both boys and girls (for schools)
5 the things a school offers outside the academic timetable
6 the first qualification you can get from a university
7 a person studying at university who hasn't graduated yet

Have your say!

- What do you think about boarding schools?

G Grammar 1

Unreal past

Look at this sentence. Does the verb in bold refer to (a) the past or (b) the present?

*It's time you **started** revising for the exam.*

After certain phrases, or in certain types of sentence, we use the past simple or past continuous to refer to now, a general situation or the future.

Second conditional:
If you paid attention in class, you'd have a much better chance of passing the exam.

***Suppose*, *Imagine* and *What if* …?:**
Suppose you saw tomorrow's exam lying on the secretary's desk. Would you look at it?

***would rather* + *you*/*he*/*she*/*we*/*they*:**
I'd rather you didn't write such long essays, Caroline.

It's (high) time:
It's high time you took your driving test.

Polite questions:
Did you want to see me now about my report, Mrs MacDonnell?

***Wish* and *If only*:**
I wish I was better at geography.

Past wishes

For wishes about the past, we use the past perfect:
I wish I hadn't failed the test yesterday.

To express criticism or complaint about an activity now, in the future or generally, we can use *wish* + *would*:
I wish you would pay more attention in class. (= I wish you paid …)

To express hypothetical ability or permission now, in the future or generally, we can use *wish* + *could*:
I wish we could sit next to each other in every lesson. (= I wish we were able to …)

See *Grammar database 31* on page 190 for more information.

1 These sentences were in the article on pages 142–143. Without looking back, choose the words or phrases that can fill each gap. Be careful! More than one word or phrase might fill the gap.

1 I wish they ________ the opportunities I had.
a had **b** have **c** can have

2 If I ________ do it all again, would I do anything differently?
a am able to **b** could **c** was able to

3 If I ________ back at prep school, I would make more of an effort to be liked.
a was **b** were **c** am

2 If a sentence is correct, put a tick (☒). If it is incorrect, correct it.

1 Imagine you had a photographic memory!
2 It's about time the bell rings.
3 I really wish we don't have to choose between doing biology and German.
4 Would you rather I don't use a dictionary so much?
5 If only I was going with you on the school trip next weekend.

3 Put the verbs in brackets in the correct form to complete the sentences.

1 If you ______________ (**be**) a teacher, how strict would you be?
2 I wish our English teacher ______________ (**not** / **give**) us so much homework all the time!
3 It's high time you ______________ (**learn**) how to tell the time.
4 If only I ______________ (**know**) the answer to number four! What could it be?
5 I wish you ______________ (**come**) on the field trip with us next month.
6 I'd rather you two ______________ (**not** / **sit**) next to each other today.
7 I wish I ______________ (**start**) studying earlier. The exam is tomorrow and I haven't finished the work yet!

4 For each situation, make a sentence beginning with the phrase in bold.

1 You are at school. You want to be at home. **I wish**
I wish I was at home or I wish I wasn't at school.
2 You've got such a lot of homework to do. **If only**
3 A friend of yours keeps copying from you in class and you think the[y] should stop. **It's time**
4 Your teacher is thinking about giving your class some extra lessons during the holidays. You don't think it's a good idea! **I'd rather**
5 You're daydreaming about being able to speak English fluently. **If I**
6 You're suggesting to a friend that they do a computer course. **What i[f]**

Have your say!

- If you had the power to change one thing about your school, what would you change and why?

V Vocabulary

Education

1 Put these people into two categories: Teachers and Learners.

apprentice • pupil • instructor • lecturer • professor
tutor • coach • trainee • trainer • undergraduate

! Be careful!

an undergraduate is doing a university degree
a graduate has a university degree
a postgraduate is doing a Master's or PhD

2 Make notes and discuss.

What's the difference between a qualification and

1 a certificate?
2 a skill?
3 a licence?
4 an exam result?
5 a degree?

! Be careful!

☒ take an exam = sit, do an exam
☒ give an exam
take an exam DOES NOT MEAN pass an exam

3 Phrasal verbs

Complete each sentence using a phrasal verb to do with education in the correct form. You will use one of the phrasal verbs twice.

cross out • get down • go over • look up
sail through • set out • work out

1 I'd thought the exam would be really difficult but in fact I __________ it.
2 Don't bother using correction fluid. If you make a mistake, just __________ it __________.
3 Shall we quickly __________ that grammar point again, or do you think you understand it now?
4 It's time you __________ to some serious studying!
5 Our tutor wants us to __________ our thoughts in a 3000-word essay!
6 It took me over half an hour to __________ the answer to that maths question.
7 I tried to take notes during the lecture, but I didn't manage to __________ everything the lecturer said __________ on paper.
8 If you don't know what a word means, __________ it __________ in the dictionary.

4 Word formation

Complete each sentence using a form of the word in brackets.

1 I never do any __________ (**revise**) the night before an exam.
2 Are you going to apply for the __________ (**scholar**)?
3 This school prides itself on its __________ (**academy**) record.
4 We'll need a copy of all your __________ (**certify**).
5 I think that watching TV can be very __________ (**educate**).
6 Do you remember being __________ (**teach**) how to tie your shoelaces?
7 If you fail the exam in June, you can __________ (**take**) it in December.
8 If someone can't read and write, they are __________ (**literate**).

5 Collocations

Match to make phrases.

1 school — **a** needs
2 special — **b** tutor
3 university — **c** by heart
4 assessed — **d** fees
5 science — **e** fashion
6 personal — **f** instructor
7 learn — **g** campus
8 parrot — **h** lab
9 driving — **i** essay

6 Use five of the phrases from exercise 5 to complete these sentences.

1 We don't have an exam at the end of this course, we just have to hand in a 5000-word __________.
2 I love doing experiments in the __________ at school.
3 Angela teaches students with __________, such as children with dyslexia or learning difficulties.
4 We had to learn the whole page and then repeat it __________ to the teacher the next day.
5 My uncle's a teacher at a boarding school. He says the __________ are really expensive.

Listening

Starting point

Apart from what they learn at school, what do children learn as they grow up?
What is your best 'learning experience' so far?

1 **Look at question 1 in exercise 2. The key words are *think* and *course*. Underline the key words in the other questions.**

> **EXAM EXPERT**
>
> **How should you do the exam practice task?**
>
> **a** Don't worry if there are words or phrases in the recording you don't know. You are not expected to know every word!
>
> **b** Don't answer the question if you didn't understand every word. You'll probably get it wrong.

3 **Look at the list A–F in exercise 4 and choose one of the statements. Tell your partner a real or imaginary short story based on that statement. Ask your partner to guess which statement you chose.**

2 4.02 exam practice

You will hear people talking in eight different situations. For questions 1–8, choose the best answer (A, B or C).

1 You hear two university students talking. What do they think about their course?
A It is confusing.
B It is boring.
C It is irrelevant.

2 You hear a woman talking about choosing a language school. What was the most important reason for her choice?
A the cost
B the location
C the timetable

3 You hear part of a radio interview with a writer. What does she say about her education?
A It was expensive.
B It was unpleasant.
C It was interrupted.

4 You hear a teenager talking about finding some information. Where did he finally find the information?
A in a magazine
B in a dictionary
C in an encyclopaedia

5 You hear a driving instructor talking to a learner driver. What does the instructor want the learner driver to do?
A revise what the road signs mean
B hold the steering wheel differently
C look in the mirror more often

6 You hear two teachers talking. What do they agree about?
A the bad behaviour of some of the students
B the high level of some of the students
C the laziness of some of the students

7 You hear a father talking about teaching his daughter to ride a bike. What happened?
A It took her a few days to learn.
B She fell in some water.
C She wanted to learn something else instead.

8 You hear a woman describing a learning experience. What did she learn?
A Honesty is the best policy.
B Money doesn't buy happiness.
C Love is the most important thing in the world.

4 4.03 exam practice

You will hear five people talking about experiences connected with learning. For questions 1–5, choose from the list (A–F) what each speaker says. Use the letters only once. There is one extra letter which you do not need to use.

A I was an underachiever.
B I was praised for my work.
C I made a bad choice.
D I prepared for months.
E I was surprised.
F I made an important discovery.

Speaker 1 ____
Speaker 2 ____
Speaker 3 ____
Speaker 4 ____
Speaker 5 ____

> **EXAM EXPERT**
>
> **How should you do the exam practice task?**
>
> **a** As soon as you think you know the answer, write it down and stop listening until the next question.
>
> **b** Even if you think you know the answer, keep listening to the end just to make absolutely sure.

Have your say!

- Which of the speakers in exercise 4 do you relate to most? Why?

Speaking

Starting point

How is being in a class different to receiving individual tuition?

1 4.04 **Listen to two candidates describing photographs in the Speaking paper of an English exam and answer these questions.**

1 Does Angie (the second candidate) answer the question?
2 Is Angie's answer too short?
3 Should Angie have been more serious?
4 On the whole, is Angie's answer successful?

2 **Look at the photos in exercise 3 and make notes to complete the tables.**

Photo	This is a picture of ...	Similarities / differences	Which situation makes learning easier? Why?
A			
B			
Photo	**This is a picture of ...**	**Similarities / differences**	**Which situation makes learning easier? Why?**
C			
D			

3 exam practice

Candidate A, here are two photographs of people being taught something. I'd like you to compare them and say which situation you think makes learning easier. You only have one minute for this.

- Which situation do you think makes learning easier?

Candidate B, here are two photographs of different classrooms. I'd like you to compare them and say how you would feel about being in these rooms. You only have one minute for this.

- How would you feel about being in these rooms?

A

C

B

Candidate B, have you ever been in situations similar to these?

EXAM EXPERT

How should you do the exam practice task?

a Speak at a normal conversational speed.
b Speak as quickly as you can because you have such a short amount of time.

See *Speaking database* on page 193.

D

Candidate A, which classroom would you prefer to be in?

Reading 2 4.05

Wordpower!

stress • anxious • panic • nightmare • pass • fail

Starting point

What are you like at exam times? Do you get nervous?
Why do some people cheat in an exam?

1 **Look at the sentences in exercise 3. Without reading the article, come up with as many possible words and phrases as you can to fill each gap.**

2 **Read the title of the article and only the first sentence of each paragraph. What sort of things do you expect the writer to say?**

3 exam practice

Complete each sentence using a word or short phrase from the article.

1 Exams are meant to ________ students but they can do the opposite.
2 Richard Cass failed to reach his ________ and suffered greatly because of exams.
3 Richard's driving test was different from school exams because the questions were based on ________.
4 The writer advises us not to delay revision until ________.
5 He warns us to avoid the ________ people who are selling essays on the internet.
6 Experienced examiners ________ work that is not your own.

You can pass exams!

With exam time looming, educational adviser Victor Harlow tells it like it is.

Exams can be a nightmare for some people. They go to pieces just at the thought of them. Others can become physically ill in anticipation of them, while others still are traumatised for life. Often, exams – the very things that are supposed to motivate us to do well – have had the opposite effect and have led to people settling for second best. 'I'd rather people thought I was a failure, just as long as I had my life back,' lorry driver Richard Cass told me. 'Never having learned how to revise effectively, I found exam time a nightmare. I couldn't sleep for days. The moment I left school, I decided; I was finished with exams.'

Richard's case is a particularly sad one, not just because he hasn't fulfilled his potential, but because he has clearly suffered. It also highlights the fact that exams are everywhere in our lives because, of course, Richard didn't leave exams behind when he left school – he had to take his

EXAM EXPERT

How should you do the exam practice task?

- **a** Search for key words from the sentences in the text. For example, for number 9 here, find the word *break* in the text.
- **b** Search for key ideas from the sentences in the text. For example, for number 9 here, find the idea of *break* in the text rather than look for the word itself.

7 You get a great ________ when you learn to do something for yourself.
8 Your work will appear ________ if you break it up.
9 Breaks are important because if you study for very long periods, you are not learning ________.
10 ________ is the key to passing exams.

driving test, twice: first in a car and then in a lorry. 'The same old feelings flooded back,' says Richard. 'Although I was 25 when I passed my second test, I felt as though I was 16 again and back at school sweating over a blank piece of paper. The only difference was that this time, the questions were common sense – they ask you about vehicle safety, and these are the things that you really need to know if you want to do that job. I knew the answers just by thinking logically.'

So how do you go about passing an exam? First of all, there is one inflexible factor – time. If you're looking for ways to get a degree in two months or to revise a year's worth of geography in three hours, you've come to the wrong article. So allow enough time because you can't afford to leave it until the last minute.

Then, you need to know your enemy. A little investigation on the internet should help you find out what you're up against. Past papers are extremely helpful. There is also probably a forum or discussion group somewhere on the net needed for people who are in the same position as you are. Don't be tempted by the many offers to help you cheat, though. There are plenty of unscrupulous people out there offering essays at a price. Just remember this: in the time it takes you to learn to cheat, you could have learned the real thing for yourself. While we're on the subject, examiners are not fools. They are very experienced at what they do and they can spot a copied essay a mile off. Don't forget that the tactics you learn for passing one exam can be used in others – you will be developing a skill for life. And of course, the sense of satisfaction you get from learning to do something for yourself is enormous. Cheating, on the other hand, is more trouble than it's worth.

Having allowed enough time and armed yourself with all the information you can find, it's time to make a plan. Divide the work up into sections and set yourself a task a day. This has the advantage of making the work seem more manageable. Be realistic about this and factor in breaks. Nobody can learn effectively for 12 hours straight. Then, just use the strategies you've heard a hundred times before – test yourself by covering the information on the page; write cards or stickers with the basic information; get a friend to test you – whatever works for you. Exams are not a mystery – they just need careful preparation.

4 Find words or phrases in the text which have a similar meaning to these words and phrases.

1 get very upset or worried (paragraph 1)
2 mentally disturbed or scarred (paragraph 1)
3 accepting less than you deserve or are capable of (paragraph 1)
4 achieved; reached; realised (paragraph 2)
5 thing which cannot be changed (paragraph 3)
6 old copies of the exam from previous years (paragraph 4)
7 include; make allowance for (paragraph 5)
8 tactics; methods (paragraph 5)

WORK IT OUT!

Find these words and phrases in the text and underline them. Can you work out what they mean from the context?

in anticipation of • highlights • a mile off
what you're up against • armed

Have your say!

- What are the main pieces of advice the writer has to offer? Do you agree with what he suggests? Can you add any advice of your own?

G Grammar 2

Participles

Which two words can be cut out of this sentence without changing the meaning?

The girl who is taking the test is dyslexic so she's been given an extra half an hour.

Present, perfect and past participles can be used as an alternative to the normal **subject** + **verb** + **object** sentence structure. Present participles end in ***-ing***. Past participles usually end in ***-ed***, although there are many irregular verbs (seen, gone, brought, etc). Perfect participles are formed using **having** + **past participle**.

Present participles can be used:

- after prepositions and conjunctions, such as **after**, **before**, **when**, **while**, **on**, **despite**.
  After revising for four hours, I took a break.
- to mean **because**.
  Being a good public speaker, Adrian had no problems getting into the school debating team. (= *Because he was …*)
- to talk about actions happening at the same time.
  Waiting for the exam to start, Carol went through her revision notes one more time.
- to replace some relative clauses.
  The teacher taking your class today is called Mrs Jenkins. (= *The teacher who is taking …*)

Perfect participles can be used:

- after prepositions and conjunctions, such as **after**, **before**, **when**, **while**, **on**, **despite**.
  After having revised for four hours, I took a break.
- to mean **because**.
  Having been a good public speaker at school, Adrian decided to join the university debating team. (= *Because he had been/was …*)
- to talk about actions happening in sequence.
  Having waited for half an hour for the exam to start, Carol nervously turned over the paper.

Past participles can sometimes be used:

- as an alternative passive form.
  Built in 1936, the school buildings are in a bad state of repair. (= *The school buildings were built in 1936. They are in a bad state of repair.*)
- to replace some relative clauses.
  A teacher called Mrs Jenkins took our class today. (= *A teacher who is called …*)

See Grammar database 32 on pages 190–191 for more information.

1 These sentences all come from the article on pages 148–149. Without looking back, write an appropriate word or phrase in each gap.

1 Never ________ how to revise effectively, I found exam time a nightmare.
2 I knew the answers just by ________ logically.
3 There are plenty of unscrupulous people out there ________ essays at a price.
4 ________ enough time and armed yourself with all the information you can find, it's time to make a plan.

2 Each of these sentences contains an extra word. Find it.

1 The boys who sitting at the back of the class were throwing paper aeroplanes!
2 All of the pupils were taught by Mr Carlton this year passed the exam.
3 Not I having studied economics at school, I had a lot of catching up to do when I started my politics degree.
4 Who's the teacher who taking us for German next year?
5 Having been done a lot of research, I found writing the essay quite straightforward.

3 Use a participle to join each pair of sentences.

1 The new girl was sitting at the front of the class. She was called Karen.
The new girl sitting at the front of the class was called Karen.
2 I opened my bag. I realised I'd left my books at school.
3 It was compiled by a team of experts. It is widely recognised as the most up-to-date dictionary in the world.
4 Adrian was handed the exam paper. Adrian realised he was in the wrong exam.
5 I had never sat in the driving seat before. I was terrified for the whole of my first driving lesson.
6 The people will mark your papers in the UK. They need to be able to read your handwriting.

Use of English

1 **Look at the gaps in exercise 2. What part of speech (noun, verb, adjective, etc) is each missing word?**

2 exam practice

Read the text below. Use the word given in capitals at the end of some of the lines to form a word that fits in the gap in the same line. Write your answers IN CAPITAL LETTERS.

Learning how to learn and think

What is the point of the (1) ____ system? Although this question **EDUCATE**
may seem (2) ____ at first sight, it's actually not as stupid as it **RIDICULE**
sounds. The reason it's worth trying to answer is that schools and
universities clearly (3) ____ academic achievement, passing exams **EMPHASIS**
and gaining (4) ____ much more than acquiring skills such as **QUALIFY**
raising children or car (5) ____ . But why is this? Why do they **MAINTAIN**
neglect to teach practical skills at school?
One answer may be that schools don't exist to help us gain useful
(6) ____ about the world. At school, what we're actually learning **KNOW**
is how to learn effectively. The idea is that we can then make use
of that (7) ____ later on in life when we come to deal with more **ABLE**
(8) ____ aspects of day-to-day living. **PRACTICE**
However, some people argue that the current system is in fact a
(9) ____ because it doesn't actually teach children how to become **FAIL**
good (10) ____ . Learning how to learn is one thing. Learning **THINK**
how to think is quite another.

EXAM EXPERT

How should you do the exam practice task?

Remember that irregular forms are **sometimes** / **never** tested in this task.

3 **Look at exercise 4. For each second sentence, decide what kind of word (noun, verb, adjective, pronoun, preposition, etc) could come immediately after the word or words given at the beginning of the sentence.**

4 exam practice

Complete the second sentence so that it has a similar meaning to the first sentence using the word given. Do not change the word given. You must use between two and five words, including the word given. Write the missing words IN CAPITAL LETTERS.

EXAM EXPERT

How should you do the exam practice task?

a If you're not sure of the answer, just write the word in bold in the gap.

b If you're not sure of the answer, look at the word in bold and make a list of all the different patterns and collocations it is associated with.

1 We really should have another parents' meeting.
high
It ____________ another parents' meeting.

2 The teacher standing in for Mrs Williams was really nice.
was
The teacher ____________ in for Mrs Williams was really nice.

3 Revising these topics again is a good idea.
go
I think you ____________ these topics again.

4 Why don't you use a dictionary to find out what those words mean?
up
Why don't you ____________ a dictionary?

5 The earthquake led to the school being demolished.
result
The school had to ____________ of the earthquake.

6 I'd rather not do my homework now.
feel
I ____________ my homework now.

7 It was unfair that Hardip was given more time to finish the test.
deserve
Hardip ____________ given more time to finish the test.

8 Although she couldn't swim very well, Sindy decided to go on a lifesaving course.
able
In spite ____________ swim very well, Sindy decided to go on a lifesaving course.

Writing: informal letter/email

Wordpower!

accommodation • cost • length • level • intensive

Starting point

If you are thinking of doing a short course somewhere (learning how to type, use a computer, learning a foreign language, etc), what things do you need to consider before you apply?

1 Read this letter and answer the questions.

1 Apart from mentioning his idea, what else did Pedro mention in his letter to Diana?
2 What information was mentioned in the advertisement Diana found?
3 What information that they need was not mentioned in the advertisement?
4 Is the letter formal or informal? Give examples.

Dear Pedro,

Thanks a lot for your letter. It was great to hear from you! I'm so glad your leg's out of plaster now.

Doing a short typing course this summer is a great idea! It'll be so much easier to write essays on the computer at university if we can type. Good thinking!!! I've actually done some research and found a course in Manchester that sounds ideal.
It's only three weeks, so it's not too long, and ______________________.

Also, they say in their ad that they can help us find somewhere to stay, which could be really useful.

There are still a few things we'll need to find out, though. They don't say how much the course costs, and they also don't say ______________________.

Let me know if you want me to find out more.

Anyway, I have to go now as I'm helping my dad in the shop.

Hope to hear from you soon.

All the best,
Diana

2 Two parts of Diana's letter are incomplete. Use your imagination to complete them in an appropriate style.

3 Using the information in the letter, the ideas you had for exercise 2 and your imagination, write a short advertisement for the typing course.

Have your say!

- If you could do a short course in something during the summer, what would you choose to study?

Plan ahead

1 exam practice: informal letter

This is part of a letter you received recently from a friend who is also learning English.

Have you got any plans for the summer? I was thinking maybe of going to a language school in the UK to improve my English. It would be a lot more fun if we went together. What do you think?

You have seen the advertisement below in a magazine and decide to write to your friend about it. Read the advertisement and the notes you have made. Then, using all the information, write a letter to your friend.

Give reasons why you should both go to Brighton and suggest what other things you both need to think about.

The Danton
School of English
BRIGHTON, ENGLAND

- summer courses at all levels
- help with accommodation offered

reasons to go to Brighton
easy to fly to (near London)
help with accommodation

things to think about
cost of course/accommodation?
dates?

EXAM EXPERT

a Learn an informal letter/email by heart before the exam and just change a few words and phrases to fit the question you are given.

b Remember that there is not just one letter/email that is appropriate for all questions so make sure you know what types of informal letter/email are possible and learn some useful phrases to use.

See *Writing database* on page 199 for further information.

2 **Read the information in exercise 1 carefully and answer these questions. Use your imagination where necessary.**

1 What's the name of your friend?
2 Apart from their idea, what did they mention in their letter to you?
3 What will you say about that in your letter?
4 What was your friend's idea?
5 What do you think of the idea?
6 What information have you found?

3 **Use the notes in exercise 1 to write two or three sentences explaining why you think Brighton is a good place to go to. Then write two or three sentences mentioning the things you have to think about further.**

4 **Make a paragraph plan. Decide what you will include in each paragraph.**

5 **Write your letter in 120–150 words. You must use grammatically correct sentences with accurate spelling and punctuation in a style appropriate for the situation. Do not write any addresses.**

6 **When you have written your letter, make sure that you have:**

- used informal English ☐
- mentioned your friend's letter in paragraph 1 ☐
- given reasons why you should both go to Brighton ☐
- mentioned the points to think about ☐
- included any other relevant information ☐
- started and ended your letter appropriately. ☐

12

The Law

Wordpower!

acceptable • desensitise • fiction
thriller • violence • whodunnit

Starting point

Is crime a problem in your area? Is it getting better or worse?
Do you think people are affected negatively by any of the following?

- crime shows on TV
- crime reports in the news
- films about crime

1 **Read paragraph 1 of the article, in which a teenager called Anita expresses her opinion about the effects of violence on TV. Note down as many arguments as you can think of that someone could use to disagree with Anita. Discuss these with the class.**

2 **Read the rest of the article and circle any crimes mentioned.**

Reading 1 4.06

3 exam practice

You are going to read an article about crime and violence on television. For questions 1–15, decide which of the people express these opinions. Choose from the list of people (A–H). Some of the people may be used more than once. When more than one answer is required, these may be given in any order.

A Anita Shar
B Alvin Shar
C Toby Bassett
D Devi Pascha
E Greg Dawson
F Liz Black
G Damon Psaropoulos
H Claire Psaropoulos

Which person expresses these opinions?

Crime on television leads to crime in society. 1 ___
Politicians have a responsibility to act in the right way. 2 ___
We must take care when using statistics. 3 ___
Television is more violent because society is more violent. 4 ___
Violence on TV is much worse than it used to be. 5 ___
Society has always had the problem of crime. 6 ___
Programmes can deter us from committing crimes. 7 ___ 8 ___
We need to know how violent our society is. 9 ___
Crime is a problem in my local area. 10 ___
We should not overreact to news of crimes. 11 ___
The public can be actively involved in solving crimes. 12 ___
Fictional criminals rarely achieve their aims. 13 ___
What is shown on television is not important. 14 ___
I haven't been affected by crime and violence on TV. 15 ___

EXAM EXPERT

How should you do the exam practice task?

Remember that when you are scanning a text it **sometimes** / **never** helps to run your finger down the page, and to follow your finger with your eyes.

4 **Write a word from the article in each gap.**

Criminals are people who (1) ___ crimes or, in other words, (2) ___ the law. The police try to (3) ___ criminals. When they do, the criminals are (4) ___ . If they are officially charged by the police, they are then taken to (5) ___ .

TV Crime
does it affect us?

A recent study has shown that there is more crime and violence on our TVs than ever before.

Abe Kowalski met with a group of sixth formers at an inner city comprehensive to find out their opinions.

Anita Shar, 17, has strong views on the subject. 'There's no doubt that violence and crime on TV have a negative impact on society,' she says. 'We've seen over the last 50 years or so a huge rise in TV violence, and a corresponding rise in violence in society. That's not coincidence. The two are clearly related.'

Anita's twin brother, **Alvin**, is not so sure. 'I must have watched hundreds of bank robberies, murders and other crimes on TV over the years,' he says. 'That hasn't made me any more likely to go out and kill someone or rob a bank myself. It's too easy to say there's a direct link between what we watch and what we do. People have been stealing and killing since the beginning of time.'

Toby Bassett, also 17, agrees with Alvin that it may not be a simple case of cause and effect. 'I think maybe Anita's got it the wrong way round. The increase in violence and crime in society is just being reflected in the programmes that are shown. And we have to be very careful. Abe mentioned this study that said there's more crime on TV than ever before, but what form is it in? Is it drama, or is it on the news? Programmes like *Crimewatch*, where they re-enact real life crimes and get people to ring in with information, help to catch criminals. They're clearly good for society. But if they're being included in the figures then that's just misleading.'

Devi Pascha, 16, believes there's little cause for concern. 'I agree that the vast majority of people can watch violent crimes on TV without wanting to commit similar crimes themselves. I'd take it one stage further, though. Programmes like that actually stop some people breaking the law. What's the message that these programmes are sending out? That crime doesn't pay. At the end of the show, the goodies win, the criminals get caught, and justice is done. Most of the programmes with crime in are police dramas. The police always come out on top in the end.'

'Programmes about crime can definitely be educational,' says 18-year-old **Greg Dawson**, 'whether the criminals get punished or not. Take *Grange Street*, which has been dealing recently with the issue of shoplifting. Yes, we saw two teenagers going into a shop and stealing some clothes, but we also saw the repercussions – their being arrested and being taken to court – and the guilt they felt. I think that particular show has stopped a lot of teenagers who might have thought about shoplifting from trying it.'

Liz Black, 18, believes we are focusing on the wrong problem. 'TV programmes are an irrelevance,' she says. 'What's more important is what people experience in their daily lives. Round here, it's not safe to get your mobile out in public because it might get nicked. We should concentrate on that before we worry about what's on TV.'

Damon Psaropoulos, 17, agrees that we should not worry about TV drama. 'To me,' he says, 'the worst kind of violence we see on TV is on the news, but it's important that it's reported, so we know what our society is like. What we must not do, though, is see one crime and think that the whole country has become a nation of criminals. It hasn't.'

Damon's sister, **Claire**, aged 16, has the final word. 'People talk about the messages that crime and violence on TV send out. What about the messages our governments send out? They're telling us all the time that it's okay to use violence under certain circumstances – when we go to war, for example. That's a terrible message to be giving to young people. They should be saying: under no circumstances is it okay to use violence.'

WORK IT OUT!

Find these words in the text and underline them. Can you work out what they mean from the context?

coincidence • reflected • re-enact
misleading • repercussions

Have your say!

- Do you think there's too much crime and violence on TV and in movies?

Grammar 1

Inversions

Look at this sentence and answer the questions.

Never has the crime rate been so low.

1 Is this sentence grammatically correct?
2 Are the subject and verb in the question form?
3 Is it a question?

When some negative adverbial words and phrases are placed at the beginning of a sentence, the subject and the verb 'invert'. This means we use the question form, even though the sentence is not a question.

Negative adverbial words and phrases we can put at the beginning of a sentence include: **Hardly, Barely, Scarcely, Never, No sooner, Rarely, Not only, Under no circumstances, At no time**, etc.

Hardly had I opened the door when I realised the flat had been burgled!

No sooner had the robber left the bank than he was arrested.

Rarely do first-time offenders get sent to prison.

Not only are criminals punished in prison, but they are also educated.

Inversions are usually formal, so they are not usually used in speech unless you are trying to make a dramatic effect.

Putting the negative adverb at the beginning of the sentence adds emphasis.

See *Grammar database 33* on page 191 for more information.

! Be careful!

Hardly/Barely/Scarcely … **when**
No sooner … **than**

1 This sentence was in the article on page 155. Without looking back, choose the correct form of the subject and verb.

Under no circumstances ***it is*** */* ***is it*** *okay to use violence.*

2 If a sentence is correct, put a tick (☒). If it is incorrect, correct it.

1 Under no circumstances are prisoners allowed to carry weapons.
2 Never there has been such a miscarriage of justice.
3 Rarely criminals get away with their crimes.
4 Hardly had the programme started when people started calling in with information!
5 No sooner the police had appealed for witnesses than someone came forward.

3 Use these words and phrases to complete the sentences.

at no time • little • nor • not • only

1 ____________ did the police interview Mrs Watkins.
2 There weren't any fingerprints on the glass, ____________ were there any traces of poison.
3 ____________ until they found the body were the police able to make an arrest.
4 ____________ did I realise how bad the conditions in prison actually were.
5 ____________ after the trial did the accused finally confess to the crime.

4 Rewrite each sentence beginning with the word or phrase given.

1 Women rarely commit violent crimes.
Rarely ____________
2 Prisoners cannot become Members of Parliament under any circumstances.
Under no circumstances ____________
3 The detective did not suspect Hitchins of having committed the robbery at any time.
At no time ____________
4 I hadn't realised how guilty I would feel.
Little ____________
5 She had only just been released from prison when she was arrested for shoplifting!
Hardly ____________
6 Davis had only just bought his Porsche when he was stopped for speeding.
No sooner ____________

5 Imagine you are a detective. You have been investigating a crime and are now writing your report. Use the notes to write sentences from the report.

Adams entered bank – pulled out gun
we found getaway car – then realised Adams was the bank robber
we had no idea – wife helping him plan crimes!
found in flat: a million euros in cash, two million euros worth of jewellery!
I've never met such an unrepentant couple!
interviewed them eight times – then they confessed!

1 No sooner ____________
2 Not until ____________
3 Little ____________
4 Not only ____________
5 Never ____________
6 Only after ____________

Vocabulary

Crime and punishment

1 Use a word in each gap to complete the text.

accused • evidence • fraud • innocent • judge
jury • solicitor • trial • verdict • witness

TRIAL OVER!

The (1) __________ at Barkingham Crown Court of Stan Pemberton, 32, collapsed today. Pemberton, who had been charged with (2) __________, was cleared of all charges. Following the testimony of an expert (3) __________, the (4) __________ dismissed the 12 members of the (5) __________ and told the (6) __________ he was free to go. Outside the court, Pemberton's (7) __________ issued a statement. 'Stan Pemberton has always said he was (8) __________ and that was the (9) __________ of the court. There was no (10) __________ that my client was in any way connected with this crime. We are glad that this is all over,' he said.

2 Phrasal verbs

Choose the correct word to complete these sentences.

1 The shoplifter was caught **making** / **doing** off with over €1,000 worth of electrical equipment.
2 Although the driver had been speeding, the police officer **let** / **gave** him off with a warning.
3 The bomb **blew** / **went** off at half past seven this morning.
4 What made you think you could **take** / **get** away with this without being caught?
5 The burglars **broke** / **made** in through a downstairs window.
6 I was **set** / **taken** up! Someone else made it look like I'm guilty!
7 If you **hit** / **beat** someone up, you can be charged with physical assault.

3 Word formation

Complete the table.

	Person		Person
crime		rob	
accuse		theft	
offence		murder	
law		convict	

4 Word patterns

Choose the correct word or phrase to complete each sentence.

1 Are you accusing me **of stealing** / **to steal**?
2 Terry denied **to drive** / **driving** the getaway car.
3 We're charging you **for** / **with** murder.
4 She was convicted **of attempting** / **to attempt** to pervert the course of justice.
5 Stella refused **cooperating** / **to cooperate** with the police.
6 I don't know why you're blaming me **to break** / **for breaking** your stereo!

! Be careful!

refuse = say you will not do something
deny = say you did not do something

Listening

Wordpower!

try cases • sentence
responsibility • plead

Starting point

What do you think the daily life of a judge is like?
Would you like to be a judge?

1 **Read through the questions in exercise 2 and next to each one, note down a word or phrase which logically and grammatically could fill the gap.**

2 4.07 exam practice

You will hear part of a talk given by a magistrate (a kind of judge). For questions 1–10, complete the sentences.

Magistrates handle less serious crimes and are local **1** ______

The magistrates are given legal advice by a **2** ______

Defendants aged **3** ______ are dealt with by the Youth Court.

The Referral Order is for defendants who plead guilty and do not have any **4** ______

The **5** ______ of the crime often attends the panel as well.

6 ______ is an example of the minor offences that magistrates deal with.

A trial is arranged if the defendant pleads **7** ______

The least severe punishment is usually **8** ______

Kathleen views sending a young offender to prison as a **9** ______

The Youth Court is not always **10** ______ in its aims.

EXAM EXPERT

How should you do the exam practice task?

a If you think there are two different possible answers, put both of them.

b If you think there are two different possible answers, just put one of them.

3 4.08 exam practice

You will hear part of an interview with a journalist who reports on crimes. For questions 1–7, choose the best answer (A, B or C).

1 What are people mostly interested in reading about in the newspapers?
A sad stories
B any kind of murder
C violent murders

2 Which aspect of the murder trial confused the journalist?
A the reason for the crime
B how the crime was committed
C the denial of the crime

3 What reason is not suggested for the murderer saying little in his defence?
A Someone had threatened him.
B He knew deep down that he was guilty.
C He hoped his other crimes would stay undetected.

4 What aspect of the police and the courts makes it difficult for a first-time offender?
A their determination to teach criminals a lesson
B their experience and professionalism
C the fact that the law is so strict

5 The arson and attempted murder case is an example of
A how stupid criminals can seem to be when they are in court.
B how accidents can easily lead to serious consequences.
C how the rate of serious crime is on the increase.

6 The journalist feels a certain amount of sympathy for the criminal because of the
A punishment they are going to suffer.
B events that led up to the crime.
C discomfort they feel when in court.

7 The journalist can get angry about the fact that
A criminals can steal your property and get away with it.
B robbers sometimes injure innocent people during their crimes.
C people don't consider the emotional distress victims suffer.

EXAM EXPERT

How should you do the exam practice task?

If you're sure you've chosen the correct answer to a question after hearing the recording once,

a use the second time you listen to check that you've got it right.

b don't bother checking you've got it right when you hear the piece again.

Have your say!

- Now you have heard what magistrates do, would you like to be one?
- What could be done to prevent crime in your local area?

Speaking

Wordpower!

a safe • be aware of/that • security code
password • car/burglar alarm • lock

Starting point

What can people do to try to prevent crimes happening to them?

1 **Read the task for exercise 3 and look at the pictures. For each picture, make notes on (1) the crime prevention idea shown in the picture and (2) why that idea might be sensible.**

2 4.09 **Listen to two candidates talking about one of the pictures in exercise 3 and answer these questions.**

1 Which picture are they talking about?
2 Do the candidates discuss the benefits of the idea?
3 Does it sound like they are having a conversation and working together?

3 exam practice

I'd like you to imagine that you are writing an article together on crime prevention for a local magazine. Here are some ideas that you are thinking of writing about. Talk to each other about the benefits of each idea and then choose the three you will mention in your article. You have about three minutes.

What are the benefits of each idea?

Which three will you mention in your article?

EXAM EXPERT

How should you do the exam practice task?

If you don't understand or are not sure what your partner or the examiner has said,

a don't admit it or you will lose marks.

b it is fine to say *What do you mean exactly?* or *Could you say that again?*

See *Speaking database* on page 193.

4 Do exercise 5 with a group of three students as the examiner and two candidates. The rest of the class should give each of the candidates a mark out of five.

EXAM EXPERT

How should you do the exam practice task?

a Try to relax and have a natural conversation. It's okay to smile and seem interested!

b Never smile because you are discussing very serious questions and you should show what a serious person you are.

5 exam practice

Can you think of any other crime prevention ideas?

Why do people commit crimes?

Is crime a serious problem in your area?

What do you think life is like in prison?

Is imprisonment the best punishment for most crimes? Why? / Why not?

MARK SCHEME

5 Engaged in a natural conversation, had eye contact with other speakers, listened to other speakers.
4 Some of 5 and some of 3.
3 Spoke too much or too little, had some eye contact with other speakers, listened to other speakers at times.
2 Some of 3 and some of 1.
1 Did not engage in a conversation, no eye contact with other speakers, did not listen to other speakers.

Reading 2 4.10

Wordpower!

dishonest • fake • fraud • genuine • illegal
immoral • pirated goods • theft

Starting point

Put these crimes in order, 1–8, where 1 is the most serious and 8 is the least serious in your opinion. Compare your answers with a partner.

- Bank robbery ___
- Burglary ___
- Forging money ___
- Keeping money you find in the street ___
- Picking someone's pocket ___
- Selling fake or pirate goods ___
- Shoplifting ___
- Stealing a car ___

The genuine article

Counterfeit or pirated goods, fakes and forgeries: they're all big business. Nicholas Snow briefly considers a life of crime and questions what we think of as honest.

What child hasn't dreamed of being able to make their own money and becoming super rich? Admit it – you've thought about it, haven't you? Well, you're not alone. In fact, last year in Britain, around 300,000 counterfeit banknotes were taken out of circulation. **1** ___ And those are just the ones they found.

Obviously, the forger has less of an incentive to make notes of smaller value because they will make less money, so the vast majority of fakes (280,000) were £20 notes. You wouldn't think, then, that forgers would bother with £1

1 **Read the article title, the words in blue under the title and look at the photos. What do you think the article is about?**

> **EXAM EXPERT**
>
> **How should you do the exam practice task?**
>
> a Read the removed sentences before you read the text to give you an initial general idea of what the text is about.
>
> b Don't read the removed sentences first as, until you've read the text, they won't make much sense.

2 exam practice

You are going to read an article about honesty. Seven sentences have been removed from the article. Choose from sentences A–H the one which fits each gap (1–7). There is one extra sentence which you do not need to use.

A You can find a fake anything these days.
B He wasn't really rich, but he lived comfortably.
C You also need a place to hide your activity.
D Being accused and then convicted of a crime has serious consequences on your life.
E The reason for the campaign was that people just didn't consider illegal downloading or copying of films to be a crime.
F They had a combined value of £6 million.
G Some of the paintings didn't sell at all but others went for high prices.
H Yet they do – in a big way.

coins, would you? 2 ___ It is said that up to 1 in 36 of those in circulation are fake. And their numbers are rising, too, in contrast with the falling number of fake banknotes.

Making your own money is a lot of fuss, and I really don't think it's for me. You need expensive specialised equipment to print the notes or forge the coins. 3 ___ It's a little difficult to explain the delivery and use of a noisy coin-cutting machine to the neighbours, isn't it? Of course, like any criminal, there is always the chance of getting caught. If you're found guilty of forgery, you could be sentenced to prison for up to ten years, which is no laughing matter.

But the real money is in counterfeit goods. 4 ___ Clothes, watches, jewellery, toys, electrical goods – just about anything can be forged, or imitated, or pirated. These goods are then sold for a fraction of the price of the genuine article. The effect on the market is calculated in hundreds of billions of dollars. Similarly, theft of copyright on such items as CDs and DVDs is said to cost the music and film industries billions. A campaign used on rented DVDs used the slogan, 'You wouldn't steal a car ... ' to emphasise that piracy is theft. However, in many people's minds, the line is not clear between what is and isn't dishonest. 5 ___ Many people still don't.

If I were to make a career change and decide to live on the wrong side of the law, I think I would quite like to be an art forger. You don't have to buy a lot of expensive equipment and you can work away quietly in your back room without arousing the suspicion of your neighbours. I once knew someone who did something like this, and he made a nice living from it. 6 ___ He used to paint in the style of certain artists, rather than copy their work. He had perfected a way of 'ageing' the paintings. This actually involved putting them in the oven so that the varnish cracked and looked old (I'm giving you ideas, here, aren't I?). Then he sent them to be sold, being careful to choose smaller art sales, thus avoiding the experts. Was this dishonest? You see, he wasn't claiming that they were genuine, but he was relying on other people thinking they were. 7 ___ Just as he had planned, people thought they had discovered a lost masterpiece. Was he breaking the law? It's a risk, isn't it? Now that I think about it, I don't think a life of crime is such a good idea. Perhaps honesty is the best policy after all.

3 Find words or phrases in the text which have a similar meaning to these words and phrases.

1. someone who copies things to make them look like the real thing (paragraph 2)
2. items that are not genuine (paragraph 2)
3. being arrested (paragraph 3)
4. jailed (paragraph 3)
5. catchy, memorable phrase (paragraph 4)
6. making people think you're committing a crime (paragraph 5)

WORK IT OUT!

Find these phrases in the text and underline them. Can you work out what they mean from the context?

the vast majority of • in contrast with
I really don't think it's for me • found guilty
a fraction of the price of • honesty is the best policy

Have your say!

- Do you think the art forger in the article was breaking the law? If not, why not? If so, what punishment would you give him?
- Do people in your country download music from the internet? Is this illegal? Explain your viewpoint.

G Grammar 2

Question tags

Circle the correct word to complete each sentence.

1 *You're going to prison, **are** / **aren't** you?*
2 *You're not going to prison, **are** / **aren't** you?*

We use question tags (1) to ask someone to agree with us and (2) to check that something is true.

When we ask someone to agree with us, our voice **goes down** at the end of the sentence. When we check that something is true, our voice **goes up** at the end.

When the main verb is positive, the question tag is usually negative.
*You **stole** that watch, **didn't** you?*

When the main verb is negative, the question tag is usually positive.
*You **didn't** do it, **did** you?*

See *Grammar database 34* on page 192 for more information.

Impersonal passive

What does 'It' in this sentence refer to?

It is said that justice is blind.

a nothing
b something in a previous sentence

Some verbs, such as ***say***, ***think***, ***feel***, ***know*** and ***believe*** can be put into the passive with ***it*** as the subject. This is a more formal way of saying ***people say***/***think***/etc.
***It has been said** that judges are not strict enough.* =
***Some people have said** that judges are not strict enough.*

Note: There is another common passive structure used with **say, suppose, think, believe, know, feel: subject + verb in passive + full infinitive.**
*This prison **is believed to be** the most secure in the country.*

See *Grammar database 35* on page 192 for more information.

1 Each of the question tags in these sentences is incorrect. Correct them.

1 You were 16 when you were first arrested, didn't you?
2 She's never been in any trouble, has she been?
3 We won't get caught, won't we?
4 Fletcher stole the diamonds, stolen't he?
5 They had a terrible time on the run, hadn't they?
6 You've got an alibi, haven't you got?
7 You're not going to tell anyone, will you?

2 Imagine you're a detective investigating a burglary. You are interviewing a suspect who you think has been lying to you. Ask questions using these question tags.

You're lying to me, aren't you?

1 … are you?
2 … were you?
3 … did you?
4 … didn't you?
5 … haven't you?
6 … can't you?
7 … don't you?

! Be careful!

☒ I am telling the truth, aren't I?
☒ I am telling the truth, amn't I?

3 Rewrite these sentences using the impersonal passive.

1 Everyone feels that she's a successful Minister of Justice.
2 People will think that the police gave her special treatment.
3 Everyone had thought that he was innocent.
4 We didn't know that he'd been in trouble as a teenager.
5 Some people have said that McGarrett received an unfair trial.
6 Nobody has ever said that the legal system is perfect.
7 People believe that he left the country and assumed a new identity.

4 Rewrite each sentence beginning with the word or words given so that the meaning remains the same.

1 People believe that education prevents crime.
It ________
Education ________
2 Everyone knows that life in prison is hard.
It ________
Life ________
3 Most of us feel that freedom is very important.
It ________
Freedom ________
4 The papers say that the police found some fingerprints at the scene of the crime.
It ________
The police ________

Use of English

1 These phrases appear in the text you are going to read in exercise 2. What do you think they mean?

a innocent until proven guilty
b beyond a reasonable doubt
c find the defendant 'not guilty'

> **EXAM EXPERT**
>
> **How should you do the exam practice task?**
>
> If you are really not sure which of the four words fills the gap,
>
> **a** pick one at random.
>
> **b** say the sentence to yourself with each word in turn and pick the word that sounds the best.

2 exam practice

Read the text below and decide which answer (A, B, C or D) best fits each gap.

Guilty or Not Guilty?

In many legal (1) ___ around the world, the defendant is considered to be innocent until proven guilty. This means in effect that it is not (2) ___ to the defendant's lawyers to prove that the defendant did not commit the crime he or she is (3) ___ of. Rather, it is the responsibility of the (4) ___ to prove beyond a reasonable doubt that the defendant did (5) ___ the law.

But what does the phrase 'beyond a reasonable doubt' mean in practice? It means that, although there may not be absolute (6) ___ , such as a video, that the defendant committed the crime, the judge or (7) ___ , after having examined all the (8) ___ , are certain that the person is guilty. If they are not certain, or, in (9) ___ words, if they believe there is a reasonable doubt, they must find the defendant 'not guilty'. In British (10) ___ , defendants are never (11) ___ innocent. The only possible (12) ___ are 'guilty' or 'not guilty'.

1	**A** structures	**B** systems	**C** constructions	**D** arrangements
2	**A** about	**B** up	**C** over	**D** round
3	**A** accused	**B** blamed	**C** charged	**D** arrested
4	**A** persecution	**B** prescription	**C** prosecution	**D** persuasion
5	**A** commit	**B** abandon	**C** break	**D** cheat
6	**A** observation	**B** sign	**C** proof	**D** demonstration
7	**A** audience	**B** jury	**C** team	**D** collective
8	**A** warnings	**B** hints	**C** confirmation	**D** evidence
9	**A** other	**B** more	**C** differing	**D** these
10	**A** exhibitions	**B** courts	**C** councils	**D** institutions
11	**A** mentioned	**B** declared	**C** spoken	**D** stated
12	**A** verdicts	**B** conclusions	**C** decisions	**D** effects

3 The story in exercise 4 is supposed to be amusing. Quickly read the text, ignoring the gaps, and explain in your own words why the situation is funny.

4 exam practice

Read the text below and think of the word which best fits each gap. Use only one word in each gap. Write your answers IN CAPITAL LETTERS.

Another unsuccessful criminal

It has (1) ___ said that ignorance is no defence in the eyes of the law, but some criminals (2) ___ to be a lot more ignorant (3) ___ others. Take the case (4) ___ the convict who broke (5) ___ of prison in Washington, DC, USA. A few days later, (6) ___ the massive police hunt for him, he decided to accompany his girlfriend to her trial (7) ___ robbery. He sat in the courtroom (8) ___ morning listening to the proceedings, and then at lunchtime (9) ___ out to get a sandwich. (10) ___ he was out, his girlfriend needed to speak to him, and so (11) ___ him paged over the court loudspeaker system. Police officers in the building recognised his name and immediately arrested him (12) ___ his return to the court – in a car he had just stolen.

> **EXAM EXPERT**
>
> **How should you do the exam practice task?**
>
> **a** If you think there are two possible different answers for a gap, write both.
>
> **b** If you think there are two possible different answers for a gap, only write one of them.

Writing: essay

Starting point

Put these crimes in order, with 1 being the most serious, 2 the next most serious, etc. If you think two or more are the same, give them the same number.

armed robbery
arson
blackmail
burglary
speeding
forgery
theft
kidnapping
manslaughter
murder
picking pockets
shoplifting

Which of the crimes above deserve these punishments?

the death penalty / capital punishment
a prison sentence
a suspended sentence
community service
a fine
a warning

1 **Read the essay written by a student in answer to the statement 'Capital punishment is an appropriate punishment for murderers' and use these words and phrases to fill the gaps. Capitalise the first letter where appropriate.**

a second argument against • firstly • hand • however
in conclusion • in other words • personally • secondly • such as

No countries in the European Union carry out the death penalty for those convicted of murder. 1 ______________, a number of countries throughout the world, 2 ______________ the USA, do still have capital punishment.

There are several arguments in favour of capital punishment. 3 ______________, it is argued that the death penalty acts as a deterrent. 4 ______________, people do not commit murder because the death penalty exists. 5 ______________, some people believe that murder is such a terrible crime that death is the only appropriate punishment.

On the other 6 ______________, it can be argued that society should show how much it values life by never killing anybody – even murderers. 7 ______________ capital punishment is that sometimes innocent people are found guilty. If they are imprisoned, they can be released. This cannot happen if they have already been put to death.

8 ______________, there are strong arguments on both sides. I 9 ______________ believe that ... ______________

2 **Make a paragraph plan for the essay.**

	Aim of paragraph	Points to make
paragraph 1		
paragraph 2		
paragraph 3		
paragraph 4		

3 **Complete the final paragraph in an appropriate formal style using your own ideas.**

Plan ahead

1 exam practice: essay

You have been doing a class project on crime and punishment. Your teacher has asked you to write an essay about the following statement:

There are far more effective punishments for criminals than prison.

EXAM EXPERT

How should you write an essay?

a Always agree completely with the statement you are given.

b Remember you can choose whether to completely agree or disagree with the statement, or present a balanced view and express your opinion at the end.

See *Writing database* on page 195 for further information.

2 Work in pairs. Make a note of the main advantages and disadvantages of each of these punishments.

	Advantage(s)	Disadvantage(s)
The death penalty / capital punishment	*It may act as a strong deterrent.*	*Mistakes can't be corrected.*
A prison sentence		
A suspended sentence		
Community service		
A fine		
A warning		

3 Read the question in exercise 1 and discuss the following.

Do you agree with the statement?
- For which crimes is imprisonment not appropriate? Give reasons.
- Which punishments are more effective? Give reasons to support your opinion.

Do you disagree with the statement?
- For which crimes is imprisonment appropriate? Give reasons.
- Explain why all other punishments are less effective and why prison is the best punishment for all crimes.

Does it depend on the crime?
- What does it depend on? Give details and examples.

4 Make a paragraph plan. Decide what you are going to include in each paragraph.

5 Write your essay in 120–180 words in an appropriate style.

6 When you have written your essay, make sure that you have:

- used a formal style ☐
- used some discursive expressions ☐
- followed your paragraph plan ☐
- checked your spelling and grammar. ☐

Check your progress! Units 11–12

1 Write a word from the box in the correct form to complete each sentence.

find • lock • left • commit • learn • give • have

1 I wish I ___ my homework at home again!
2 It's high time you ___ to tie your own shoelaces!
3 Almost everyone wishes they ___ more money.
4 I bet people in prison wish they ___ any crimes.
5 I'd rather you ___ me your composition tomorrow, not now.
6 Suppose you ___ some money in the street. Would you keep it?
7 If only I ___ the window before I left, the burglar wouldn't have got in.

7 marks

2 Write a form of the word in brackets in each gap to complete each sentence.

1 The man denied the ___ (**accuse**) of blackmail.
2 Is committing a crime ___ (**accept**) in some situations?
3 You'll need to do quite a lot of ___ (**revise**) before the exam.
4 Our ___ (**intense**) summer course only lasts six weeks but it's very demanding.
5 Guess what? I've won a ___ (**scholar**) to go to college in the UK!
6 The media are starting to ask questions about the ___ (**fail**) of the police investigation.
7 Everyone thought the woman was guilty, but there wasn't enough ___ (**evident**).
8 When the fake banknotes were traced back to him, the man was charged with ___ (**forge**).

8 marks

3 Choose the correct word to fill the gap in each sentence.

1 My elder brother is a(n) ___ at the University of Essex.
A pupil **B** undergraduate **C** apprentice **D** beginner
2 The police asked to see the man's driving ___ .
A licence **B** degree **C** certificate **D** pass
3 It's amazing that we can learn to ___ a foreign language.
A compress **B** compare **C** comprehend **D** compact
4 Nancy and I had both bought exactly the same kind of schoolbag without knowing it. It was a complete ___ .
A coincidence **B** chance **C** luck **D** fortune
5 I think people who ___ the law should be punished.
A break **B** commit **C** misbehave **D** undo
6 My dad had to go to court because he was a(n) ___ to a crime.
A spectator **B** viewer **C** observer **D** witness
7 Don't forget to set the ___ alarm when you go to bed tonight.
A criminal **B** burglar **C** thief **D** police
8 The judge looked very serious as he read out the ___ of the jury.
A saying **B** result **C** verdict **D** sentence
9 Warning! People parking in this area will be ___ .
A persecuted **B** prescribed **C** persuaded **D** prosecuted
10 My dad's really angry with my mum because she was caught ___ last week when she was driving to work.
A running **B** accelerating **C** speeding **D** chasing

10 marks

4 Write a word from the box in the correct form in each gap to complete the sentences. Use one of the words twice.

break • go • work • beat • get • cross

1 Reports are coming in that a bomb has ___ off in the city centre.
2 Paul was finally expelled for ___ up one of his classmates.
3 When you have finished your composition, simply ___ out any notes you have made by putting a line through them.
4 Miss, could you ___ over what you just said about the unreal past again, please?
5 When we got to school, we realised that someone had ___ in during the night.
6 I think I probably have to ___ down to learning some more vocabulary before the exam.
7 Can't you ___ out the meaning of the word from the context?

7 marks

5 Write a question tag to complete each sentence.

1 You've never been arrested by the police, __________?
2 There will always be criminals in society, __________?
3 Let's get together at my house to do some revision together, __________?
4 It can be quite an educational experience to visit another country, __________?
5 Our parents' generation had a much harder time at school, __________?
6 Your sister doesn't think she's going to fail the exam, __________?
7 We'd better get down to some hard work, __________?
8 We'd really miss our teacher if she left, __________?

8 marks

6 Complete the second sentence so that it has a similar meaning to the first sentence, using the word given. Do not change the word given. You must use between two and five words, including the word given.

1 I don't want to study for the exam next week.
feel
I don't ________________ for the exam next week.
2 People believe that London has a lot of crime.
have
London ________________ a lot of crime.
3 I was three years old when I learned to read.
age
I learned to read ________________ three.
4 Please don't chew gum during the lesson.
rather
I ________________ chew gum during the lesson.
5 Don't you think you should start revising for the exam?
about
Isn't it ________________ revising for the exam?
6 Please don't keep boasting about the grade you got in the exam.
stop
I wish ________________ about the grade you got in the exam.
7 The criminal was convicted and then sentenced to ten years in prison.
been
Having ________________ sentenced to ten years in prison.
8 I found the grammar rule in the back of the book because I couldn't remember it.
up
I couldn't remember the grammar rule ________________ in the back of the book.
9 When he took the driving test, my brother passed it easily first time.
sailed
My brother ________________ at the first attempt.
10 Ian might not say much, but he's very intelligent.
spite
Ian is very intelligent, ________________ much.

20 marks

Total: 60 marks

Revision 2

Reading

Starting point

Describe the plot of either a book you have read or a film you have seen about sport.

1 Look at the questions and multiple-choice options in exercise 2 and find words to complete these sentences.

1 Jenny __________ me of the time we played baseball together.
2 I'm not really sure how to __________ to people who ask personal questions.
3 If people laugh at you when you lose, the best thing is to __________ them.
4 You look __________. Are you worried about tomorrow's match?
5 Players usually wear numbers on their backs so that the crowd can __________ them.

2 exam practice

You are going to read an extract from a short story. For questions 1–7, choose the answer (A–D) which you think fits best according to the text.

1 What is Jake reminded of by Ben at the start of the extract?
A a mistake he made
B a time when they were not friends
C an enjoyable time they spent together
D an occasion when Ben hurt himself

2 How do the boys respond to Mr McIver?
A They ignore what he says.
B They find his comments amusing.
C They don't think he means what he says.
D They begin to get ready more quickly.

3 Why does Jake check his boots?
A He wants to make sure he is completely ready.
B He feels slightly uncomfortable with the situation.
C He wants to show Ben how easy he finds it.
D He is trying to make Ben feel more comfortable.

4 What does Jake not understand at first?
A what Ben is referring to
B what being in the sixth form really means
C how much Ben has changed
D why they have to work so hard

5 Why is Ben in a thoughtful mood?
A He wants to go to university.
B He is sorry that Jake doesn't like Sean.
C He thinks Sean is making the wrong decision.
D He is about to be parted from someone he loves.

6 Ben is pleased by the fact that
A Jake feels the same as he does about the situation.
B his explanation is clear enough for Jake to understand.
C Jake is able to explain things in a way he understands.
D Jake knows how he feels without being told.

7 Why does Ben point to the school building?
A He wants to show how it never changes.
B He wants Jake to identify the students.
C He hopes that he can get away from Jake.
D He sees something through one of the windows.

3 Find words in the text which have a similar meaning to these words and phrases.

1 pieces of metal or plastic on the bottom of football boots (paragraph 1)
2 speaking in a proud way about one's achievements (paragraph 1)
3 smiling widely (paragraph 1)
4 turned red in the face (paragraph 1)
5 tired, exhausted (paragraph 1)
6 in a shy way (paragraph 1)
7 slightly uncomfortable or nervous (paragraph 2)
8 moving slowly in air or water (paragraph 2)
9 annoying, upsetting (paragraph 3)
10 steps (paragraph 4)

Changes

Jake finished tying his boots, stood up and stamped his feet on the tiled floor of the changing room. The noise of his studs was lost in the chaos of ten other boys getting changed, shouting insults, boasting about what they were going to do in the match. Jake looked up as a towel flew past his head. 'Think you can get it in their net this week?' It was Ben, grinning as he pulled his number nine shirt over his head. Jake blushed briefly as he remembered the own goal he had scored in the last match. He knew Ben meant no real harm, but the memory of the weary silence from his own team-mates and the laughter and celebrations of their opponents hurt anyway. He threw the towel back to cover his embarrassment. Mr McIver, the PE teacher, stuck his head around the door. The noise level fell a little. 'All right, lads,' he said. 'I want a hundred per cent out there today. And that means you, Smithy.' The boy he was referring to smiled sheepishly. 'I want all of you out there in two minutes. Get a move on!' He disappeared and there was a new sense of urgency about the changing room, with those boys who had not yet put on their boots starting to rush.

Ben sat down next to Jake with a thoughtful look on his face, his elbows on his knees and his head in his hands. It made Jake slightly uneasy and he started to check his boots, which he already knew were perfectly fine. Jake liked to keep things on a light, joking level and tried to avoid getting too serious, too emotional, as if he was afraid of opening a door somewhere because of what he might find inside. A few of the boys started to disappear out of the door, their boots clicking as they walked. Ben watched them leave and then spoke. 'It's all changing, isn't it?' Jake looked around the room, which looked the same to him as it had always done and then realised that Ben was talking about something else. Ben stood to look out of the small window, shouts from the first boys to reach the pitch drifting back into the room. 'They don't know it yet, but it's all changing. Two months, then the summer, then we'll be in the sixth form and everything will be different.' The sixth form meant more work, more exams, but they were used to that, so Jake couldn't see what Ben was getting at. Things changed every year. Why was Ben in this mood?

'I suppose so,' said Jake, finally. Then he remembered that Ben's brother, Sean, was going away to university that year. Ben was very close to Sean, closer even than he was to Jake, and Sean's leaving would turn his world upside down. Jake watched the last of the other boys leave. 'Maybe we'd better go out,' he said, quietly. Ben looked at him. 'Yes, maybe,' he said after a moment, but made no move towards the door. Jake stood and kicked a sock across the room. 'He'll be back,' he said and Ben nodded, grateful that Jake had understood what was bothering him without needing an explanation.

'I know,' Ben said. They began to walk out of the changing room, along the short corridor and out into the sunshine. The sound of shouts and a whistle came down to them from the pitch. Ben put his hand on Jake's shoulder and stopped him. 'Look,' he said, and pointed back the way they had come. Jake looked at the school building. He saw nothing unusual about the red-brick walls, with their high windows, or the entrance to the building, where one or two students he recognised stood chatting. 'What? Looks just the same as ever to me,' he said. As he turned, he realised that Ben had already started to run towards the pitch. As he ran, Ben turned, running backwards for a few paces, facing Jake. 'Exactly!' he shouted, then turned again as he reached the pitch and lost himself in the excited mass of boys chasing the ball.

Listening

1 4.11 exam practice

You will hear part of a radio phone-in programme about television programmes. For questions 1–10, complete the sentences.

Sound Off is unusual for a **1** ______

Sound Off does things that people normally associate with **2** ______

The presenter of Sound Off has been criticised by journalists for his **3** ______

Some people think that Charles Wilson doesn't show enough **4** ______

Nancy thinks famous people shouldn't expect to have **5** ______

According to Nancy Girl Power is a bad example of **6** ______

Girl Power was broadcast for **7** ______

News Review is unusual because it is made outside **8** ______

Nancy is not interested in **9** ______

Nancy suggests that News Review should be on at **10** ______

2 4.12 exam practice

You will hear a radio programme about education. For questions 1–7, choose the best answer (A, B or C).

1 What was the point of the experiment?
- **A** to show what school used to be like
- **B** to punish some school pupils
- **C** to teach the importance of freedom

2 One thing Mark liked about the clothes he had to wear was
- **A** they were very attractive.
- **B** they stayed cleaner for longer.
- **C** they were practical.

3 What does Mark say about the work he had to do?
- **A** It was quite varied.
- **B** It seemed irrelevant.
- **C** It was confusing.

4 How has learning French changed, according to Hannah?
- **A** Pupils now learn language that is more useful.
- **B** Pupils now learn less vocabulary than in the past.
- **C** Pupils now are much better at learning languages.

5 What did Hannah and her classmates find funny about the maths lesson?
- **A** They were used to questions at a higher level.
- **B** They had no idea how to answer the questions.
- **C** They had to ask each other questions.

6 What does Gareth say teachers no longer do in the classroom?
- **A** care about their pupils' development
- **B** merely focus on what the book says
- **C** sit facing a group of students

7 How does Gareth say that relationships between pupils have changed since the fifties?
- **A** Pupils helped each other more back then.
- **B** Boys and girls understand each other more now.
- **C** There was more bullying then.

Have your say!

- Would you like to try the educational system of 60 years ago?
- What would be the main differences between this and today's system?

Speaking

1 Ask and answer the following questions.

- Do you have any ambitions for the future?
- What kind of work would you like to do?
- Do you know what qualifications you need to do that job?
- How important is it to you to earn a high salary?
- Are there any jobs you would never do?

2 Read the examiner's instructions and do the task.

Candidate A, here are two photographs of people doing different jobs. I'd like you to compare them and say which job you think is more satisfying? You only have one minute for this.

- Which job do you think is more satisfying?

Candidate B, which job would you prefer to do?

Candidate B, here are two photographs of different offices. I'd like you to compare them and say which office you would prefer to work in. You only have one minute for this.

- Which office would you prefer to work in?

Candidate B, which office looks more comfortable?

3 Read the examiner's instructions and do the task.

I'd like you to imagine that a teenage friend of yours, John, has asked for your advice on summer jobs. Here are some jobs that your friend is considering. Talk to each other about what doing these different jobs would be like and then choose the job you think would be suitable. You only have three minutes for this.

- What would doing these different jobs be like?
- Which job would be suitable for your friend?

4 Ask and answer the following questions.

- Should teenagers work part-time to earn money?
- Do people nowadays work too hard?
- What are the best ages to start and stop working?
- Apart from money, what else is important to people in their working lives?

Use of English

1 exam practice

Read the text below and think of the word which best fits each gap. Use only one word in each gap. Write your answers IN CAPITAL LETTERS.

Identity theft

For three months, Joanna Sugden was the victim of a crime (1) _________ she didn't even know was being (2) _________ . Joanna had (3) _________ her identity stolen. Someone was going around the UK (4) _________ to be her – forging her signature in (5) _________ to take money out of her bank account, and buying things online with her credit card.

'If I (6) _________ not checked my credit card bill carefully,' says Joanna, 'they might still (7) _________ using my identity and stealing (8) _________ me today. The amounts on the bill didn't (9) _________ any sense to me, so I contacted the credit card company. They started to investigate, and it turned (10) _________ this had been going on for ages. They contacted the police, and the next time the thief tried to take money out of my account, she was arrested and charged (11) _________ theft. (12) _________ I haven't got all the money that was stolen back yet, I'm hopeful that I will eventually.'

2 exam practice

Read the text below. Use the word given in capitals at the end of some of the lines to form a word that fits in the gap in the same line. Write your answers IN CAPITAL LETTERS.

Want to work in the media?

Bravo, the brand-new magazine for teens, is looking	
for (1) ___ , creative and energetic youngsters to join	**ENTHUSE**
its team of trainee (2) ___ . If you are aged between	**JOURNAL**
thirteen and sixteen, then our (3) ___ wants to hear from you!	**EDIT**
You must have excellent (4) ___ skills. The ability to use a computer and the internet would be	**COMMUNICATE**
an advantage, as you will be given (5) ___ for researching and writing stories and making initial	**RESPONSIBLE**
(6) ___ to interview people.	**ARRANGE**
Under the (7) ___ of experienced members of staff,	**SUPERVISE**
you will learn all aspects of magazine (8) ___ , perfect for those of you thinking about finding	**PRODUCE**
(9) ___ in the media in the future.	**EMPLOY**
All (10) ___ should contact us in writing at the address below.	**APPLY**

3 exam practice

Complete the second sentence so that it has a similar meaning to the first sentence, using the word given. Do not change the word given. You must use between two and five words, including the word given. Write the missing words IN CAPITAL LETTERS.

1 I think you should start eating more fruit and vegetables.
high
It _________ eating more fruit and vegetables.

2 We pay Linda to wash our car every Sunday.
have
We _________ Linda every Sunday.

3 I wish you would decide what programme you want to watch!
mind
I wish you would _________ what programme you want to watch!

4 Some people say that Pelé was the greatest footballer ever.
said
It _________ that Pelé was the greatest footballer ever.

5 Could you pass me my medicine, please?
mind
Would _________ me my medicine, please?

6 Cheating in exams is not acceptable under any circumstances.
no
Under _________ in exams acceptable.

7 Do you regret lying to your parents?
wish
Do you _________ to your parents?

8 Many people believe that fast food is unhealthy.
thought
Fast food _________ unhealthy.

Writing: email

1 Look at the task in exercise 2 and answer these questions.

1 Who are you writing to?
2 Is this the first time you have written to him?
3 How formal/informal should your email be?
4 How are you going to start and end your email?

2 exam practice: email

You help to run a basketball team for young people. A similar team from abroad is coming to your country on a tour, during which they would like to arrange a match with your team. You have been exchanging emails with Leroy, the manager of the team, discussing the possibility of having a match.

Read Leroy's latest email, and the notes which you have made. Then write a reply to Leroy, giving all the necessary information.

write reply send

From: Leroy
Sent: 12th April

Subject: Basketball match

Thanks for your email.

I think all we need to do now is decide exactly where and when we'll play. I'll leave the final details up to you, but it should be a Saturday at the end of June or the start of July. Some information about where we're playing would be useful, as well as how to get there. We don't want to get lost!

Thanks.

Yours,
Leroy

suggest Sat 5th July at Sports Centre

Sports Centre facilities - changing rooms, café, swimming pool

follow motorway to our town, then signs to Sports Centre

my mobile number 6975552189

3 Write your email in 120–150 words. You must use grammatically correct sentences with accurate spelling and punctuation in a style appropriate for the situation.

4 When you have written your email, make sure that you have:

- checked your spelling and grammar ☐
- used paragraphs ☐
- given all the necessary information ☐
- used an appropriate level of formality/informality ☐
- started and finished your email in an appropriate way. ☐

Grammar database

1 Present simple and past simple

We use the *present simple*:

- for habits.
  *My dad **talks** in his sleep.*
- to show how often things happen or don't happen.
  ***I don't see** my cousins very often.*
- for permanent situations.
  *She **lives** in Switzerland.*
- for general truths, facts and abilities.
  *Anne **is** married.*
- for states.
  ***Does** Rod **have** a girlfriend at the moment?*
- for the future (in timetables).
  *Term **starts** next Monday.*
- for the future (in time clauses).
  *I'll call you when **I get** back.*

We use the *past simple*:

- for habits in the past.
  *I **talked** in my sleep when I was a child.*
- to show how often things happened or didn't happen.
  ***I didn't see** my cousins very often when I was growing up.*
- for single completed actions.
  *I **bought** my dad's birthday present yesterday.*
- for permanent situations in the past.
  *She **lived** in Switzerland.*
- for general truths and facts about the past.
  *They **were** married for seventy years.*
- for past states.
  *Roula **had** long hair a few years ago.*
- for the main events in a story.
  *I **went** downstairs and made the kids their breakfast.*

Emphatic present simple and emphatic past simple

When we want to emphasise an action or situation, particularly to emphasise that it actually happens/happened, or that it is/was different to what someone else thinks, we can use the emphatic present simple, with *do* or *does*, or the emphatic past simple with *did*.

You haven't got a sister, have you?
*Actually, I **do** have a sister, but she lives abroad.*
You didn't agree with Joanne, did you?
*Actually, I **did** agree with her.*

Note: We **don't use** the emphatic present simple or emphatic past simple with the verb *to be*.

Stative verbs

Some verbs are not normally used in continuous tenses because they don't describe actions. These are called 'stative verbs'. For example, we say *I love you*, not *I am loving you*.

Stative verbs often refer to …

- thinking (eg *believe, imagine, know, understand*)
- emotions (eg *hate, like, love, prefer, satisfy, want*)
- the human senses (eg *hear, see, smell, sound, taste*)
- appearance (eg *appear, look, resemble, seem*)
- relationships between things (eg *belong to, consist of, include, involve, own*).

! BE CAREFUL!

Some verbs are stative with one meaning and non-stative with another meaning.

be:
*Dave **is** thirteen years old.* (state)
*You**'re being** silly!* (action)

have:
*Sheila **has** a headache at the moment.* (state)
*Sheila **is having** a bath at the moment.* (action)

think:
*What **do** you **think** of this book?* (state)
*What **are** you **thinking** about?* (action)

2 Present perfect simple and past perfect simple

We use the *present perfect simple*:

- for actions and situations continuing up to now.
  *We**'ve been** engaged for the last six months.*
- for a series of actions continuing up to now.
  *We**'ve had** an argument every day this week!*
- for completed actions at a time in the past which is not mentioned.
  ***Has** he ever **told** you that he loves you?*
- for completed actions where the important thing is the present result.
  *I**'ve finished** my homework so I'm free now.*

The present perfect simple is often used with words and phrases like: *just, yet, already, still, this is the first time …, ever, never, for, since, so far, up to now, recently, lately, before*, etc.

We often use the present perfect simple with the superlative and with ordinal numbers (first, second, third, etc).
*She's the nicest person I'**ve** ever **met**. It's the second argument we'**ve had** today!*

The present perfect simple can also be used to refer to the future in time clauses after *when*, *as soon as*, etc.
*I'll invite Tracy round when we'**ve finished** dinner.*

! BE CAREFUL!

*Carl **has been** to Paris. = Carl is not in Paris now.*

*Carl **has gone** to Paris. = Carl is in Paris or is on his way to Paris now.*

We use the *past perfect simple*:

- for actions and situations continuing up to a moment in the past.
  *They'**d been** engaged for three years before they got married.*
- for completed actions before a moment in the past.
  *I'**d asked** Sam to go out with me several times before he finally said yes!*
- for completed actions where the important thing is the result at a moment in the past.
  *We'**d** just **had** some bad news so we decided not to go to the party.*
- in reported speech.
  *Charlotte said she'**d** never **met** such nice people.*
- in third conditional sentences.
  *If you'**d told** me you were in trouble, I'd have offered to help.*
- for wishes about the past.
  *I wish I **hadn't split up** with Jenny.*

The past perfect simple is often used with words and phrases like: *before, after, when, already, as soon as, it was the first time …*, etc.

Note: We can often choose between using the past perfect simple and the past simple, as there is little or no difference in meaning.

☒ *They'd been engaged for three years before they got married.*

☒ *They were engaged for three years before they got married.*

Note: After we have used the past perfect simple to show that we are talking about a past time before the main past time of a narrative, we often use past simple instead of continuing to use past perfect.

*I **had met** the Grangers only once before. They **seemed** a very interesting couple …*

3 Present continuous (*am/is/are -ing*) and past continuous (*was/were -ing*)

These two tenses often have a similar meaning, although the present continuous refers to the present and the past continuous refers to the past.

We use the *present continuous*:

- for events happening at a particular moment.
  *Don't make so much noise! I'**m working**!*
- for temporary situations or events.
  *We'**re living** with my grandparents until our house is finished.*
- for changing and developing situations.
  *The traffic in this town **is getting** worse.*
- for future arrangements.
  *We **are having** a test next Monday.*
- to refer to annoying habits (usually with always).
  *You **are** always **interrupting** me! Stop it!*

We use the *past continuous*:

- for events happening at a particular moment in the past.
  *What **were** you **doing** at nine o'clock last night?*
- for temporary situations or events.
  *My brother **was working** as a waiter last summer until he found a better job.*
- for changing and developing situations.
  *The situation at work **was becoming** very stressful, so I left.*
- for future arrangements in the past.
  *I was very excited because we **were going** to the zoo the next day.*
- for two actions in progress at the same time.
  *While I **was studying**, my brother **was playing** his trumpet.*

The past continuous and past simple can be used together to show that one action interrupts another:
*I **was watching** TV when suddenly a face **appeared** at the window.*

Present perfect continuous (*has/have been -ing*) and past perfect continuous (*had been -ing*)

We use the *present perfect continuous*:

- for events and actions continuing up to the present moment or stopping just before it.
  *I'm bored because I'**ve been working** all day.*

We use the *past perfect continuous*:

- for events and actions continuing up to a particular moment in the past or stopping just before it.
  *Tom was tired when I saw him because **he had been playing football**.*

4 so, such, too, enough

We use *so*, *such* and *enough* to show the results of a situation:

so

… so …	adjective adverb many/much + noun	… that …

She's ***so*** *clever* ***that*** *she learned Russian in three months!*

Matt kicked the ball ***so*** *hard* ***that*** *he broke his toe.*

I've got ***so*** *many hobbies* ***that*** *I don't have time for all of them.*

such

… such …	a/an + adjective + singular noun adjective + plural noun a lot of + noun	… that …

I got ***such*** *a low mark* ***that*** *I failed the exam.*

Jill and Denise are ***such*** *good friends* ***that*** *they're always together.*

I've got ***such*** *a lot of homework* ***that*** *I can't come out tonight.*

enough

… not …	adjective adverb	*enough* + *for* and/or full infinitive

There isn't ***enough*** *time for us to contact Ben before the meeting.*

I think Zoe is old ***enough*** *to be left at home on her own now.*

We use *too* to refer to something that has a negative effect because it is more than enough or more than is necessary.

too

… too …	adjective adverb many/much + noun	+ *for* and/or *full* infinitive

I'm afraid you're ***too*** *young to see this film without an adult.*

We got there ***too*** *late for the start of the concert.*

If you eat ***too*** *many sweets, you'll damage your teeth.*

Note: When we want to refer to something that is large and positive, we do not use *too*. Instead, we use *very*, *really*, *extremely*, etc.

You look really nice in that dress.

5 used to, would, be/get used to

We use *used to*:

- for past states.
  I ***used to*** *live in Germany.*
- for past habits.
  We ***used to*** *come here on holiday every year when I was a child.*

Note: The negative of *used to* is *didn't use to* or *never used to*.

We use *would*:

- for past habits.
  My Grandma ***would*** *read to me every night when I was very young.*

Note: *Would* is not used to talk about past states, only actions which are repeated. *Used to* and *would* are not usually used for the recent past.

We use *be/get used to*:

- for situations that are now familiar or no longer strange.
  It took me a while to ***get used to*** *my new school.*

Note: *Be used to* refers to the state of being familiar with something, while *get used to* refers to the process of becoming familiar with something.

6 The future

There are a number of different ways of expressing the future in English, such as *will*, *be going to*, *present simple*, *present continuous*, *future perfect*, and *future continuous*. For some situations, more than one choice is correct.

will and *be going to*

There is sometimes very little difference in meaning between *will* and *be going to*. It is often just a matter of formality. *Will* is generally more formal than *be going to*.

We can use either *will* or *be going to* for:

- facts about the future.
  Technology ***will*** *continue to develop.* (more formal)
  *Technology****'s going to*** *continue to develop.* (more informal)
- predictions not based on present evidence.
  In a thousand years, there ***won't*** *be any wars. (more formal)*
  In a thousand years, there ***aren't going to*** *be any wars. (more informal)*

- decisions made at the moment of speaking.
  *I know! I'**ll** buy Mum a CD for her birthday.*
  *I know! I'**m going to** buy Mum a CD for her birthday.*

Note: *will* emphasises the decision, whereas *be going to* emphasises the intention. The meaning, however, is basically the same in both sentences.

We can also use *will* for:

- most first conditional sentences.
  *If you help me, I'**ll** finish more quickly.*
- offers, suggestions and requests.
  *I'**ll** help you.*
  ***Will** you help me?*

! BE CAREFUL!

With offers and suggestions in the question form, we do not use *will* with *I* and *we*. We use *shall*.

☒ Will I help you set up the new DVD player?
☒ Shall I help you set up the new DVD player?

We can also use *be going to* for:

- plans and intentions (which you already have when you speak).
  *I'**m going to** be a scientist when I grow up.*
- predictions based on present evidence. Watch out!
  *You'**re going to** drop that box!*

Present simple

We can use the *present simple*:

- for timetables, arrangements and fixed events (which the speaker cannot change).
  *The tour of the museum **starts** at 11 o'clock.*
- after *if* in first conditional and zero conditional sentences.
  *If robots **start** driving taxis, what will all the taxi drivers do?*
- after certain time expressions, such as *when* and *while*.
  *I'll call you when I **get** there.*

Present continuous

We can use *present continuous* for:

- arrangements made before the moment of speaking
  *They'**re driving** to Paris next week.*

! BE CAREFUL!

We cannot say: *I'm being a scientist when I grow up.* because it is not an arrangement.

Modals

We can use *modals* for:

- predictions which we are not so sure about.
  *It **might** rain tomorrow.*
- predictions which we are almost certain about.
  *Carl **can't** be playing tomorrow. He's got a broken leg.*

Future perfect simple

We use the *future perfect simple* for:

- actions which are completed some time between now and a point in the future.
  *I **will have finished** my homework by eight o'clock.*

Future perfect continuous

We use the *future perfect continuous* for:

- actions in progress up to a point in the future.
  *At nine o'clock, I **will have been playing** this computer game for five hours!*

Future continuous

We use the *future continuous* for:

- actions in progress at a point in the future.
  *This time next week, I'**ll be travelling** round Switzerland.*
- habits or repeated actions at a point in the future.
  *In a hundred years' time, we'**ll** all **be having** holidays on other planets.*

7 Articles

We use *a* and *an* (indefinite articles) with:

- singular countable nouns (when we are not being specific).
  *Have you got **a** DVD player?*

! BE CAREFUL!

An comes before words with a vowel sound. It is the sound that is important, not the spelling. So, we say 'an umbrella' but 'a uniform'.

We use *the* (the definite article) with:

- singular countable nouns (when we are being specific).
  *That's **the** woman who won the lottery!*
- singular countable nouns (for general groups or categories).
  ***The** calculator makes maths a lot easier.*
- plural countable nouns (when we are being specific).
  ***The** DVDs are in the cupboard.*
- uncountable nouns (when we are being specific).
  ***The** ice cream is in the fridge.*

We don't use an article with:

- plural countable nouns (when we are not being specific).
  Videos are cheaper than DVDs.
- uncountable nouns (when we are not being specific).
  Ice cream is more popular in the summer.

BE CAREFUL!

Be careful! There are a lot of phrases and other rules that determine which article we use. Pay particular attention to the following:

- entertainment:
  a programme on television, on the radio, watch (the) TV, listen to music, play football, play (the) piano, go to the cinema
- time:
  in 2013, in the 1990s, in the 21st century, in the morning, at night, in April, in (the) winter
- geographical features:
  Mount Everest, the Mediterranean, Crete, the Thames, London, Greece, America, the USA, the UK, Mars, the Earth, the Sun, the Moon
- people and work:
  a doctor, a teacher, the President, become President, the Queen, go to work, be at work, have a job
- nationalities:
  She's French, the Germans
- organisations:
  the army, the police, the Scouts
- buildings:
  the bank, the post office, go to prison/hospital, be in prison/hospital, go to the prison/hospital (as a visitor)
- health:
  have toothache, (the) flu, a headache, a cold
- travel:
  go by bus, take the bus, on foot, take a taxi, go home
- education:
  go to school, go to the school (as a visitor), *be in the fifth year, be in Class 5, maths*

8 Time clauses

With first conditional sentences, we do not use *will* or *be going to* immediately after *if*, even though we are referring to the future. We use a present tense.

*If you **see** Adam tomorrow, ask him to call me.*

The same thing is true with these time words and phrases. We use a present tense (present simple, present continuous or present perfect) and not *will* or *be going to* to talk about the future.

- *when:*
  *Tell me when you **finish**/you **have finished** the exercise.*
- *as soon as:*
  *I'll tell you as soon as I **finish**/I **have finished**.*
- *before:*
  *Don't open your books before you **finish**/you **have finished** the test.*
- *after:*
  *I'll collect the papers after you **finish**/you **have finished**.*
- *until/till*
  *Don't open your books until you **finish**/you **have finished** the test.*
- while:
  *I'll mark these compositions while you **do**/you **are doing** the test.*

9 Conditionals (1): zero, first, second

Many sentences with *if* are conditionals: they express a condition and a result. We use different tenses and different structures, depending on what we are trying to express.

We use the zero conditional (*if* + a present tense + a present tense):

- for general or scientific truths.
  *If you **burn** plastic, it **produces** a bad smell.*

We use the first conditional (*if* + a present tense + *will* + bare infinitive):

- for real or likely situations in the present or the future.
  *If you **work** hard, you **will pass** the exam.*

Note: A common mistake is to use *If you/she/etc will…* when referring to the future. Remember that we use a present tense for the future in this kind of sentence.
If you call Debbie next Monday, she will tell you about the party.

Note: Instead of *will*, we can also use *may, might, can, could, shall, should, ought to* and *have to*.

We can also use the *first conditional* with an imperative (*if* + a present tense + imperative):

- for giving instructions about real or likely situations in the present or the future.
  *If you **make** a mistake, **use** an eraser.*

We use the *second conditional* (*if* + past (simple or continuous) + *would* + bare infinitive).

- for impossible, unlikely or hypothetical situations.
  *If I **won** the lottery, I **would buy** a new house.*

- Instead of *would*, we can also use *might* and *could*.
  *If I had more time, I **might/could** take up a new hobby.*
- We can also use *could* in the *if* clause.
  *If I **could** go anywhere on holiday, I would go to the Bahamas.*

Note: All these conditional sentences can also be written with the *if* clause in the second half of the sentence. Notice that when the *if* clause comes first, we use a comma and when it comes second we don't.
*Use an eraser **if** you make a mistake.*
*I would buy a new house **if** I won the lottery.*

10 *unless, in case, as long as, provided that*

- *Unless* means 'except if' or 'if … not'.
  *We're having a picnic in the morning, **unless** it rains.* (= … except if it rains or … if it doesn't rain.)
- *In case* means 'because it/he/etc might'.
  *Take your mobile **in case** I want to call you.* (= … because I might want to call you.)
- *As long as* and *provided that* both mean 'only if'.
  ***As long as/Provided that** everyone comes, the party will be a great success.*

We can also use *so long as* with the same meaning.
*You'll pass the exam **so long as** you're careful.*

11 Countable and uncountable nouns

Nouns can be either countable or uncountable. Countable nouns are ones we can count (*one car, two cars, three cars,* etc). Uncountable nouns are ones we can't count (*truth, water, advice,* etc). Uncountable nouns include abstract ideas (*information*), materials (*iron*) and collections of things (*luggage*).

With countable nouns, we:

- use *a/an* and *some*.
  *We've got **a** dog. I need **some** potatoes.*
- use *many* (usually in questions and negative statements).
  *Does this bank have **many** branches outside the city centre?*
- use a plural verb, when the noun is plural.
  *Your books **are** on the table.*

With uncountable nouns, we:

- use *some*, but not *a/an*.
  *Let me give you **some** advice.*
- use *much* (usually in questions and negative statements).
  *We don't have **much** information about the accident yet.*
- use a singular verb.
  *My money **is** in my wallet.*

Note: After *so, as* and *too* we can use *much* and *many* in affirmative statements.

*There are **so many** things I want to tell you!*
*He's got **too much** baggage to carry by himself.*

Here are some common uncountable nouns, all of which take a singular verb: *information, furniture, advice, news, luggage, baggage, knowledge, money, travel, paper.*

With some of these nouns, we can use phrases such as *a piece of …, an item of …, a sheet of …,* etc.

There are also some plural uncountable nouns. Common ones include: *clothes, jeans, scissors, trousers, groceries, spectacles,* etc.

With plural uncountable nouns, we:

- use *some*, but not *a/an*.
  I need some new trousers. (**not** … a new trouser ☒)
- use *many*.
  *You didn't get **many** groceries, did you?*
- use a plural verb.
  *Where **are** my jeans?*

Note: Some nouns can be countable with one meaning and uncountable with another (*glass, a glass*). This often happens when we talk about a material or substance and a thing made out of it: *chocolate* (the substance), *a chocolate* (one from a box), *paper* (the substance), *a paper* (a newspaper), *coffee* (the substance), *a coffee* (a cup of coffee), etc.

12 Quantifiers

- *Many* is used for countable nouns, usually in negative sentences and in questions.
  *We don't have **many** visitors to the hotel at this time of year.*
- *Much* is used for uncountable nouns, usually in negative sentences and in questions.
  *Have you got **much** free time these days?*
- In positive statements, we usually use *lots of* and *a lot of* for both countable and uncountable nouns.
  *He's won **a lot of/lots of** prizes/money.*

- With countable nouns, we can also use the phrase *a large number of* and with uncountable nouns we can use *a large amount of* or *a great deal of*.
  *Simon has **a large number of** friends.*
  *The police have **a large amount of/a great deal of** information about the criminal.*
- *Few/A few* are used for countable nouns. *Few* means 'not many'.
  *We get **few** visitors to the hotel at this time of year.*
  A few means 'some'.
  *The shop still has **a few** copies of the book left.*
- *Little/A little* are used for uncountable nouns. *Little* means 'not much'.
  *We can't meet for coffee next week because I have **little** free time.*
  A little means 'some'.
  *We can meet for coffee next week because I have **a little** free time.*

Note: The phrase *only a few* … means 'not many' and *only a little* … means 'not much'.

13 Modals (1): ability, permission, advice/criticism, obligation

We can use modals (*can, could, may, must, should*) and semi-modals (*have to, ought to*) to express *permission, ability, obligation, advice* and *criticism*.

- *have to* has a similar meaning to *must*
- *ought to* has a similar meaning to *should*

! BE CAREFUL!

While *modals* and *ought to* have only one form (*I should, he should*, etc), *have to* changes its form depending on person and tense.
*She **has to** go home now.*

! BE CAREFUL!

Modals are never followed by the full infinitive (with to). Use the bare infinitive.
*She **could play** the guitar when she was three.*

ability

- Use *can* to talk about ability now or generally.
  *The doctor **can** see you now. Terry **can** speak Arabic.*
- Use *can* to talk about decisions made now about future ability.
  *We **can** go to the concert tomorrow, if you like.*
- Use *will be able to* to talk about future ability.
  *You **will be able to** take your driving test after a few more lessons.*
- Use *could* to talk about ability in the past.
  *Tammy **could** read when she was two years old.*
- Use *could* to talk about present, future or general hypothetical situations.
  *I wish I **could** go with you tomorrow.*
- Use *could* + *have* + past participle (modal perfect) to talk about past hypothetical situations.
  *I **could have bought*** (= was able to buy) *a more expensive shirt, but I didn't want to.*

! BE CAREFUL!

Can cannot be used as an infinitive. Use *to be able to*:

☒ *I'd love **to be able to** go on a round-the-world cruise.*

☒ *I'd love to can go on a round-the-world cruise.*

permission

- Use *can, could* or *may* to ask for and give permission now, for the future, or generally. They mean the same thing, but *could* is more polite than *can*, and *may* is more polite than *could*.
  ***Can/Could/May** I go on the school trip next week?*
- To talk about *past permission*, we don't usually use a modal.
  ☒ *I **was allowed** to go on the school trip.*
  ☒ *I **could** go on the school trip.*

Note: We do use *could* to talk about past permission in reported speech.
*My parents said I **could** go on the school trip.*

advice

- Use *should* or *ought to* to ask for and give advice now, for the future, or generally. They have a very similar meaning, but *should* is much more common in spoken and written English (both formal and informal) than *ought to*.
  *You **should/ought to** eat less fast-food.*

criticism

- Use *should* or *ought to* + *have* + past participle (modal perfect) to make criticisms about past behaviour.
  *You **should/ought to have studied** harder for the test*

obligation

- We often use *must* for personal obligation now, in the future, or generally.
  *I **must** remember to get Dad a birthday present.*
- We often use *have to* for external obligation now, in the future, or generally.
  *I **have to** study for a test tonight.*

- We can also use *will have to* for future obligation.
  ***I'll have to** be more careful in future.*
- For personal or external obligation in the past, use *had to.*
  *I **had to** tidy my bedroom last night.*

Note: It is very unusual to use *must* for questions. We usually use *have to.*
*Do I **have to** be home by midnight?*

! BE CAREFUL!

*You **mustn't** eat that! = Don't eat that!*

*You **don't have to** eat that. = You can eat it if you want to but it isn't necessary.*

! BE CAREFUL!

Must cannot be used as an infinitive. Use *to have to:*

☒ *I'd hate **to have to** go to school on Sundays.*
☒ *I'd hate to must go to school on Sundays.*

14 Comparatives and superlatives

We use *comparative adjectives* and *adverbs* to compare things or people that are different and separate from each other.
*This computer is **better than** those computers.*
*Tom drives **more carefully** than his sister.*

We use *superlative adjectives* and *adverbs* to compare one member of a group with the whole group.
*This is **the best** computer in the shop.*
*Of all the people in my family, Tom drives **the most carefully**.*

Note: superlative adverbs are not used very often in English.

Adverbs			
type of adverb	**adverb**	**comparative**	**superlative**
regular adverbs	*slowly*	more/less + adverb *more slowly*	most/least + adverb *most slowly*
irregular adverbs	*early* *late* *far* *fast (drive fast)* *hard (work hard)* *well (do well)* *badly* *often*	*earlier* *later* *further/farther* *faster* *harder* *better* *worse* *more often*	*earliest* *latest* *furthest/farthest* *fastest* *hardest* *best* *worse* *most often*

Adjectives			
type of adjective	**adjective**	**comparative**	**superlative**
regular adjectives with one syllable	*old*	*+er* *older*	+ *-est* *oldest*
regular adjectives with one syllable (ending in vowel+ consonant)	*big*	double final letter + *-er* *bigger*	double final + *-est* *biggest*
regular adjectives with two syllables ending in *-y*	*happy*	replace *-y* with *-ier* *happier*	replace *-y* with *–iest* *happiest*
other regular adjectives with two or more syllables	*comfortable*	more/less + adjective *more comfortable*	most/least + adjective *most comfortable*
irregular adjectives / quantifiers	*good* *bad* *far* *little* *much* *many*	*better* *worse* *further* *less* *more* *more*	*best* *worst* *furthest* *least* *most* *most*

- To compare two or more things that are similar or the same, we can use *as* + adjective/adverb + *as.*
  *My story is (nearly) **as funny as** yours.*
  *Paul did **as well as** Carol and Angela in the test.*
- We can also use the negative form of this: *not as* + adjective/adverb + *as.*
  *My story **isn't as funny as** yours. (= Your story is funnier.)*

15 Questions

to be **– main verb and auxiliary verb**

- With the verb *to be* (as a main verb or an auxiliary verb), we form questions by inverting the subject and verb.

Main verb: ***Is this book*** *interesting?*
Auxiliary verb: ***Were you*** *given any homework?*

to have **– auxiliary verb**

- With the verb *to have* as an auxiliary verb, we form questions by inverting the subject and verb.
  Have you *ever* ***been*** *to France?*

to have **– main verb**

- When *to have* is the main verb, we form questions using the verb *to do.*
  Do you have *any brothers or sisters?*

all other verbs

- With all other verbs, we form questions using the verb *to do.*
  Does she go *out often?*
  Did you do *your homework last night?*

Question words

With the question words *who* and *what*, whether we use *to do* or not depends on whether the question word refers to the subject or object of the verb.

Compare:

Who told you? (= *Someone told you something.*)

Who did you tell? (= *You told someone. Who was it?*)

Note: Adverbs immediately before a main verb take the same position in a question as they do in a statement.
Statement: *I* ***still*** *want to go with you.*
Question: *Do you* ***still*** *want to go with us?*

16 The passive

The passive is formed by using the verb *be* in the correct form with the past participle of the main verb of the sentence. The verb *be* may be in a tense, such as the present perfect, or it may be some other form of the verb, such as the full infinitive. We normally put the person/thing the action is done to *before* the verb, and the person/thing doing the action *after* the verb (when it is necessary).

Our mail ***is delivered*** *every morning.* (simple present)

David ***is being told off*** *by the Head.* (present continuous)

The tickets ***were booked*** *by a travel agent.* (simple past)

We did some shopping while our car ***was being washed.*** (past continuous)

My wallet ***has been stolen!*** (present perfect)

I ***had been invited*** *to the party, but I didn't go.* (past perfect)

An announcement ***will be made*** *when we have more information.* ('will' future)

All compositions ***should be left*** *on my desk at the end of the lesson.* (other modals)

I can't stand ***being insulted*** *in public like that!* (-*ing* form)

Terry refused ***to be interviewed*** *by the local newspaper.* (full infinitive)

Note: We do not normally use the passive in the present perfect continuous or the past perfect continuous.

We use the passive:

- when we don't know who does/did/etc the action.
  My car ***has been stolen!***
- when we aren't interested in who does/did/etc the action.
  The monkeys ***are fed*** *every day at three.*
- when it's obvious who does/did/etc the action.
  A man ***was arrested*** *last night in a local park.*
- for emphasis, formality and impersonal style.
  Passengers ***will be informed*** *of any delay as soon as possible.*

Some verbs can take two objects: a direct object and an indirect object.
My doctor gave ***me a prescription.***

In the passive, we usually use the person as the subject
I *was given a prescription* (by my doctor).

When we want to say who did the action, we normally use *by.*
The burglar was spotted ***by*** *a neighbour.*

Note: We usually say who does/did/etc an action only when it is necessary.

When we want to describe something used to do an action, we normally use *with.*
This rope has been cut ***with*** *a knife.*

Note: Some verbs are not normally used in the passive. They include intransitive verbs (without objects), eg *disappear, vanish, consist, seem, appear,* and some common transitive verbs such as *have, let, lack, resemble, fit and suit.*

Note: When an adjective is followed by a full infinitive, we do not normally use the passive.

✓ *It is easy to play Snakes and Ladders.*
✗ *It is easy to be played Snakes and Ladders.*

17 *-ing* form or infinitive

After some verbs, nouns and adjectives, we use the full infinitive. These verbs include: *afford, agree, appear, arrange, ask, attempt, be pleased/able/etc, choose, decide, expect, fail, happen, help, hope, intend, learn, manage, offer, plan, prepare, pretend, promise, refuse, seem, tend, want, wish, would like.*

I've arranged ***to meet*** *Diana outside the library.*
Did you manage ***to speak*** *to Mrs Harris?*
I can't promise ***to be*** *there, but I'll try.*

After some verbs and phrases and after prepositions, we use the *-ing* form. These verbs and phrases include: *admit, appreciate, avoid, be capable of, be good/bad at, be interested in, can't help, can't stand, consider, delay, deny, discuss, dislike, enjoy, feel like, finish, give up, imagine, involve, look forward to, mention, mind, miss, practise, succeed in, suggest, talk about, think of.*

The young man admitted ***lying*** *to the police.*

It's hard to imagine ***standing*** *on the Moon and seeing the Earth above you.*

I would suggest ***asking*** *your teacher for some advice.*

After modal verbs, *make* and *let*, we use the *bare infinitive.*

You can ***send*** *the information to me by email.*
I hate it when people make me ***wait****.*
Why don't you let James ***join*** *you?*

Note: In the passive, make is followed by the full infinitive.
All the students at our school are made ***to wear*** *a cap.*

Some verbs can be followed by both the *-ing* form or the full infinitive without a change in meaning. These verbs include: *begin, continue, hate, intend, love, prefer, start.*

With some other verbs, using the *-ing* form of the full infinitive changes the meaning. These verbs include:

remember

- have a picture in your mind of a past event.
  I remember ***seeing*** *Mount Everest for the first time.*
- do something you are/were planning to do.
  I forgot the butter, but at least I remembered ***to get*** *some milk!*

forget

- always remember (usually I'll never forget).
  I'll never forget ***arriving*** *at school on the first day.*
- not do something you are/were planning to do.
  Oh, no! I forgot ***to lock*** *the front door!*

try

- do something as an experiment to solve a problem.
  If you're cold, why don't you try ***putting*** *a sweater on?*
- make an effort to achieve something.
  I'm going to try ***to join*** *the school football team.*

stop

- stop an action.
  Will you please stop ***making*** *so much noise?*
- interrupt an action to do something else.
  I'm tired of driving. Why don't we stop ***to have*** *a cup of coffee?*

go on

- continue.
  It started raining, but we went on ***playing*** *football.*
- stop one action and start another.
  After doing my French homework, I went on ***to do*** *my maths homework.*

like

- enjoy.
  I like ***collecting*** *stamps.*
- be in the habit of, think it right to do.
  I like ***to get up*** *at six so that I can be at work by eight thirty.*

regret

- be sorry about what has happened.
  Don't you regret ***leaving*** *university before finishing your degree?*
- be sorry about giving somebody bad news.
  We regret ***to inform*** *passengers that the train to Doncaster has been cancelled.*

18 prefer, would rather, had better

Prefer and *would rather* are both used to express preferences.

Had better is used for saying what someone should do.

We can use *prefer* in the following ways:

- *prefer* + noun/*-ing* form + *to* + noun/*-ing* form
  *I **prefer** adventure films **to** romantic comedies.* (general preference)
  *I **prefer** watch**ing** adventure films **to**/**rather than*** (watching) *romantic comedies.* (general preference)
- *would prefer* + full infinitive + *rather than*
  *I **would prefer to watch** an adventure film **rather than** a romantic comedy.* (specific preference, on this occasion)

Note: We do not usually say *I don't prefer …*. We normally use *I prefer not to …*.
***I prefer not to** stay up too late during the week.*

We can use *would rather* in the following ways:

- *would rather* + bare infinitive + *than* + bare infinitive
  ***I would rather paint than draw** with a pencil.* (general or specific preference)
- *would rather* + person + verb (in past tense)
  ***I would rather** you **didn't tell** everyone my secrets.* (general or specific preference)

We can use *had better* in the following ways:

- *had better* + bare infinitive
  *You **had better ask** Colin what time the meeting is.* (advice)

19 Modals (2): degrees of certainty

When we *make deductions* (form an opinion based on evidence), we use different modals to show how sure we are.

For *deductions about the present*, the modal is followed by the bare infinitive.

For *deductions about the past*, the modal is followed by the perfect infinitive (*have* + past participle).

We use *must*, *canvt* and *couldn't* for deductions we think are almost certainly correct:
*Sharon reads books in English quite often so she **must enjoy** them.*
*You **must have felt** very satisfied when you passed the exam.*
*John's in America, so that **can't be** him at the door.*
*I haven't received Amy's email yet, so she **can't/couldn't have sent** it.*

We use *should* and *ought to* for deductions we think are probably correct
*Liam's trained very hard, so he **should/ought to** win the match.*

We use *could*, *may* and *might* for deductions we think are possibly correct:
*Mum's late. She **could/may/might** be stuck in traffic.*
*Didn't Paula call you? She **could/may/might** have forgotten.*

20 Prepositions of time and place

The prepositions *at*, *on* and *in* are all used to refer to times and to places. They are also used in different phrases.

We use *at* to refer to:

- a specific time: *at one o'clock/midnight/6.30*
- a public holiday: *at Christmas/Easter/New Year*
- a specific location or building: *meet at the airport/McDonald's/the cinema*
- group activities: *be at a match/party/concert*
- other phrases: *at the weekend, at work, at night, at dawn*, etc

We use *on* to refer to:

- days: *on Monday/Friday morning/my birthday*
- positions on a surface: *on the table/a bridge/the road*
- islands: on *Tenerife/Crete/the Isle of Man*
- other phrases: *on TV, on the phone, on time*, etc

We use *in* to refer to:

- periods longer than a day: *in 1996/the first week of March/summer*
- parts of the day: *in the morning/afternoon/evening*
- inside rooms, buildings or large areas: *in the cinema/London/the centre of town*
- other phrases: *in a week's time, in time*, etc

Note: We can use different prepositions with the same place with slightly different meanings.
*I'll meet you **at** the library.*
(I'll meet you outside the library or at the entrance to the library.)
*I'll meet you **in** the library.*
(I'll meet you inside the building.)

Note: *On time* means 'at the right time, not late'.
*Please be **on time** for your interview.*
In time means 'early enough'.
*We got to the bus station just **in time** to catch our bus.*

21 Indirect questions

Direct questions use inverted word order, begin with a question word and end with a question mark:

*How **are you**?*
*What **are you** thinking about?*
*How much **are those shoes** in the window?*

Indirect questions are more formal than direct questions. They are formed using an introductory phrase, normal word order, and may or may not end with a question mark.

Common introductory phrases are:

***Could you tell me** where the 501 bus leaves from?*
***Do you know** what time it is?*
***I wonder if you** could send me a catalogue.*
***Would you mind** telling me when the interview will take place?*
***Could I ask** where the Head's office is?*
***Do you think you could tell me** what the job involves?*

Each introductory phrase is followed by a question word clause. Notice the word order.

*Could you tell me **where I can find Ms Archer?***
*I wonder if you could let me know **who is in charge here**.*

When the question has a 'yes/no' answer, we use *if* or *whether*.

*Could I ask **if/whether** the salary includes travel expenses?*

When an indirect question begins with a question form, it needs a question mark at the end. Otherwise, we do not use a question mark. Compare:

Would you mind telling me where the hotel manager is?
I wonder if you could tell me where the hotel manager is.

22 Reported speech

- We use *reported speech* when we want to say what someone else said.
  Phil said he was going to come to the party.
- *Tenses*, *pronouns*, and *time and place words* are often different in *reported speech* compared to direct speech.

Tense changes

If the reporting verb is in the past (eg *said*), we usually have to change the tense of what the person actually said.

- *simple present ➡ simple past*
  *'I **am** upset,' said Adrian.*
  *➡ Adrian said (that) he **was** upset.*
- *present continuous ➡ past continuous*
  *'I **am studying** Chinese,' said Don.*
  *➡ Don said (that) he **was studying** Chinese.*
- *present perfect simple ➡ past perfect simple*
  *'I **have passed** the test,' said Sally.*
  *➡ Sally said (that) she **had passed** the test.*
- *present perfect continuous ➡ past perfect continuous*
  *'I've **been phoning** people all morning,' said Rich.*
  *➡ Rich said (that) he **had been phoning** people all morning.*
- *simple past ➡ past perfect simple*
  *'I **went** to a private school,' said Alex.*
  *➡ Alex said (that) he **had gone** to a private school.*
- *past continuous ➡ past perfect continuous*
  *'We **were talking** about football,' said Miriam.*
  *➡ Miriam said (that) they **had been talking** about basketball.*
- *am/is/are going to ➡ was/were going to*
  *'We'**re going to** eat soon,' said Mrs Taylor.*
  *➡ Mrs Taylor said that they **were going to** eat soon.*

Note: *past perfect simple* and *continuous* do not change tense.
*'I'**d been standing** there for an hour,' said Gareth.*
*Gareth said (that) he **had been standing** there for an hour.*

Note: We often don't make any changes to the verb tense when we are reporting a scientific fact or when something is still true.
'Italy is in Europe,' said the geography teacher.
➡ The geography teacher said that Italy is in Europe.

Modal changes

If the reporting verb is in the past (eg *said*), we also usually have to change some modals.

- *will ➡ would*
  *'I'**ll** be there at eight,' said Rod.*
  *➡ Rod said (that) he **would** be there at eight.*
- *can ➡ could*
  *'I **can** swim,' said Bob.*
  *➡ Bob said (that) he **could** swim.*
- *must/have to ➡ had to*
  *'I **must** go soon,' said Fiona.*
  *➡ Fiona said (that) she **had to** go soon.*
- *may ➡ might*
  *'I **may** need some help,' said Tanya.*
  *➡ Tanya said (that) she **might** need some help.*

Pronoun changes

We also usually have to change some pronouns (and other words that are similar to pronouns).

- *my* ➡ *his/her*
  *'I'll tidy **my** room later,' said George.*
  ➡ *George said (that) he would tidy **his** room later.*
- *this/that + noun* ➡ *the* or *that*
  *'I love **this** movie', said Angela.*
  ➡ *Angela said (that) she loved **the/that** movie.*
- *this/that + verb* ➡ *it*
  *'**That** is fantastic!' said Steve.*
  ➡ *Steve said (that) **it** was fantastic.*
- *these/those + noun* ➡ *the* or *those*
  *'I'm going to sell **these** old books,' said Mr Fisher.*
  ➡ *Mr Fisher said (that) he was going to sell **the/those** old books.*
- *these/those + verb* ➡ *they*
  *'**Those** are fantastic!' said Steve.*
  ➡ *Steve said (that) **they** were fantastic.*
- *verb + these/those* (without an object) ➡ *them*
  *'I'm going to take **these**,' said Courtney.*
  ➡ *Courtney said (that) she was going to take **them**.*

Time and place changes

We also usually have to change words connected to time and place.

- *here* ➡ *there*
  *'I wish Jason was **here**,' said Adam.*
  ➡ *Adam said (that) he wished Jason was **there**.*
- *now/at the moment* ➡ *then* or *at that moment*
  *'I'm doing it **now**,' said Dawn.*
  ➡ *Dawn said (that) she was doing it **at that moment**.*
- *today* ➡ *that day*
  *'I'll call Bill **today**,' said Ben.*
  ➡ *Ben said (that) he would call Bill **that day**.*
- *tomorrow* ➡ *the following day* or *the next day*
  *'I'll do it **tomorrow**,' said Monica.*
  ➡ *Monica said (that) she would do it **the following day**.*
- *tonight* ➡ *that night*
  *'I'll do it **tonight**,' said Barbara.*
  ➡ *Barbara said (that) she would do it **that night**.*
- *next week/month/year* ➡ *the following week/month/year*
  *'I'll see you **next week**,' said Fred.*
  ➡ *Fred said (that) he would see me the **following week**.*
- *yesterday* ➡ *the day before* or *the previous day*
  *'I passed my driving test **yesterday**,' said Narinda.*
  ➡ *Narinda said (that) she had passed her driving test **the day before**.*
- *last week/month/year* ➡ *the previous week/month/year* or *the week/month/year before*
  *'I went there **last year**,' said Gloria.*
  ➡ *Gloria said (that) she had been there **the year before**.*
- *ago* ➡ *before*
  *'I finished an hour **ago**,' said Francis.*
  ➡ *Francis said (that) he had finished an hour **before**.*

Note: We often don't make any changes to time and place words when the information is still true at the moment of speaking/writing.
*'I'll see you all **tonight**,' said Terry.*
➡ *Terry said that he'll see us **tonight**.*

23 Reported questions

We use *reported questions* when we want to say what someone else asked.
Phil asked if he could come to the party.

We use the *same rules* regarding tense, pronoun and time and place word changes with *reported questions* as we do with reported speech.

have, do or *be* and modal questions

If a direct question begins with the verbs *have*, *do* or *be* (usually as auxiliary verbs), or a *modal* (*will*, *can*, etc), we use *if* or *whether* in the reported question. This is the kind of direct question which requires the answer yes or no.
'Have you seen Placebo in concert, Jake?' asked Carl.
➡ *Carl asked Jake **if/whether** he had seen Placebo in concert.*

Note: In direct questions we use the question form and question marks (*Have you seen …?*). In reported questions we do not use the question form or question marks (*asked if I had seen*).

Wh- questions

With questions beginning with *what, who, which, when, where, why* and *how* we do not use *if* or *whether*. We use the same question word as we used in the direct question, but we do not use the question form and we do change tenses, modals, etc.
*'**Why did you go** there?' asked Alan.*
➡ *Alan asked me **why I had gone** there.*

24 Reporting verbs

Different reporting verbs take different grammatical patterns.

- + *noun* (or noun phrase)
  deny: Sam denied ***the accusation****.*
  say: When she said ***the answer****, I knew she had won.*
  suggest: I suggest ***pizza for tonight****.*
  tell: (certain phrases) *I want you to tell* ***the truth****.*
- + *that clause*
  claim: Are you really claiming ***(that) you're innocent****?*
  deny: Do you deny ***(that) you were there****?*
  say: He says ***(that) he's happy****.*
  state: He stated ***(that) it was the truth****.*
  suggest: I suggest ***(that) we have pizza tonight****.*
- + *-ing*
  deny: Do you deny ***stealing*** *the money?*
  suggest: I suggest ***getting*** *a pizza tonight.*
- + *full infinitive*
  agree: They agreed ***to come on*** *Thursday.*
  claim: He claimed ***to be*** *a police officer.*
  refuse: She refused ***to talk*** *to anyone.*
- + *someone* + *full infinitive*
  ask: Could you ask ***John to come*** *in for a moment?*
  beg: I beg ***you to stop****!*
  command: I command ***you to stop****!*
  order: I order ***you to stop****!*
  tell: I told ***them to be*** *quiet!*
- (+ *to someone*) + *for* + *-ing*
  apologise: Don't forget to apologise (to your teacher) ***for being*** *late.*
- *someone* + noun
  ask: I asked ***James a question****.*
  tell: (certain phrases) *I told* ***Chris the truth****.*

25 *although, even though, in spite of, despite, however*

Although, even though, in spite of, despite and *however* are all used to express contrast, and so are similar in meaning to but.

although/even though

Although and *even though* have a very similar meaning but *even though* is more emphatic than *although*. They both take the same grammatical structure: *even though/although* + subject + verb.
Although/Even though *I did a lot of revision, I didn't pass the exam.*

Note: We can also put *although* and *even though* in the middle of the sentence.
I didn't pass the exam ***although/even though*** *I did a lot of revision.*

in spite of/despite

In spite of and *despite* mean exactly the same thing and take the same grammatical structures:

- *in spite of/despite* + *-ing* form, subject + verb.
  In spite of/Despite *doing a lot of revision, I didn't pass the exam.*

Note: We can also use the perfect *-ing* form to show that the action happened before the result.
In spite of/Despite ***having done*** *a lot of revision, I didn't pass the exam.*

- *in spite of/despite* + *the fact (that)* + subject + verb, *subject + verb.*
  In spite of/Despite *the fact (that) I did a lot of revision, I didn't pass the exam.*
- *in spite of/despite* + noun, subject + verb.
  In spite of/Despite *all my revision, I didn't pass the exam.*

Note: For all of these structures, we can also put *in spite of/despite* in the middle of the sentence.
I didn't pass the exam ***despite*** *doing a lot of revision.*

! BE CAREFUL!

With *in spite of/despite* + *-ing* form, the subject of the main verb must also carry out the action of the *–ing* verb.

☒ *Despite* ***doing*** *a lot of revision, I didn't pass the exam.*

☒ *Despite* ***doing*** *a lot of revision,* ***the exam*** *was impossible. (= the exam did a lot of revision!)*

however

However can be used at the beginning or end of a sentence, or in the middle under certain circumstances.
I did a lot of revision. ***However****, I didn't pass the exam.*
I did a lot of revision. I didn't pass the exam, ***however****.*
I did a lot of revision for the exam. I didn't pass, ***however****, so I'm going to have to take it again in December.*

26 Relative clauses

There are two types of relative clause: *defining* and *non-defining*. With both types, we use different *relative pronouns* depending on what we are referring to:

- *who* for people (and animals when we want to give them a personality).
  The girl ***who*** *won the dance competition was called Janie.*
- *which* for things (and animals when we don't want to give them a personality).
  The trophy ***which*** *she won was made of silver.*
- *when* for times.
  That was the summer ***when*** *we went to Kenya.*
- *where* for places.
  New York, ***where*** *he grew up, used to be well known for its crime rate.*
- *why* for reasons.
  The reason ***why*** *I couldn't come with you is rather complicated.*
- *whose* the possessive of *who*.
  That's Mrs Davis, ***whose*** *husband is also a teacher here.*

Note: We can also use *in which*, *to which*, *at which*, etc instead of *where* and *when*. The choice of *in*, *at* or *to*, etc depends on the preposition the verb or noun usually takes. So, you grow up **in** a place – we can use *in which*; you go **to** a place – we can use *to which*; you arrive **at** a building – we can use *at which*, etc.

☒ *That's the house* ***where*** *Daryl used to live.*
☒ *That's the house* ***which*** *Daryl used to live* ***in****.*
☒ *That's the house* ***in which*** *Daryl used to live.* (more formal)

! BE CAREFUL!

When the subject before the relative pronoun is the subject of the verb after the relative pronoun, we do not repeat the subject.

☒ *The boy* ***who won*** *the poetry competition is in the fifth year.*
☒ *The boy* ***who he won*** *the poetry competition is in the fifth year.*

Defining relative clauses

Defining relative clauses give us essential information. We cannot remove the relative clause and still understand the sentence.
The colour ***which I love most*** *is green.*
If we remove the relative clause, the sentence doesn't make any sense:
The colour is green. Which colour? We don't know.

With *defining relative clauses*, we:

- cannot use commas.

☒ *The colour, which I love the most, is green.*

- can replace *who*, *which*, *when* and *why* with *that*.

☒ *The colour* ***that*** *I love the most is green.*

Note: When the subject of the defining relative clause is different to the subject of the rest of the sentence, we can usually leave out the relative pronoun completely.

The ***colour which I love*** *the most is green.*
The ***colour that I love*** *the most is green.*
The ***colour I love*** *the most is green.*

Non-defining relative clauses

Non-defining relative clauses give us extra information. We can remove the relative clause and still understand the sentence.

This computer game, ***which I bought yesterday****, is called Road Rage 3000.*

If we remove the relative clause, the sentence still makes sense:

This computer game is called Road Rage 3000.

With *non-defining relative clauses*, we:

- must use commas. (Think of the commas as brackets/parentheses, giving extra information.)

☒ *This computer game which I bought yesterday is called Road Rage 3000.*

- cannot replace the relative pronoun with *that*.

☒ *This computer game, that I bought yesterday, is called Road Rage 3000.*

- cannot ever leave out the relative pronoun.

☒ *This computer game, I bought yesterday, is called Road Rage 3000.*

27 The causative

The *causative* is a grammatical structure we can use to show that someone pays or asks someone else to do something for them.

- The causative = *have/get + object + past participle* (*by/with*).
  The newsagent delivers our newspaper every morning.
  ➡ *We* ***have/get*** *our newspaper delivered every morning.*
- If we use *by*, we say who is actually going to do the work.
  She had the dress made ***by a professional dressmaker****.*
- If we use *with*, we say which tools or materials they used.
  They had their house painted ***with a special paint****.*

- *get* is usually more informal than *have*.
  *We **get** our newspaper delivered every morning.* (more informal)
  *We **have** our newspaper delivered every morning.* (more formal)
- We can also use this structure with *get*.
  *We **get** the newsagent to deliver our newspaper every morning.*

Note: The causative can also sometimes be used for unpleasant situations which we did not arrange.

*Mum **had** her handbag **stolen** on holiday.*

Choosing the right tense

If you are not sure what tense *have* or *get* should be in, think of the sentence as a normal subject + verb + object sentence and use the same tense.

*The newsagent **delivers** our newspapers.* (present simple)
➡ *We **have/get** our newspapers delivered.* (present simple)

*The newsagent **is going to deliver** our newspapers.* (*be going to* future)
➡ *We **are going to have/get** our newspapers delivered.* (*be going to* future)

28 Conditionals (2): third, mixed and inverted

Sometimes we want to imagine a different past. We can use the *third conditional* for this.

The third conditional:

- is formed using *if* + past perfect + modal + *have* + past participle.
- refers to a hypothetical (unreal or imaginary) past.
  ***If** I **had known** you were ill, I **would have called** you.* (= *I didn't know you were ill so I didn't call you.*)
  ***If** you **had tried** harder, you **might have won** the game.* (= *You didn't try very hard and that might be why you lost the game.*)

Sometimes we want to imagine how a different past could change things in the present. We can use a *mixed conditional* for this.

This mixed conditional:

- is formed using *if* + past perfect + modal + present.
- refers to a hypothetical (unreal) past condition and a present result.
  If I **had revised** more, I **would know** the answers to these questions. (= *I didn't revise enough* (past) *so I don't know the answers to these questions* (present).)

Sometimes we want to imagine how changing something about the present could have changed things in the past. We can use another *mixed conditional* for this.

This mixed conditional:

- is formed using *if* + past (simple or continuous) + modal + *have* + past participle.
- refers to a hypothetical (unreal) present condition and a past result.
  ***If** I **had** a car, I **would have taken** you home last night.* (= *I don't have a car so I didn't take you home last night.*)

We can make second and third conditional sentences more formal by using an *inversion*. Instead of using *if*, we use the same word order as we use in questions.

***Were** I the President, I would make sure people obeyed the law.* (= *If I were the President, I would make sure people obeyed the law.*)

***Had I known**, I would have done something about it.* (= *If I had known, I would have done something about it.*)

29 Direct and indirect objects

Some verbs can be followed by both a *direct* and an *indirect object* (usually a person). These verbs include: *bring, buy, get, give, lend, make, offer, owe, pass, promise, send, show, take, teach, tell, write*, etc.

*Mr Johnson gave **my brother*** (indirect object) ***some old magazines*** (direct object).
*My mum bought **me*** (indirect object) *a **DVD*** (direct object).

Sentences like this can also be written with the indirect object last. When this is the case, we usually use a preposition (often *for* or *to*).

*Mr Johnson gave some old magazines **to** my brother.*
*My mum bought a DVD **for** me.*

When these verbs are used in the passive, the subject of the sentence is usually the indirect object of the active sentence and not the direct object.

My brother was given some old magazines by Mr Johnson.

(***Some old magazines** were given **to my brother** by Mr Johnson* is not very natural.)

*I was bought **a DVD** by my mum.*

(*A DVD was bought **for me** by my mum* is not very natural.)

30 Infinitives of purpose

When we want to talk about someone's purpose (the reason they do something), we can use the full infinitive:

*I called Andrea **to ask** her about the homework.*

We can also use:

- *in order* + full infinitive
  *I called Andrea **in order to ask** her about the homework.*
- *so as* + full infinitive
  *I called Andrea **so as to ask** her about the homework.*

Note: We can also express the same idea using *so that.*
*I called Andrea **so that I could** ask her about the homework.*

With a negative purpose or with stative verbs, we don't normally use the infinitive alone.

⊠ *We'd better hurry up **in order/so as not to be** late.*
⊠ *We'd better hurry up **not to be** late.*

Note: With the verb *try* we can use *and* instead of the full infinitive with a similar meaning.

*Why don't you **try and jump** over this wall?*

This is more informal than the full infinitive. We only use this structure to express a purpose with the base form of the verb, not with *tries*, *tried*, etc.

I try and help my friends when I can. (= *I try to help my friends when I can.*)

31 Unreal past

A past tense does not always refer to past time. In some sentences and with some verbs or phrases we use a past tense to refer to the present or the future or to a general situation.

These sentences include ones that contain:

- a second conditional:
  *I could take a taxi if I **had** more money.*
- *Suppose* and *What if … ?*:
  *What if life **existed** on other planets?*
- *would rather + you/he/she/we/they*:
  *I'd rather you **didn't call** me 'Bob'. I prefer 'Robert'.*
- *It's (high/about) time*:
  *It's high time you **made** up your mind.*
- polite questions:
  ***Did** you **want** me to speak to Sandra for you?*
- *wish* and *if only*:
  *If only I **was** better at sport.*

We use different structures with *wish* (and *if only*), depending on exactly what we want to express. For wishes:

- about the present, we use a *past tense.*
  *I wish I **was learning** the piano, instead of the guitar.*
- about the past, we use a *past perfect tense.*
  *I wish I **had known** about the test! I haven't revised!*
- criticising other people or complaining about a situation now, in the future or generally, we use *wish + would.*
  *I wish you **wouldn't** talk with your mouth full.*
- expressing hypothetical ability or permission now, in the future or generally, we can use *wish + could.*
  *I wish I **could** come with you next week.*
- expressing desires in a formal way, we use the *full infinitive.*
  *I wish **to speak** to Mr Spencer.*

Note: We do not normally say
*I wish **I** would/wouldn't …*

Note: To express desires about the future, we often use the verb *hope.*
*I **hope** to go to university.*
We do not use *I wish I will …*

32 Participles

Present, perfect and past participles can be used in a number of different clauses and sentence structures as an alternative to the normal *subject + verb + object* sentence structure. Present participles end in *-ing*. Past participles usually end in *-ed*, although there are many irregular verbs (*seen*, *gone*, *brought*, etc). Perfect participles are formed using *having* + past participle.

Present participles and perfect participles can be used:

- after *prepositions* and *conjunctions*, such as *after, before, when, while, on, despite.*
  *After **driving** all day, I was really tired.*
  *After **having driven** all day, I was really tired.*
- to mean *because.*
  ***Being** tall, I had no problem getting into the basketball team.* (= *I had no problem getting into the basketball team because I am tall.*)

Present participles can also be used:

- to talk about actions happening at the same time.
  Standing *on the edge of the cliff, I began to feel dizzy.*
- to replace some relative clauses.
  The architect ***designing*** *our new house is very experienced. (= The architect who is designing our new house is very experienced.)*

Perfect participles can also be used:

- to talk about actions happening in sequence.
  Having *finished my homework, I went to meet my friends. (= I finished my homework and then went to meet my friends.)*

Past participles can sometimes be used:

- as an *alternative passive* form.
  Arrested *for murder, the man denied everything. (= The man was arrested for murder. He denied everything.)*
- to replace some *relative clauses.*
  The student ***chosen*** *to carry the flag felt very proud. (= The student who had been chosen to carry the flag felt very proud.)*

Note: You have to be careful that the participle and the rest of the sentence both refer to the same subject.

☒ *Driving to work, a horse ran across the road.*
☒ *Driving to work, I saw a horse run across the road.*

Both present and past participles can be used as adjectives:

The book was very ***interesting****.*
I was very ***interested*** *in the book.*

We can sometimes use these participles as adjectives before nouns:

Police have found the ***missing*** *child.*
Many people in ***developing*** *countries want to move to the* ***developed*** *world.*

However, you have to be careful because there are many verbs where the participle can't be used like this.

☒ *The* ***found*** *child was glad to get back home.*

In these cases, you have to say it in another way, often by using a relative clause:

The child ***who had been found*** *was glad to get back home.*

33 Inversions

When some negative adverbial words and phrases are placed at the beginning of a sentence, the subject and the verb 'invert'. This means we use the question form of the verb, even though the sentence is not a question.

Normal sentence order:
I have never seen *such bad behaviour before!*

Inversion:
Never have I seen *such bad behaviour before!*

Inversions are usually formal, so they are not usually used in speech unless you are trying to make a dramatic effect. Putting the negative adverb at the beginning of the sentence adds emphasis.

Negative adverbial words and phrases we can put at the beginning of a sentence include:

- *Hardly* (*… when*):
  Hardly ***had we set out*** *when the car broke down!*
- *Barely* (*… when*):
  Barely ***had we set out*** *when the car broke down!*
- *Scarcely* (*… when*):
  Scarcely ***had we set out*** *when the car broke down!*
- *Never*:
  Never ***have I heard*** *such an unbelievable story!*
- *No sooner* (*… than*):
  No sooner ***had we set out*** *than the car broke down!*
- *Rarely*:
  Rarely ***do we get*** *any visitors here.*
- *Seldom*:
  Seldom ***do we get*** *any visitors here.*
- *Not only* (*… but also/too*):
  Not only ***did you cheat*** *in the exam, but you lied about it too!*
- *Under no circumstances*:
  Under no circumstances ***should you talk*** *to strangers.*
- *At no time*:
  At no time ***did he admit*** *he was guilty.*
- *Little* (in certain phrases):
  Little ***did I realise/know/understand*** *how much trouble I was in.*
- *Not until* (Note: It is the *second* verb in the sentence which inverts with this structure):
  Not until we got home ***did we remember*** *we'd left Grandma in the town centre!*
- *Only then*:
  Only then ***did we remember*** *we'd left Grandma in the town centre!*
- *Only after*:
  Only after the robbery ***did I appreciate*** *how important the photographs were to me.*

34 Question tags

We can use *question tags* to:

- ask someone to agree with us.
  *It's cold today, **isn't it?***
  (Note: When we are asking someone to agree with us, our voice goes *down* at the end of the sentence.)
- check that something is true.
  *You were born in Israel, **weren't you?***
  (Note: When we are checking that something is true, our voice goes *up* at the end of the sentence.)

With most question tags, if the verb is negative we use a *positive question tag*. If the verb is positive we use a *negative question tag*.

be + *have* (as auxiliary verb) + modals

In sentences where the verb is *be* (either as a main verb or as an auxiliary verb), *have* (only as an auxiliary verb) or a *modal*, we make question tags using the same verb or modal in the same person and tense.

*You'**re** the new assistant, **aren't** you?*
*He **hasn't** done something stupid, **has** he?*
*Diana **can** help us, **can't** she?*
*We **won't** get in any trouble, **will** we?*

Other verbs

With all other verb forms, we use the verb *do* in the question tag in the same person and tense as the first verb.

*She **goes** to the same school as Ben, **doesn't** she?* (present simple)

*Phil and Carl **had** an argument, **didn't** they?* (past simple)

! BE CAREFUL!

You have to be careful with the verb *have*.

If it's being used as an auxiliary verb, we use *have* in the question tag.

If it's a main verb and there's no other auxiliary verb, we use *do* in the question tag.

*You'**ve** got a computer, **haven't** you?* (auxiliary verb)
*They **had** an argument, **didn't** they?* (main verb)

Unusual question tags

Pay particular attention to these question tags:

- *Let's … shall we?*
  Let's** get a pizza, **shall we?
- *I'm* (NOT followed by *not*) … *aren't I?*
  I'm** coming with you, **aren't I?
  (BUT: ***I'm** not coming with you, am I?*)
- *Don't … will you?*
  Don't** tell Mum, **will you?

Note: In sentences with a negative word like *never, no, nobody*, etc, we use a positive question tag.

*He **never** tells the truth, **does he?***

Note: If the subject of the main verb is *someone, nobody*, etc, we use *they* in the question tag.

Someone** will have to pay for the damage, won't **they?

35 Impersonal passive

Some verbs, such as *say, think, feel, know, believe* and *understand*, can be put into the passive with *it* as the subject.

This is a more formal way of saying *people say/think/* etc.

The subject *it* here does not refer to anything.

It has been said (that) money is the root of all evil.
*(= **People have said** money is the root of all evil.)*

It is thought (that) he escaped in a helicopter.
*(= **People think** he escaped in a helicopter.)*

It has been said (that) judges are not strict enough.
*(= **Some people have said** (that) judges are not strict enough.)*

It was felt (that) the punishment was too strict.
*(= **Some people felt** the punishment was too strict.)*

Note: There is another common passive structure used with *say, suppose, think, believe, know, feel* and *understand*: subject + verb in passive + full infinitive.

*This judge **is said to be** very strict!* (= *People say this judge is very strict!*)

*The punishment **was felt to be** appropriate.* (= *People felt the punishment was appropriate.*)

*He **is thought to have escaped** in a helicopter.*
(= *People think he escaped in a helicopter.*)

Speaking database

Greetings and farewells

- Hello.
- Good morning/afternoon.
- How do you do?
- Pleased to meet you.
- Nice to have met you.
- Goodbye.

Talking about yourself

- I've lived here all my life/for (ten) years and …
- I used to live in …
- There are (four) of us in my family. There's me, …
- My dad works as a … and my mum is a …
- I'm in the (third) year of secondary school/high school, etc.
- One of my favourite subjects is …
- I don't have much free time, but …
- I enjoy listening to music/collecting stamps, etc.
- I've been studying English/playing tennis, etc for …
- In the future, I'd like to …
- I haven't really decided yet, but …
- One of my ambitions is to …

Comparing / Expressing preference

- This is a photograph of … , while the other is of …
- In the picture, there's a …
- To begin with, …
- The first point I'd like to make is …
- Another similarity is that …
- Similarly, …
- On the one hand, …
- On the other hand, …
- … whereas …
- … while …
- A key difference is that …
- Another way in which they differ is that …
- I can't quite make out …
- I'm not absolutely sure, but …
- As for which I would prefer …
- Myself, I think I would prefer …
- Although … , I think I would go for …
- As far as I'm concerned, …

Problem solving

To the interviewer:

- I'm sorry. Do you think you could explain it again, please?
- I'm sorry. I didn't catch what you said.
- Do you want us to … ?

To the other candidate:

- Would you like me to begin?
- What do you think about … ?
- What about … ?
- How about … ?
- I'd say that …
- One possibility is …
- I'd suggest …
- I completely agree, and …
- Absolutely, and would you agree that … ?
- In a way, you are right.
- I partly agree with you, but …
- I agree to a certain extent, but …
- You have a point, although …
- I'm afraid I have to disagree because …
- I don't really agree. Don't you think … ?
- So, which do you think we should choose?
- Personally, …
- To sum up, then, we've chosen …

Discussing

- That's an interesting question. I suppose …
- To be honest, I haven't thought about it before, but I think …
- As I/(John)/you said earlier, …
- Despite what (John) says, I would say that …
- To my mind, …
- If you ask me, …
- Well, I don't really know much about it, but I imagine …
- I'd like to make two points. Firstly, …
- I tend to think that …

Writing database

Article

Example question

You see this announcement in an international magazine.

What does the future hold?

What will life be like for our grandchildren?
Will we be living on the Moon in fifty years' time?

What do you think? Write us an article, giving your suggestions.
The best article will be published in our magazine.

Write your article.

Example answer

Give your article a title

What the future holds

You can ask rhetorical questions to get your readers' attention.

Speak directly to your readers.

What will life be like in fifty years' time? It's impossible to know for certain, but there's one thing we can be sure of. In some ways, life for our grandchildren will be very different from life today. Let's just imagine some of the possibilities.

Introduce your first point.

Use humour where appropriate.

Give examples where appropriate

One thing that is changing very rapidly is technology. You can bet that our grandchildren will live in a world where everything and everybody relies on computers. Transport will also change, and perhaps we'll have cars that fly. Maybe our grandchildren will find themselves stuck in traffic jams in the sky!

Introduce further points.

Yet another way in which life will be different is the environment. It doesn't look like we're going to solve the problems of pollution soon, so our grandchildren may live in a world where many species have become extinct. Sadly, they might never see animals like pandas, apart from in books and zoos.

Conclude and summarise.

Give your opinion where appropriate.

So, like the present, I believe the future will have its good points and its bad points. I, for one, can't wait to find out!

Useful phrases for articles:

- **Rhetorical questions:** *Have you ever …?, Are you one of those people who …? What do you think about …?*
- **Introducing first point:** *Firstly, First of all, In the first place, To begin with, One thing to consider is …*
- **Introducing further points:** *Secondly, In addition (to this), Yet another …, Apart from that …*
- **Introducing final points:** *So, In conclusion, To sum up, To conclude*
- **Introducing your opinion:** *In my opinion, If you ask me, To my mind, Personally, I believe that …, In my view*

Essay

Example question

You have recently been doing a project on sport, and your teacher has asked you to write an essay giving your opinions on the following statement:

The best sports are competitive.

Write your essay.

Example answer

The first paragraph should be a general introduction to the subject.

Give examples where possible.

Millions of people around the world, both as spectators and participants, enjoy sport on a regular basis. Many of the sports they enjoy, for example football or tennis, are competitive. There are many other sports, however, such as fishing and skiing, which are not.

Use some complex sentence structures.

Use formal language.

Competitive sports, whether they are team games like rugby or one-on-one games such as squash, are appealing because we all have the desire to win. They force us to do our best, and allow the winner to celebrate a victory. However, whenever there is a winner there is also a loser. For this reason, some people believe that non-competitive sports are better, as no-one has to lose.

Develop your argument in the middle paragraphs.

Don't use contractions (*There's*, etc).

Use a variety of discursive words and phrases (see below).

There is no doubt that non-competitive sports can be highly enjoyable. Skateboarding is extremely popular, and often people skateboard for fun rather than to beat another skateboarder. Nevertheless, it may well be true that when watching a sport, it is more exciting when people compete.

Give reasons to support the argument.

Sum up your argument in the final paragraph.

To conclude, both competitive and non-competitive sports are popular. I personally believe that we cannot say which type is better. They both have positive aspects and it should be up to the individual to choose the sport that is right for them.

The final paragraph is often the best place to express your opinion clearly.

Useful phrases for essays:

Presenting two (dis)advantages together: *not only … but … also*

Presenting two opposing views: *on the one hand, on the other hand*

Expressing contrast: *however, but, although, even though, in spite of, despite*

Expressing results: *because of this, for this reason, as a result, therefore, thus*

Giving examples: *for example, for instance, such as, like*

Expressing someone else's opinion: *According to, Some people say (that), It is said (that)*

Formal letter/email

not true – many types of game: sports, puzzle, adventure

no proof

When will we ever learn? These computer games present a world where violence is everything. Teenage crime is on the increase as a direct result of these games and exam results are falling. How many hours are wasted on this rubbish, hours that could be spent studying? Too many. I'm sure all responsible parents will join me in calling for a ban on these products.

Another problem facing today's youngsters is the advertising aimed at them by...

bad idea – educate people instead

Example question

You have just read an article in a local newspaper about computer games. You decide to write a letter to the newspaper, disagreeing with the writer of the article.

Read the extract from the article on the left, together with the notes you have made. Then write to the editor of the newspaper, giving your opinion.

Write your letter. You must use grammatically correct sentences with accurate spelling and punctuation in a style appropriate for the situation. Do not write any addresses.

Example answer

Use an appropriate greeting.

Dear Sir/Madam,

Explain your reason for writing.

I am writing with regard to an article that appeared in your newspaper recently. This article claimed that computer games are a waste of teenagers' time and lead to crime. I strongly disagree with this point of view.

Introduce your first point.

First of all, it is not true that all computer games are violent. Many games, including sports games, puzzle games and adventure games, contain no violence. In fact, some of these games can be very educational.

Cover all the points in any notes you are given.

Introduce further points.

Secondly, there is no proof that playing video games leads to an increase in the crime rate. Most young people who play these games are normal, honest teenagers.

Introduce your final point.

Finally, the writer of the article calls for a ban on these games. In my view, this would be a mistake. Instead, we should educate young people about the problems of a small number of these games.

Introduce any opinons or suggestions you make.

End the letter in an appropriate way.

I look forward to hearing other readers' views.

Yours faithfully,
James Powell

Write both your first and last names.

End with 'Yours faithfully' after 'Dear Sir' and 'Yours sincerely' when you use the person's name.

Useful phrases database for formal letters/emails

There are a number of different kinds of formal letters/emails. Make sure you know who you are writing to, and why.

Include all the points from the prompts you are given and use an appropriate style.

General useful phrases:

- **Greetings:** *Dear Sir, Dear Madam, Dear Sir/Madam, Dear Mr/Mrs/Ms Smith, etc*
- **Reason for writing:** *I am writing with regard to/in response to …*
- **Ending the letter:** *I look forward to …-ing, Yours faithfully/sincerely,*

Complaining:

- **Reason for writing:** *I am writing in order to complain about …*
- **Introducing first complaint:** *First of all, In the first place, The first problem is … , My first complaint is …, The first thing I would like to draw to your attention is …*
- **Introducing further complaints:** *Not only … but also …, In addition (to this), The … was also unacceptable.*
- **Demanding action:** *I suggest that you replace the item. I would be grateful if you could give me a refund.*
- **Ending the letter:** *I look forward to hearing from you/receiving your explanation/receiving a full refund.*

Making suggestions:

- **Reason for writing:** *I am writing to suggest/arrange/make arrangements …*
- **Making first suggestion:** *First of all, My first suggestion is …, I would like to suggest …*
- **Making further suggestions:** *Secondly, Another/A further possibility is …,*
- **Offering a choice:** *either … or …, Would you mind choosing between …?*

Requesting information:

- **Reason for writing:** *I am writing to enquire/request further information about …*
- **Requesting first piece of information:** *The first thing I would like to know is …, I wonder if you would mind telling me first of all …*
- **Requesting further information:** *Do you think you could also inform me …? Would you mind also telling me …? Do you know …? I would like to know if/whether …, I hope you can also let me know about …*
- **Thanking for information:** *I would like to thank you/Thank you in advance for this information.*

Giving information:

- **Reason for writing:** *I am writing to request information about …*
- **Providing first point:** *The first thing I wish to inform you of is …, I would like to begin by informing you that …*
- **Providing further points:** *Another piece of information you may find useful is that …, I would also like to inform you that …*
- **Ending the letter:** *If you require further information, please do not hesitate to ask.*

Requesting permission:

- **Reason for writing:** *I am writing to request permission for …*
- **Making first request:** *I wonder first of all whether/if you would mind …, The first request I would like you to consider is …*
- **Making further requests:** *I would be grateful if you would also consider …, I wonder if it might be possible for us to …, I would also like to request permission for …*
- **Thanking for permission:** *Thank you for considering these requests.*

Review

Example question

You recently saw this notice in an English-language magazine called *Entertainment Monthly*.

> **Reviews wanted!**
>
> Have you been to the theatre recently? If you have, could you write us a review of the play you saw? Include information on the story, characters and production and say whether you would recommend the play to other people.
>
> The best reviews will be published in the next issue.

Write your review.

Example answer

'Back Together' –
Central Theatre, Plymouth

What happens when two school friends meet up twenty years after they last saw each other? In 'Back Together', by Alma Shapiro, the answer is a lot of fun and a few tears.

'Back Together' stars Alan Taylor as Dave and Maureen Lipton as Debbie. Best friends at school in the 1980s, they meet up again by chance in 2008 and arrange to go out to dinner. Much has changed in their lives since their schooldays, and they have a lot of catching up to do. But can they still be friends, and do they have anything in common?

This is not an easy play to put on, as we see Dave and Debbie as they were in the 1980s and in 2008. Both Alan Taylor and Maureen Lipton manage to jump backwards and forwards in time. The wonderful costumes – showing the changes in fashion – help them achieve this.

This is an entertaining and thought-provoking play that would appeal to most teenagers and adults. If you get a chance to see it, don't miss it!

Choose an appropriate title.

Use a friendly, chatty style.

Use appropriate descriptive language.

Conclusion and your recommendation

Introduction: main information about what's being reviewed.

Start a new paragraph for each main point you want to make.

Give your opinion.

It's acceptable to use contractions (I've, etc).

Useful phrases for reviews:

- **What I (dis)liked most was:** *I was disappointed by/with … , I was pleasantly surprised by … , would appeal to … , If you get a chance to …*
- **Reviews of books:** *main character, is set in, comedy/thriller/science fiction/etc, author/written by, believable, ending, chapter*
- **Reviews of films, TV programmes and plays:** *lead (role), star, starring, X plays a … , written by, is set in, ending*
- **Reviews of restaurants, hotels, etc:** *location, service, setting, owned/run by, reasonable prices, book in advance*

Informal letter/email

Example question

You have received an email from your English-speaking friend Harry. Read Harry's email and the notes you have made.

Then write an email to Harry, using all your notes.

write reply send

From: Harry Parker
Date: 10th May

Subject: Summer plans

Just wondering what your plans are for the summer. I've decided to go on an adventure holiday this summer, and I'd love it if you could come with me. It's in Wales, and should be great fun. They have loads of different activities to do. I'm going for two weeks, from the 7th to 20th July. If you can't come for the whole two weeks, maybe you could come for one week.

Let me know what you think!

Hope to hear from you soon!

Harry

Sounds great! Cost? (must be less than € 200!)

Ask best way to get there from London.

2nd–sister's wedding during first week.

rock climbing? canoeing?

Write your email. You must use grammatically correct sentences with accurate spelling and punctuation in a style appropriate for the situation.

Example answer

write | reply | send

To: Harry Parker
Date: 10th May

Subject: Summer plans

Dear Harry,

Thanks for your email! It's great the summer's nearly here, isn't it?

The adventure holiday you mentioned sounds like a great idea! Do you know if they offer rock climbing and canoeing? I hope so!

I'd love to come for two weeks, but my sister's getting married during the first week so I – obviously! – have to be here. I could come for the second week, though. You didn't say how much it costs. I can only afford €200, so I hope it's not more than that!

One more question for now – what's the best way to get to Wales from London? Is there a train or a bus that goes near the place?

Well, I'd better go now as I've got an exam tomorrow.

Hope to hear from you soon!

All the best,

Adam

Start with Dear + first name,

Use informal language.

Use chatty, informal expressions.

Introduce your first point.

Use some informal punctuation, such as exclamation marks.

Start a new paragraph for each main point you want to make.

Make sure you use all the information from the question.

Give a reason for ending your letter/email.

Use a closing expression.

Use an expression to sign off.

Only write a first name

Useful phrases for informal letters/emails:

- **Greetings:** *Dear Mary/John/etc*
- **Asking about health:** *How are you? How are things? I hope you're well. Hope you're well.*
- **Referring to someone's news:** *Glad to hear … , I was very happy to hear/read … , Great news about your …*
- **Introducing points:** *Well, Oh, and another thing! By the way, Listen, Let me tell you about … , Guess what!*
- **Ending the letter/email:** *I have to go now. Got to go. Take care. Write soon! Love, Lots of love, All the best, Yours*

Report

Example question

You work for your local tourist office. Your manager asked you to visit a new tourist attraction (for example a theatre, museum or disco) in your area. Now you must write a report for your manager.

Write your report. Describe the attraction, say what it has to offer to tourists and comment on its good and bad points.

Example answer

To: Ms Carlton
From: Monica Phillips
Subject: Bakeworth Toy Museum
Date: 24th June

Introduction

As requested, I have visited the new Bakeworth Toy Museum at 24, Pensilva Street, Bakeworth. My findings are presented below.

Entrance fees

Entrance is free for children under eight. For those aged eight to sixteen, entrance costs £1.50. The fee is £2.50 for adults.

The museum

Having been recently renovated, the building is in extremely good condition. The museum is large, with over twenty rooms full of toys and games from the past hundred years. There are many toys for visitors to actually touch and play with, so many tourists – children and adults alike – will find the museum interesting and entertaining.

Other facilities

There is a café on the fourth floor, which serves snacks and cold drinks. Prices are reasonable and there is plenty of seating.

Conclusion

The Bakeworth Toy Museum is an excellent tourist attraction. The entrance fees are reasonable and there is plenty for people to do there. I believe we should recommend the museum to tourists, particularly those with children.

Always start with To: and think of an appropriate name for the person who will read the report.

Put from: on the line below then add your name.

Put Subject: on the next line. Choose a heading that clearly describes what the report is about.

You do not need to put the date, but you can if you want to.

Every paragraph should have a heading which clearly explains what the paragraph is about.

Use key report phrases.

Do not use contractions (*I've*, etc).

Use a variety of grammatical structures.

Use formal language.

Some paragraphs can be quite short.

We often make or talk about recommendations in a report. These are usually in the final paragraph.

Useful phrases for reports:

- **Introductory information:** *To: From: Subject: Date:*
- **Headings:** *Introduction, Conclusion or Recommendation(s)*
- **Introductory paragraph:** *As requested, This involved + -ing, My findings are presented/ outlined below.*
- **Recommending:** *I would like to suggest/ recommend … , I therefore (do not) suggest/ recommend … , I believe we should (not) recommend … , You may wish to consider …*

Story

Example question

You have decided to enter a short story competition. The competition rules state that the story must begin or end with the following sentence:

What was I going to do?

Write your story for the competition.

Example answer

It is a good idea to give your story a title.

Coming Home

My flat was being redecorated so my friend Julie, who was away on holiday, had kindly said I could stay at her house. I moved in on Tuesday night.

When I arrived home from work on Wednesday, it was dark. I got my key out of my jacket pocket and put it in the lock. It didn't fit. I tried again and again.

I finally realised why. It was the key to my flat, not Julie's house. 'Oh no!' I said to myself. 'I left her key on the kitchen table. How am I going to get in?' I walked round the house, trying all the windows and doors downstairs. Everything was locked, but I could see that the bathroom window was open. I knew there was a ladder in the garage, so I got it and leaned it against the wall. I was halfway up the ladder when a voice shouted, 'Freeze! You're under arrest!'

The neighbours had called the police. They didn't know I was staying there and, unfortunately, I didn't have any identification on me. How could I prove I wasn't a burglar? What was I going to do?

Use past continuous for background information.

Use past simple for the main events.

It is acceptable to use contractions (*didn't*, etc). However, a story should not be as informal as a letter to a pen friend, for example.

Try to include some direct speech.

Use connectors and conjunctions (*so*, *but*, *although*, etc) to make some sentences longer.

Try to include one or two descriptive adjectives or adverbs.

Make sure you have at least four main paragraphs. You may wish to follow this guide. Paragraph 1: background information. Paragraphs 2 and 3: the main part of the story. Paragraph 4: the climax (key moment) of the story OR what happened after the climax.

Don't just use the verb *say* with direct speech.

You cannot change the words you are given in the question at all. Always read the question carefully – sometimes you have a choice whether to start or finish the story with the words they give you. Sometimes you do not have a choice.

Useful phrases for stories:

- **Time phrases:** *It all began, Meanwhile, Shortly afterwards, A little later, Some time later, Eventually, Finally, In the end*
- **Dramatic devices:** *Suddenly, All of a sudden, without warning, Just like that, Just at that moment, out of the blue*
- **Direct speech:** *'…,' said X.*
- **Verbs with direct and/or indirect speech:** *say, tell, ask, shout, whisper, scream, think, cry, promise*
- **Concluding:** *It had all been … , When it was all over, After everything that had happened, Looking back now, In the end*

Key word database

able	(dis/in)ability, unable, disabled
academy	academic, academically
accept	acceptance, (un)acceptable, accepted, accepting
accuse	accusation, accused, accuser, accusing(ly)
achieve	achievement, (un)achievable
act	actor, actress, acting, action, activate, (in)activity, (in)active(ly)
addict	addiction, addictive
advertise	advertisement, advertising, advertised, advertiser
allergy	allergic
allow	allowance, disallow
amuse	amusement, amusing(ly),amused
announce	announcement, announcer
appear	disappear, (dis)appearance
apparent	apparent(ly)
apply	applicant, application, (in)applicable, applied
appreciate	appreciation, (un)appreciative(ly)
argue	argument, argumentative(ly)
arrange	arranged, arrangement
arrive	arrival
assist	assistant, assistance
attend	attendance, attention, attendee, (in)attentive(ly)
attract	attraction, (un)attractive(ly)
benefit	beneficial
bore	boredom, boring
broad	broaden
care	carer, caring, careful(ly), careless(ly)
certify	certificate, certified
choose	choice
comfort	discomfort, (un)comfortable, (un)comfortably
ommerce	commercial, commercialise, commercialised, commercially
ommunicate	communicator, communication, (un)communicative(ly)
ompete	competitor, competition, competitive
onverse	conversation, conversant, conversely
onvict	conviction
orrespond	correspondence, corresponding
reate	creator, creation, creativity, creative(ly)
rime	criminal(ly)
ulture	cultural(ly)
anger	endanger, endangered, dangerous(ly)
ay	daily, everyday
ecide	decision, (in)decisive(ly)
edicate	dedication, dedicated
evelop	developer, development, developing
iffer	difference, (in)different(ly)
irect	director, direction, (in)direct(ly)
iscover	discoverer, discovery
iscuss	discussion
ish	dishwasher
stant	distance
onomy	economist, (un)economical(ly)
lit	editor, edition, editing
ucate	education, educator, educated, educational(ly)
nphasis	(de)emphasise
nploy	(un)employment, employer, employee, (un)employed, (un)employable, self-employed
joy	enjoyment, (un)enjoyable
enter	entrance
entertain	entertainer, entertainment, entertaining
enthuse	(un)enthusiasm, (un)enthusiastic(ally)
environment	environmentalist, environmental(ly)
equip	equipment, (un)equipped
Europe	European
evident	evidence, evidently
excite	excitement, exciting, (un)excited(ly)
expensive	expenses, (in)expensive(ly)
fact	factual(ly)
fail	failure, failing, failed
fame	(in)famous(ly)
fashion	(un)fashionable, (un)fashionably
finance	finances, financial(ly)
fit	unfit, fitness
forge	forgery, forger
fortune	misfortune, (un)fortunate(ly)
freeze	freezer, freezing, frozen
friend	befriend, friendship, (un)friendly
globe	global
grow	growth, grown, grower
happy	(un)happiness, (un)happily
harm	harmful(ly), harmless(ly)
help	helper, helping, (un)helpful(ly), helpless(ly)
honest	dishonest, (dis)honesty, (dis)honestly
humour	humorous(ly)
ill	illness
improve	improvement, improved
industry	industrial(ly), industrialist
infect	infection, infected
inhabit	inhabitant, inhabited
inject	injection
injure	(un)injured, injury
intense	intensive(ly)
interest	disinterest, (un)interested, (dis) interested, (un)interesting(ly)
introduce	introduction
invent	inventor, invention, (un)inventive(ly)
invest	investment, investor
jealous	jealousy, jealously
journal	journalist, journalism
kind	(un)kindness, (un)kind(ly)
know	knowledge, (un)known, knowledgeable
law	lawyer
like	alike, unlike, likeness, (un)likeable, dislike
literate	illiterate, (il)literacy
lose	loss, loser, losing, lost
maintain	maintenance
manage	manager, management, managing
medal	medallion, medallist
mix	mixture, mixer
murder	murderer, murderous, murdered
nature	(un)natural, naturalist
nervous	nervousness, nervously
obey	(dis)obedience, (dis)obedient(ly)
offence	offender, (un)offensive(ly)
operate	operator, operative, operation, operating
oppose	opponent, opposing, opposition, opposite
pay	payment, payable, (un)paid
perform	performance, performer
person	people, (im)personal , personality, personalities, impersonate
poison	poisonous
pollute	pollution, (un)polluted, polluter

poor	poorly, poverty
popular	(un)popular(ity)
practice	practise, practising, (im)practical(ly)
prepare	preparation
produce	producer, product, production, (un)productive(ly)
qualify	qualification, (un)qualified
real	reality, really, unreal, realise, realisation
recover	recovery
relate	relation(ship), relative(ly)
report	reporter
respond	response, (un)responsive(ly)
responsible	(ir)responsibility, irresponsible, (ir)responsibly
revise	revision, revised
revolution	revolutionary
ridicule	ridiculous(ness)
rob	robber, robbery
rude	rudeness, rudely
say	saying(s)
scholar	scholarship, scholarly
science	scientist, scientific(ally)
solve	solution
spectate	spectator, spectacle
strong	strength, strengthen, strongly
style	stylist, stylish(ness), stylishly
success	succeed, (un)successful(ly)
supervise	supervisor, supervision, supervising
surgery	surgeon, surgical(ly)
take	retake
teach	teacher, teaching(s), taught
theft	thief
think	thought, thoughtless(ness), thinker, (un) thinkable
tour	tourist, touring
train	trainer, trainee, trained
treat	treatment
true	untrue, truly, truth, (un)truthful(ly)
value	(in)valuable, (in)valuably, valueless, valued
work	worker, (hard)working, (un)workable
world	worldwide, worldly

Phrasal verb database

beat up	hit (a person) repeatedly and violently
break down	stop working (for machines, cars, etc)
break in	enter a building illegally
break out	(of diseases, fires, etc) appear suddenly
bring out	release, publish (a new product, magazine, etc)
bring up	mention (a subject); raise (children)
bump into	meet by chance
call off	postpone; cancel
calm down	become less excited or upset
carry out	do, conduct (research, an investigation, etc)
catch on	become popular
catch up	reach the same point
catch up with	reach; learn the latest news about
check in	sign the register at a hotel; tell the airline you have arrived at the airport ready to travel
cheer up	become happier, make someone happier
clear up	become brighter (for the weather)
close down	stop doing business
come about	happen
come across	find (often by chance)
come between	cause trouble or disagreement (between people)
come down	lower, decrease (for prices, etc)
come down with	get a minor illness
come into	inherit
come off	leave (a stage, football pitch, etc)
come on	develop, improve
come out (on top)	win
come out	be published, be released (for magazines, CDs, etc); become known
come over	arrive from another country (usually to live)
come to	regain consciousness after fainting
come up	appear (on screen, etc); be going to happen
come up with	have, create, invent, think of (an idea)
cross off	put a line through an item on a list
cross out	put a line through
cut down	cut until it falls (for trees)
cut down on	do/eat less of something
cut off	disconnect
die out	become extinct
dig up	remove from the ground
do without	manage to survive without
drop out	leave a course, etc before the end
eat up	reduce, decrease (profits, etc)
end up	finally arrive at a particular place or in a particular situation; finally do
fill in	complete (an application form, etc)
find out	discover
fit in	be accepted as a member of a group
flick through	turn over and look at the pages (of a magazine, etc) quickly
get away	leave home, work, etc in order to take a break
get back (to someone)	reply, respond, contact again
get back	return
get back together	start a relationship again after having split up
get by	survive on little money
get down	to start doing seriously (work, revision, et
get in	arrive (for trains, buses, etc)
get off	leave (a bus, etc)
get on (well, badly, etc) (with)	have a (good, bad) relationship (with)
get on (with)	continue doing sth
get out of	remove (clothes)
get over	recover from, deal with
get round	move from the start to the finish of a trac course, etc
get through	connect (to someone on the phone)
give back	return something you have been given
give off	produce (a smell, a gas, etc)
give up	stop making an effort; stop doing something (smoking, etc)
go for	choose
go off	stop being fresh

go off	explode (for bombs)
go on	continue; become
go out (with friends, etc)	do social activities outside the house
go out (with someone)	be the boyfriend/girlfriend of
go over	explain the main points of
go through	experience
grow up	become older
hand in	give (a form, test, etc) to someone so they can read or correct it, etc
hang around	stay at a place doing nothing important
hang up	end a phone call
help out	help someone to do some work, etc
hold (someone) up	delay (someone)
hurry up	do something faster
join in	take part in an activity
keep up with	make sure you know the latest about (developments, news, etc)
lead to	cause
let down	disappoint
let off	not punish
live up to	fulfil (potential, someone's expectations, etc)
lock out	prevent someone from entering a building (often by locking the doors)
log on	gain access to a computer system, etc; get a computer, etc ready to use
look after	take care of
look back on	think about the past
look down on	not respect, treat as an inferior
look into	examine
look round	explore and look at (a place, building, etc)
look up	find something in a reference book, such as a dictionary
look up to	respect
make off	escape
make up	create; form a part of
meet up	meet (usually socially)
pass out	faint, lose consciousness
pay back	return money, etc you have borrowed; take revenge on
pay off	produce a benefit or success
pick up	collect
pop up	appear suddenly
pull out	remove, reveal suddenly
put in (for)	apply (for promotion, a pay rise, etc)
put in	install (a piece of equipment, etc)
put off	arrange for a later time; make one dislike something
put on	start wearing (for clothes, jewellery, etc)
put through	connect (on the phone)
put up	provide accommodation; place on a wall
put up with	tolerate, stand
rip off	cheat
roll up	wrap into the shape of a cylinder (for paper, etc)
run away	leave (home, etc) secretly (because you are unhappy)
run into	meet by accident
run out	have no more left
sail through	pass a test, etc easily
save up	avoid spending money to keep it for a particular purpose
see off	say goodbye at a train station, airport, etc to someone leaving
send out	give, send, transmit (for messages, information, etc)
set about (doing)	start doing in an energetic way
set off	start a journey
set out	start a (long and difficult) journey
set up	start (a business, club, etc); make (a piece of equipment, computer, etc) ready for use; put an innocent person in a situation where it appears they are guilty
show off	demonstrate in a proud way how good you are
slow down	decrease speed
sort out	solve; arrange
speed up	increase speed
splash out	spend a large amount of money (on a luxury item)
split up	end a relationship
stand for	mean (for letters, abbreviations, etc)
stand in for	take the place of
stand up	start standing
stay on	continue to go to school after you are old enough to leave
stay out	not go home
stay up	not go to bed
stick up (for)	support, defend
storm off	leave angrily
take (time) off	spend time doing something other than work, etc
take after	resemble, be similar to (an older person in the family)
take away	remove
take back	return something to the place you got it from
take down	write what someone says
take off	leave the ground (for planes, etc); become popular; remove clothing
take on	employ (staff); agree to do (work, etc)
take out	arrange to be given or receive a licence, insurance policy, etc
take over	take control of (a company, etc)
take to	begin to do something regularly
take up	use, need, fill (time, etc)
take up	start (a sport, hobby, etc)
throw away	get rid of (rubbish, etc)
tidy up	make a room, etc clean and neat
turn down	reject, not accept
turn into	change to become (a different thing)
turn off	make a machine, etc stop working
turn on	make a machine, etc start working
turn out	be finally discovered
turn over	change (TV channel, etc)
turn to	ask, go to (for advice, help, etc)
turn up	arrive, appear (often unexpectedly); increase (the volume, level, etc)
wash up	wash plates, etc after a meal
work out	solve, calculate; do physical exercise in order to get or remain fit

Laser Writing Planner **1** — Informal email

Complete the chart. Be careful! Do NOT write your email until your teacher has seen your notes here.

	Purpose	Your notes	Useful expressions
First line	greeting	Dear ________, *or* Hi ________!	
First paragraph	thank your friend for their email and say you're looking forward to meeting Adam and his family		Thanks so much for your email. / I can't wait …
Second paragraph	describe your interests; remember to mention skateboarding and say what music you like		Let me tell you what I like doing. I'm into … / It's cool that you like … / I've never … / I also really love …
Third paragraph	answer Adam's question		You asked me … / I'd love to … if possible / Are there …?
Fourth paragraph	ask any other questions you want to ask, and make any final points (eg that you've attached a photo of yourself)		While I'm here, I was wondering … / Could you let me know …? / What do you think? / I've attached …
Ending the email	end the email in an informal way		That's all for now! / Have to go now! / Write back soon! / Take care! / Bye for now!
Final line	give your first name		

Laser Writing Planner **2** — Review

Complete the chart. Be careful! Do NOT write your review until your teacher has seen your notes here.

	Purpose	Your notes	Useful expressions
Title	give the name of the hotel		
First paragraph	describe the hotel in general (where it is, what it looks like from the outside, your general positive/negative impressions)		one of the most popular … / a modern/beautiful/large/etc building / it looks … / I felt that …
Second paragraph	describe the main facilities		The hotel offers … / There are also … / Guests can … / Other facilities include …
Third paragraph	describe further relevant aspects (such as prices / level of service / nearby attractions / quality of food in restaurant etc)		One thing to bear in mind is … / Another positive aspect of the hotel is … / One major drawback is …
Fourth paragraph	conclusion and recommendation		In conclusion, / to conclude, / I'd definitely recommend … / I wouldn't recommend … / (not) particularly suitable for …

Laser Writing Planner 3 — Article

Complete the chart. Be careful! Do NOT write your article until your teacher has seen your notes here.

	Purpose	Your notes	Useful expressions
Title	write the title exactly as stated in the question		
First paragraph	introduce the topic in a general way		Are you crazy / mad about ...? / I am! I'm a huge fan of ...
Second paragraph	describe the most important two or three benefits of technology; remember to give examples		One of the main advantages ... / Another positive aspect ... / What's more, / For example, / For instance / such as
Third paragraph	describe further benefits; you may want to talk about technology in the future		
Fourth paragraph	conclude your article		In short, / There's no doubt that ... / I strongly believe that ...

Laser Writing Planner 4 — Essay

Complete the chart. Be careful! Do NOT write your essay until your teacher has seen your notes here.

	Purpose	Your notes	Useful expressions
First paragraph	introduce the subject		It is generally agreed that ... / It is clear that ... / Some people claim that ... / I would like to argue that ...
Second paragraph	present your first main points agreeing or disagreeing with the statement, with examples and supporting details		Firstly, ... / First of all, / The evidence shows that ... / In addition, ... / As a result, ... / However, ... / Despite this, ...
Third paragraph	present further main points, with examples and supporting details		Another important point is that ... / We should also bear in mind that ... / ... such as ... / In particular, ...
Fourth paragraph	present further main points, with examples and supporting details		Finally, ... / This means that ... / This is shown by ...
Fifth paragraph	come to a conclusion, summarise your opinion		To conclude, ... / In conclusion, ... / To sum up, ... / My view is that ...

Laser Writing Planner **5** — Letter

Complete the chart. Be careful! Do NOT write your letter until your teacher has seen your notes here.

	Purpose	Your notes	Useful expressions
First line	greeting	*Dear Sir or Madam,*	
First paragraph	give your general opinion of the festival and the reason for writing		I recently attended … / In my view, the festival was … / I would like to offer a number of suggestions to …
Second paragraph	make your first suggestions, including reasons why		The first improvement I would like to suggest is … / The reason for this is that … / As a result, …
Third paragraph	make further suggestions, including reasons why		In addition, … / Another idea to improve the festival would be to … / Because of this …
Ending the letter			I look forward to hearing from you. / Yours faithfully,
Final line	give your full name		

Laser Writing Planner **6** — Article

Complete the chart. Be careful! Do NOT write your article until your teacher has seen your notes here.

	Purpose	Your notes	Useful expressions
Title	write the title exactly as stated in the question		
First paragraph	ask a question to get your readers' attention; introduce the subject		Have you ever …? / Are you one of those people who …? / Do you worry about …?
Second paragraph	make your first suggestions, including reasons why		What we could do is … / One great idea would be to … / I'm sure students would enjoy … / That would mean that … / Another fantastic idea is that we could … / Why don't we start …? / That would be great because then …
Third paragraph	make further suggestions, including reasons why		
Fourth paragraph	make further suggestions, including reasons why		
Fifth paragraph	conclude your article		So, why not …? / You can help by … / Together, we can …

Webquests

Unit 1

Find the answers online! Then use the information to write a paragraph about Facebook.

1 When was Facebook founded?

____

2 Who was the main founder of Facebook?

____

3 When was he born?

____

4 Where was he born?

____

5 Where was he studying at the time he started Facebook?

____

6 Before Facebook, he created a website with a similar name. What was it called?

____

7 How many users did Facebook have by April 2012?

____

8 Which film, released in 2010, tells the story of the founding of Facebook?

____

Unit 2

Find the answers online! Then use the information to write a paragraph about Chicago.

1 Which state is Chicago in?

____

2 What is the population of Chicago?

____

3 Where does the name 'Chicago' come from?

____

4 What disaster happened in Chicago in 1871?

____

5 What is the average temperature in July in Chicago?

____

6 What is the average temperature in January in Chicago?

____

7 What are the two tallest buildings in Chicago?

____

8 Which two baseball teams come from Chicago?

____

Unit 3

Find the answers online! Then use the information to write a paragraph about the history of photography.

1 In which year did the Frenchman Joseph Niépce produce the first permanent photograph?

___

2 When was the first colour photo taken?

___

3 Which camera did George Eastman produce for sale in 1888?

___

4 He also produced the popular Brownie camera. When did it first appear?

___

5 Which camera, introduced in 1948 by Edwin H. Land, produced instant images?

___

6 When was the digital camera invented?

___

7 Tim Berners-Lee published the first photograph on the web in which year?

___

8 Flickr, a popular image website, first appeared in which year?

___

Unit 4

Find the answers online! Then use the information to write a paragraph about the English billionaire, Richard Branson.

1 When was Richard Branson born?

___

2 Where was he born?

___

3 His first business produced a magazine. What was it called?

___

4 How old was Branson when he produced that magazine?

___

5 He started a chain of record shops in 1972. What were they called?

___

6 Which company did he form in 1984?

___

7 Which company did he form in 1999?

___

8 In 1991, Branson broke the record for crossing the Pacific Ocean in what?

___

Unit 5

Find the answers online! Then use the information to write a paragraph about the Sydney Opera House.

1 The Opera House is in Sydney, in which Australian state?

____

2 Which famous bridge is it near?

____

3 Which Danish architect designed the Opera House?

____

4 His design won a competition in which year?

____

5 When was the Opera House completed?

____

6 Who officially opened the Opera House?

____

7 How much, in dollars, did the Opera House cost to build?

____

8 The Opera House is the home of which orchestra?

____

Unit 6

Find the answers online! Then use the information to write a paragraph about the WWF.

1 The letters WWF used to stand for World Wildlife Fund. What do they stand for now?

____

2 In which year did the WWF change its name?

____

3 In which year was the WWF formed?

____

4 In which country was the first WWF office?

____

5 Who was the first president of the WWF?

____

6 The WWF protects endangered animals, such as the one they chose for their symbol. Which animal is that?

____

7 Which country does that animal come from?

____

8 Approximately how many supporters does the WWF have worldwide?

____

Unit 7

Find the answers online! Then use the information to write a paragraph about rugby.

1 Who is usually credited with creating the game of rugby?
___

2 Where?
___

3 In which year?
___

4 How many players are there in a rugby league team?
___

5 How many players are there in a rugby union team?
___

6 In football, you score a goal. In rugby, you score a…
___

7 How many points does a team get for scoring in rugby union?
___

8 How many points does a team get for scoring in rugby league?
___

Unit 8

Find the answers online! Then use the information to write a paragraph about the world's first stamp.

1 What is the name of the world's first adhesive postage stamp?
___

2 How many of these stamps were ever printed?
___

3 Which museum has the only complete sheet of these stamps?
___

4 In which year were these stamps first introduced?
___

5 Who was responsible for this?
___

6 Before stamps, who paid the postage?
___

Unit 9

Find the answers online! Then use the information to write a paragraph about British politics.

1 The British Prime Minister is also known as the First Lord of ___
2 Some countries have a Finance Minister but in Britain the person with this job is called the
___

3 Some countries have a Foreign Minister but in Britain the person with this job is called the Foreign
___

4 In British politics, what does MP stand for? ___
5 Each MP in Britain represents a different geographical area. This area's called a
___

6 MPs debate issues in the House of ___
7 The MP who's responsible for making sure all the other MPs follow the rules is called the
___

Unit 10

Find the answers online! Then use the information to write a paragraph about nursing.

1 A woman with the surname Nightingale made an enormous contribution to nursing. What was her first name?
____

2 In which year was she born?
____

3 In which year did she die?
____

4 Which war started in 1853 and ended in 1856?
____

5 During this war, she was known as 'The Lady with the
____________________.'

6 In which year did she start the world's first official training programme for nurses?
____

7 What was it called?
____

8 At which hospital in London was it based?
____

Unit 11

Find the answers online! Then use the information to write a paragraph about the University of Warwick.

1 In which city is the University of Warwick?
____

2 In which year did the university first start teaching undergraduates?
____

3 In which year did Warwick Medical School open?
____

4 What's the name of the main concert hall in the Arts Centre?
____

5 What's the name of the sculpture in front of the Arts Centre at Warwick?
____

6 Who created this sculpture?
____

7 In which year did Warwick buy this sculpture?
____

Unit 12

Find the answers online! Then use the information to write a paragraph about Frank Abagnale and the film.

1 Which film is based on the life of Frank Abagnale Jr.? ____________________

2 In which year did it come out? ____________________

3 Who directed it? ____________________

4 What was the main type of crime that Abagnale committed? ____________________

5 Which organisation did the man hunting him, Carl Hanratty, work for? ____________________

6 Who plays Abagnale in the film? ____________________

7 Who plays Hanratty in the film? ____________________

Macmillan Education
4 Crinan Street
London N1 9XW
A division of Macmillan Publishers Limited
Companies and representatives throughout the world

ISBN 978-0-230-43381-6

This edition published 2013
Second edition published 2008
First edition published 2004

Original design by Peter Burgess
Page make up by Greg Sweetnam Design Solutions
Illustrated by: Oxford Designers and Illustrators
Cover design by Peter Burgess
Picture research by Susannah Jayes

Authors' acknowledgements
Malcolm and Steve would like to thank the staff at Macmillan for all their hard work bringing this project to fruition, and all the many people around the world – too many to mention – who continue to support and provide feedback on the *Laser* series.

The authors and the publishers would like to thank the following for permission to reproduce their photographs:

Alamy/john angerson p157, Alamy/Stuart Aylmer p122(cm), Alamy/Vince Bevan p75(bl), Alamy/Blend Images p102, Alamy/David Cook/blueshiftstudios p32(tmrr), Alamy/Blue Jeans Images p49(br), Alamy/Holger Burmeister p121(D), Alamy/CamEl Creative p97(E), Alamy/tom carter p90(cl), Alamy/Corbis Cusp p97(G), Alamy/Corbis Flirt 76(cl), Alamy/Chris A Crumley p64(tr), Alamy/James Davies p92, Alamy/Melanie Eldred Photography p23(br), Alamy/Extreme Sports Photo p94(A), Alamy/F1online digitale Bildagentur GmbH p43(tm), Alamy/Peter Forsberg p29, Alamy/Gaertner p90(tml), Alamy/Goddard Automotive p88, Alamy/Golden Pixels LLC p43(tr), Alamy/Jeff Greenberg p81(tr), Alamy/Hemis p87(D), Alamy/scenicireland.com/Christopher Hill Photographic p69, Alamy/Image Source pp19,96(B), Alamy/James Ingram p97(C), Alamy/JohanH p32(tr), Alamy/Christina Kennedy p58(tcmll), Alamy/Lucia Ladomerszky p44(tcl), Alamy/Oleksiy Maksymenko Photography p32(tm), Alamy/Patti McConville p171(A), Alamy/Gianni Muratore pp80-81, Alamy/Myrleen Pearson p6(tl), Alamy/Charles Polidano p89, Alamy/PYMCA p49(bm), Alamy/Andres Rodriguez p96(A), Alamy/Alexey Romanov p160(cl), Alamy/Sophotographie pp21(tcr),87(C), Alamy/Stockbroker p121(A), Alamy/Travel Pictures p28, Alamy/vario images GmbH & Co.KG p58(cl), Alamy/Bartosz Wardziak p129; **Bananastock** p6(tr); **Corbis** p38(cr), Corbis/Arctic-Images pp24(br),25, Corbis/David Aubrey p76(tcl), Corbis/Brian Bailey p101, Corbis/Hugh Beebower p36(tcl), Corbis/Benelux p17, Corbis/Jose Luis Pelaez Inc/Blend Images p48, Corbis/Leverett Bradley p21(tr), Corbis/Rolf Bruderer p18(cmll), Corbis/Reg Charity p40, Corbis/Jim Craigmyle p44(cl), Corbis/Jim Cummins p169, Corbis/George Diebold p77, Corbis/Duomo p95(tr), Corbis/Wael Hamzeh/epa p103, Corbis/ER Productions p107, Corbis/Randy Faris pp94(tr),138, Corbis/Firefly Productions p76(cmll), Corbis/Owen Franken p49(tm), Corbis/Roger De La Harpe;Gallo Images p70(cl), Corbis/Patrik Giardino p173, Corbis/Tim Hale Photography p58(cmll), Corbis/Brownie Harris p54(tm), Corbis/John Henley p152, Corbis/Ted Horowitz p68, Corbis/Image Source pp97(D),135, Corbis/Mark Karrass p165, Corbis/Michael Keller p171(cmll), Corbis/Helen King p105(tl), Corbis/Bob Krist p70(cmll), Corbis/Matthias Kulka p38(tm), Corbis/Claudia Kunin p100, Corbis/Dann Tardiff/LWA p67, Corbis/Mango Productions p151, Corbis/Lawrence Manning p171(B), Corbis/James Marshall p22, Corbis/Joe McBride p64(tcmll), Corbis/Gideon Mendel p111, Corbis/Mika p139, Corbis/Ocean pp10(tcmll),36(cmll),74,105(br),159, Corbis/Gabe Palmer p131, Corbis/Jose Luis Pelaez, Inc p134(cm), Corbis/Anthony Redpath p62, Corbis/Chuck Savage p64(tcl), Corbis/George Shelley pp10(bcmll),94(cr), Corbis/Hugh Sitton p12, Corbis/Ariel Skelley p118, Corbis/Sylvain Sonnet p87(B), Corbis/Tom Stewart p117(tm), Corbis/Jared Sych p171(bcmll), Corbis/Tetra Images/p24(tr), Corbis/David Turnley pp142(tmr),147(D), Corbis/Mike Theiss/Ultimate Chase p42(tr), Corbis/Franco Vogt pp21(tmr),50, Corbis/Patrick Ward p147(B), Corbis/Nik Wheeler p153; **FLPA** p76(tcmll);**Getty Images** pp27,32(tmr),126, Getty Images/AFP pp52,93(tl), Getty Images/altrendo images p95(bl), Getty Images/Asiaselects p143, Getty Images/Bruce Ayres p128, Getty Images/Blend Images p94(C), Getty Images/Carlos Cazalis p121(B), Getty Images/Comstock p117(tl), Getty Images/Doug Corrance p148, Getty Images/Custom Medical Stock Photo p134(tm), Getty Images/Danita Delimont p79, Getty Images/George Doyle p47, Getty Images/Jon Feingersh p10(cmll), Getty Images/Flying Colours Ltd pp145,147(C),150, Getty Images/fotog p121(C), Getty Images/Blend Images/Hill Street Studios p85, Getty Images/ISC Archives p127(tr), Getty Images/Christina Kennedy p42(tcr), Getty Images/KidStock p142(tml), Getty Images/Alexander Manton p51, Getty Images/Marie-Reine Mattera p98, Getty Images/Ryan McVay pp147(A),149, Getty Images/Doug Menuez p90(tmrr), Getty Images/Joos Mind p164, Getty Images/Moviepix p15, Getty Images/Photo Nadieshda p36(cl), Getty Images/Erin Patrice O'Brien pp54-55, Getty Images/Andrew Olney p49(tr), Getty Images/Sebastian Pfuetze p108, Getty Images/David Pinkerton p16, Getty Images/Marc Romanelli p94(B), Getty Images/Andersen Ross pp23(bcr),120,122(tm), Getty Images/Stockbyte pp72,73,75(bmll,tr,cr),97(H), Getty Images/David Stoecklein p92(bl), Getty Images/Tetra Images p97(F), Getty Images/rey torres p18(cl), Getty Images/Travel Ink p87(A), Getty Images/Universal Images Group p41, Getty Images/Gari Wyn Williams p160(cm), Getty Images/Yellow Dog Productions p117(tr), Getty Images/David Young-Wolff p163; **Macmillan Publishers Ltd** p127(tl,tm); **Rex Features** p106, Rex Features/Clive Dixon p10(cl), Rex Features/Everett Collection p60, Rex Features/ITV p154 (cl,bcl), Rex Features/Frederic Sierakowski p61; **Science Photo Library**/Imane p43(tl); **Woldingham School Association** p112.

Printed and bound in Spain

2022 2021 2020 2019 2018
20 19 18 17 16 15 14